Native
Religious
Traditions

edited by Earle H. Waugh and
K. Dad Prithipaul

Joint International Symposium
of Elders and Scholars,
Edmonton, Alta., 1977,

Published for the Canadian Corporation for Studies in Religion / Corporation
Canadienne des Sciences Religieuses by Wilfrid Laurier University Press

Canadian Cataloguing in Publication Data

Joint International Symposium of Elders and Scholars,
Edmonton, Alta., 1977.
    Native religious traditions

(SR supplements ; 8)

Proceedings of the symposium held in Edmonton,
September 15-17, 1977.
Includes index.
ISBN 0-919812-10-4 pa.

1. Indians of North America − Religion and mythology
− Congresses. 2. Indians of North America − Rites
and ceremonies − Congresses. I. Waugh, Earle H.,
1936-   II. Prithipaul, K. Dad, 1927-
III. Title. IV. Series.

E98.R3J65 1977   299'.7   C79-094692-0

Cover design by Michael Baldwin MSIAD

Order from:
Wilfrid Laurier University Press
Wilfrid Laurier University
Waterloo, Ontario, Canada   N2L 3C5

Table of Contents

Native Religious Traditions:
The Proceedings of the Joint International Symposium of Elders and Scholars held in Edmonton September 15 - 17, 1977

An Introduction

On September 22, 1877 at Blackfoot Crossing, the chiefs of the Blackfoot Confederacy, David Laird of the Government and Lieutenant Macleod of the North West Mounted Police signed Treaty 7. Under its terms, the bands in what is now Southern Alberta ceded 42,900 square miles of land to the government in exchange for annuities, treaty gifts, reserve land and other government obligations. A measure of the importance of the signing is that, in conjunction with Treaties 6 and 8, it paved the way for the establishment of the Province of Alberta.

A number of programmes were developed by the native people to commemorate these Treaties, with support and financial aid from both provincial and federal agencies. The majority of these, quite properly, related to local bands and organizations and drew on local talent. Necessarily their impact was confined. It seemed to the Department of Religious Studies at the University of Alberta that this centennial occasion provided an excellent opportunity for reflection on the significance of native culture as a humanistic expression.

Whether the government of the time had envisaged it or not, one implication of the treaties was that native culture was a continuing and necessary element in Canada's makeup; even years of paternalism and benign neglect could not eradicate that reality. Despite the prejudices and disputes that have plagued European-Native interaction, it seemed essential that intellectual tools be developed that could not only bridge the impasse, but provide the possibility for incorporating the insights of native traditions into the viewpoints of contemporary religious studies.

We were all too aware of the popular folklore of the 'noble savage' that still has serious repercussions on much critical analysis of native traditions. We were also conscious of the current nostalgic mood that has succeeded in reviving trends and lifestyles of by-gone days. No one is more aware of the fallacies of these views than the natives themselves.

In order to counter these influences and to present the legitimate viewpoint of practitioners of these traditions, we sought out religious leaders from various native groups. It is safe to say that a good many of them were sceptical. Nevertheless we hoped that a conference situation, with a mix of papers and group seminars, would provide a format for creative interchange between them and scholars. The main consensus at the conclusion of the conference was that this was moderately successful, but that there were models that should be tried were the conference to be repeated.

On the other hand, one of the frequent criticisms from scholars participating in conferences with natives is that little new ever comes out of them. We took this complaint seriously and sent already published data to each of those elders invited, asking them to respond to a series of questions. A list of the material and the questions can be found in the appendix. As can be seen in the taped sections, this drew a mixed reaction from the native discussants. In a section on September 16, Mr. Emil Piapot, Cree elder from Piapot Reserve, refused to discuss some of the material, much to the consternation of many participants. Unfortunately an equipment malfunction meant that the section was not taped and so could not be reproduced here. Clearly some of the reasons for his refusal were based on the fact that such stories and sacred subjects either could not be discussed in the presence of women or only during winter. Moreover, there is always a special time and place where they could be the subject of analysis, but the secular situation at the university was not one of them. Implicit in the refusal was the view that sacred knowledge was not of the kind that could be taught or discussed openly—it had to be learned at the level of personal discovery and intuition. Almost as important was the geniune religious conviction that some truths are secret, by their very nature open to only an elite and limited group. It remains one of the crucial issues for Religious Studies scholars of how to cope with phenomena that by their very religious nature resist the attempt to present them in a situation other than religious.

Another problem was brought immediately home to us as the conference was about to begin: how fragile is our link with this knowledge. Pius Dustyhorn, an elder from Saskatchewan, died only days before the conference was to begin. These individuals represent the repository of learning and cultural achievement of their people—as someone said, they are the museums and archives of native society. Much of this culture has been lost forever to mankind, certainly a tragedy of no little dimension, and it continues to disappear at an alarming rate. In some cases, as the tapes show, there is little of it left. Still the elders regarded this with that quiet reserve which has become almost a stereotype of native response. They saw quite clearly that religion was much more than an ideology held by a group of people. Indeed it ultimately had to find allegiance within the life-experience of people themselves and if contemporary North American culture did not elicit the emotional response necessary to sustain the old ways, there was little sense in wringing one's hands over it. No amount of sentimentality, scholarly or otherwise, could generate the religious attitude if it was not there. The view disturbed the renaissance naturalists in our midst, but it was refreshing and honest. It added a welcome contextual dimension to the debates.

The symposium was originally organized to consider native mythology on the first day and ritual on the second. We have retained the format only among the scholars' papers, principally because the dimension appeared to the elders to be part of our scholarly tradition rather than of the actual world in which they lived. Certainly Luckert's paper is one indication that scholars too recognize the limitations imposed by our entrenched distinctions. But of greater significance was the individual problems that were aired. Readers will note that one area of contention among the scholars concerned the viability of Western European modes of time. Prof. Luckert made the point that the movement from so-called whiteman's time to native time was not an impossible step and that European language could be adapted to encompass the meaning of that time. Prof. Sam Gill was much less convinced of this, citing studies that indicated much more complex time presuppositions than western tenses of past, present and future. The observer in this discussion could see at least two important issues at stake. How much is understanding or comprehension tied to linguistic structures? And is there a qualitative and evaluative difference in the way time is seen by Western Europeans and natives? This is not the place to debate these issues, but we can point out how the conference related to them. Some debate arose over the meaning of medicine man, holy man and elder. "Elder" was acceptable to the natives involved because they related it with age and the wisdom that presumes to bring. But there was some disagreement among them about more precise nuances implied in the term. Many of the Cree held elder to be related to age, at least in the common understanding, and argued for other words if we were talking about individuals with gifts and talents in medicine or prophecy or insight. Some Sioux-related participants thought elder had a religious overtone, already implying a professional concern with religious tasks such as medicine or foresight, and thus could not see it being used exclusively with age-related meaning. They argued that a young person who had received many significant religious experiences and who showed obvious medicine abilities should also be called an elder.

Religiously talented individuals could be called medicine men or holy men by all natives, but even people like Emil Piapot with his obvious religious talents balked at being referred to as holy man. Holy men were very sacred people, who held tremendous powers in bygone days and who had proven themselves in leadership for many years. He did not feel the term should be used except to refer to those who might legitimately be called holy.

While we must admit there is ambiguity in the way anthropologists and historians of religion have used these terms, it is clear that there is significant difference in the way natives view religious leadership. Perhaps we could conclude that the cultural tradition of the tribe defined the linguistic structures, which in turn provided the concepts for understanding. It does not follow that it would be impossible to comprehend the basic meaning of a term, but we would have great difficulty in understanding all the nuances that could be built into it without much more training in the cultural context. This could be extended to the problem of Western European scholars' understanding of native concepts. Certainly some depth of acquaintance with a culture would be a prerequisite before we could spell out just what a key word meant. To that must be added the position or role that particular term plays in the culture, since it may be valued differently when viewed from another culture's system.

The question about evaluation of time, can be answered both positively and negatively. A glance through the native materials will show that the representatives at the conference fully comprehended the linear time Europeans use, especially when discussing their own life-span. What was not so evident was that this is the *most important* way of viewing time. Among some, the discovery of identity during the vision quest was more properly a discovery of significant time, because that became the basis for their development as an *individual* whose talents could have tribal impact. Every authentic experience after that was a new discovery of truth, adding to their insight and wisdom. Creation, then, could not be viewed from a natural or material standpoint, since the spiritual creation had at least as great an impact as the physical. Moreover the truths of the spiritual realm had to do with the way things are, and are not subject to development. In that sense they are timeless, or belong to an eternally present time.

One result of this perception of time is that finality is modified. Where creation in the western sense begins, proceeds along a purposeful track and ends at some time in the future, this perception removes the sharpness of the ultimate goal and shifts importance to a continuous discovery process. It is in the experiencing of new creations that insights come, not in one exemplary event.

Another area of disagreement among the scholars was over the division between myth, legend and fairy tales. Almost everyone agreed with Prof. Hultkrantz that myth was an unfortunate word, whose nuances of "fabrication" and "untrue" severely distorted the scholar's meaning. But the distinction between myth and other kinds of material was more contentious. Luckert argued that the distinction was fine in the library but that it was of little help in the field where materials from each type could be found interwoven during a religious ceremony. Prof. Waida, of the University of Alberta, suggested that abandoning the structure would be of little value but that scholars might regard it more as a helpful tool than as a characteristic of the data. The problem was raised in another context when scholars discovered how artificial some of their discussion appeared to natives. It led to an awareness that academics have certain acceptable ways of treating material, some of which are buried in antiquity, and not a few of which may be no more verifiable than any other Western European intellectual tradition. Prof. Newbery moved back to the creation myth as the model for a religious story that could not be modified by tales or cultural developments, and, although that position is defensible, the whole discussion raised important questions about cultural conditioning and scientific objectivity.

The objectivity was challenged another way. A young native leader stormed out of one session denouncing the conference as a charade and another attempt by whiteman to denigrate the native. Since we thought our purpose had been the exact opposite, it came as somewhat of a shock. His first point was obvious enough: we had no right to treat anything but our own traditions. This is an issue that many of us who deal with non-Christian traditions have faced many times. It ultimately becomes whether one who does not 'believe' in a religion can really discuss it with sympathy. A good deal of this young man's opinion related to the many papers written by sociologists, historians and psychologists on the ills of the native. He was disgusted with the blanket of science thrown over prejudicial writing. He made the perfectly valid point that western science cannot be very scientific if its conclusions are only rationalizations for European-American prejudice. Moreover he saw no reason why scholars should be any more eligible to receive secrets of the natives than others of the tribe who do not and cannot receive them.

He was willing to agree that science was itself progressing and that some moves had been made recently to overcome the biased reporting concering native ceremonies that had been the norm in the past, but he was not ready to admit that a scholar could be impartial in the categories and structures he used. While he would modify his blanket condemnation, he would not move on the latter point. He also insisted that our scientific objectivity could not deal with elements such as "power". He was quite right in suggesting that we knew the myths could lose their power if they were not treated circumspectly, or the taboos associated with them not respected. Where, he asked, was the objectivity then. Talking about the myths in anything but the proper place violated them—it was clearly a conflict between whiteman's view that he had a right to all knowledge and the native view that only proper situations could be the locale for information exchange. He was also opposed to anthropologists and others who spend years getting to know the people just so they could gain tribal secrets. He thought that morally wrong. In short, he saw no justification for the European model of intellectual inquisitiveness, especially since it had such ramifications. Learning was a sacred business, subject to sacred laws.

The exchange was very fruitful because it highlighted a problem of significance not only for this conference but for all research among the so-called pre-literate cultures. It raised a host of issues that should be explored by scholars as they modify the meaning of science into the twenty-first century.

This seems an appropriate place to terminate our overview of the Symposium. All that remains is to mention those without whom the Symposium would never have been held, some of whom worked tirelessly behind the scenes. First to our sponsors whose

contributions not only brought about the Symposium but this publication. They are:
Alberta Conference of the United Church of Canada
Alma Mater Fund
Canada Council
City of Edmonton
Imperial Oil
John McFarlane
Morning Star Educational Society (St. Paul, Alta.)
Newman Theological College
Prudham's Building Supplies
Religious Studies Department
St. Joseph's College & Archdiocese of Edmonton
University of Alberta Conference Committee
Then to the members of the Department of Religious Studies who steadfastly supported the project, and contributed their time to it, Profs. Cahill, Prithipaul, Waida and Morgan. Special recognition of the work of Mrs. Margaret Bolt, the department secretary, should be given; she handled the whole gamut of myriad details flawlessly. We are all in her debt. Stan Cuthand and John McFarlane both helped us as moderators although unscheduled and were splendid. Our thanks to all those who attended the sessions and, finally, our gratitude to Emil Piapot who opened our symposium in the proper religious way, and closed it with prayer.

This publication is one tangible result of the symposium; we appreciate the co-operation of all the elders and scholars in making this material available to you. Mr. Tom Porter was not available for September 16, so only the Mohawk seminar for September 17 is presented here, as is the Cree seminar for the reason noted earlier. Slavey material was only discussed on September 16. On September 17, Stan Cuthand made an excellent slide presentation of his Sun Dance which, obviously, could not be reproduced here. Ms. Shirley Kovacs prepared the Index and, once again, our grateful acknowledgement to Mrs. Bolt for her typing. Our appreciation to Ms. Debbie Reinhart and Printing Services of the U. of Alberta for preparing the camera-ready copy. We trust that the good that this conference generated will continue as "long as the sun shines, the river flows and the grass grows."

Earle H. Waugh

Native Seminars

Blackfoot Seminar

September 16

[*Blackfoot Indian talking (Allan Wolf Leg translates)*]

This is Lewis Running Rabbit, this is Joe Poor Eagle, and my name is Allan Wolf Leg. These people have been involved in various societies, as members, and they have received the knowledge of such societies. In regard to this morning's presentation—and I don't like to put tags on things—but words were used which people stumbled over. For example, "culture" is an English term for traditions which does not fit in with our life and language. It does not come close to defining what it attempts to define. Joe Poor Eagle here is fortunate enough to have had 30 or 40 years apprenticeship training under a person we commonly call Medicine Man, but whom in our terms is like your Bishop, a holy person. In Christian Churches you have higher-ups too, and in this sense our Medicine Men are Bishops, Deacons or what have you.

Joe Poor Eagle was trained and taught by Amos Leather, who officiated at various ceremonies: transfers of bundles, pipes—there are different types of pipes, Long-time pipe and several others—transfers of tipi designs, of memberships and societies. He was also the main impetus behind—let's say—the sponsoring of sun dances. Joe Poor Eagle was Amos Leather's aid, and is now looked upon by the Blackfoot as the main resource person for such ceremonies and activities—rituals, or what have you. In order to help your understanding of this morning's presentation, I would like to lay a format down in your minds.

We live east of Calgary—this is Blackfoot country. South of these, near Mcleod, are the Piegans—we call them the North Piegan—and those further south are the Blood Indians; and the South Piegans, in Brownie, Montana. These four tribes are Blackfoot, a part of the Blackfoot nation, the later Blackfoot Confederacy, and all speak Blackfoot. Among the different tribes in Arizona, or among the Coastal Indians or Eastern Indians, you will find the basic religion about the same. The real difference is the locality, the environment. People like Wissler or McLintock wrote about the Blackfoot in Montana, but it is a common mistake to say: "Well, if these are Blackfoot, all Blackfoot are the same." In each locality the original ceremonies and activities are slightly different. An example is the medicine pipe. This ceremony is one in which Blackfeet women imitate the Buffalo, attaching horns to the bundle—we are called Blackfeet in Montana, Blackfoot in Canada. When the women imitate the Buffalo in Canada, they drink berry soup when they approach the Beaver bundle. Also, a very aggressive person may sometimes, as the years go by, overrule some of the members of the society, and change rituals and activities. So all these things must be considered when you are looking at the Indian people as a whole. Environment has a lot to do with it—so does language.

Now this morning's presentation dealt with language, and in the mind of the speaker I could see all the influences he has received from books, colleagues, friends, informants—all these people. But two scholars doing the same research, who do not look at each other's work, will come up with different results, because they use different informants. One thing you must keep in mind is that informants are human beings, as are the researchers and scholars.

Today there is a lot of interference in our way of life; in the old day it was different. O.K., I think a little differently than these two, (i.e. Joe Poor Eagle and Lewis Running Rabbit). They are less influenced than I am, and they have a better concentration, a better understanding of what is involved in these ceremonies, because the ceremonies have been a part of their life. I, myself, was born in the Indian way of life but I was put into another, the white way of life, and then came back. As a result I am between two lives. When they talk about the moon I automatically think about those who have landed on the moon. I have a hard time—even though I believe what they say—when they talk about what the moon means to them, and this other half of me thinks of the astronauts. So it is with religion. Protestants have certain teachings from the Bible, and in a situation you go back to the Bible to find out how to get out of it. And when you ask too many questions they tell you, "Don't question, don't question, just believe", and in that faith there is a God, one God, Jesus Christ and white people. In the Indian religion there is God, the Indian people, and Nature in between. We do not have Jesus Christ, yet on the other hand he existed among those people who made up Christianity. The same God, the same human beings, though of a different race, but this has Christ, that has nature. So what did they call this? Paganism.

When Father Lacombe came here in the 1800's, all of a sudden he heard that another Minister, Rev. Tibbs, was coming through.

Father Lacombe headed south and told the Bloods to let the Short Robe through—"Don't bother him, don't listen to him". He told Crowfoot to let him pass through, and to not let him stay. (The Blackfoot called the Catholics Long Robes, and the people from the Church of England Short Robes). When Rev. Tibbs came through the Blood reserve from Fort Bent he headed up the Bull River, Blackfoot Crossing, to meet Crowfoot. He said to Crowfoot, "I bring the word of God to you people", and in the mind of Crowfoot he was a man of God, he carried the word of God. Crowfoot couldn't refuse Father Lacombe, so he told Rev. Tibbs: "Maybe go and see my friend Old Sun". Old Sun said, "I'll help you build your church, you are a man of God". But in the diaries it says: "I was face to face with a heathen, a sunworshipper, a devil-worshipper", and it hasn't changed today, despite the amount of research that has been done on Indian religions. People who write papers like this morning's presentation do not take the time to look at themselves; part of the answer lies in themselves. These are some of the things Joe Poor Eagle was telling me before you came in.

Before white man came God had given us directions on how to pray, but we did not have a Church like the white people. O.K., our Church was the land, the sky, the stars; our altar, the strongest object that God created, the sun. I have read that the Blackfoot believe the sun made the earth, the sun was the Creator, right off the bat. This shocked the hell out of the Christians, but I could say that Catholics and Protestants are bronze-worshippers or whatever, because they worship what is in front of their church. Then again I could say that the crucifix is a substitute for God; compare the crucifix and the sun—one is a reminder of sin and death, the forgiveness of sins, and the other is a giver of life, strength, growth, birth.

The presentation also dealt with legends, myths. To the Indian there are no legends, no myths. These are directives, and we understood them without need of explanations. There was a lot more ceremony or action than verbal instruction in Indian activities, like the medicine pipe ceremony. In the Protestant Church there is a lot of verbal direction and less action. O.K., the instructions were written in the white word—but people have a hard time interpreting the Bible. The story of the creation of the world was not written down for the Indians. It was *property*, or it was like this tape-recorder here. Give me 50 bucks and you can have it, or do something for me and I'll give it to you. But Indian

meaning worked differently. If somebody offers Joe Poor Eagle a
smoke from his pipe, he will smoke the pipe, if he wishes to, and
set the date for the transfer. The act had the meaning. The value
put on the transfer is not a price tag, only that it be four things:
four blankets, four horses, eight horses, forty horses. In the old days
there were lots of such concepts, and people could not understand
these concepts, because of the differences between the Indian and
the white ways of life. This is one of the things that strike us about
the presentations.

I read parts of the material in these pages to Joe Poor Eagle and
he was able to pick out little differences by the locality of the
ceremonies. As I said, language is another big factor. If I was an
English speaking person and I worked like hell for 15 to 20 years to
be able to speak Blackfoot just like my dad, there would still be a
big difference. I would not feel the language, but I would be able
to communicate with it. I might be able to express myself in English,
the knowledge of these people, but I do not feel the English
language when I speak. I have to think back in my own language
and recall the closet word. This is important when you want to set
something down in writing.

You asked them, "Is this a story you have remembered?" It is
not actually so. The question should have been: "Is this how you
were told it?" Elders were told many things, and shown many
things, and when they relate them for you, all of a sudden they will
stop, and you look at them, and they say, "No, I can't add anything
because that is all I was told." They will not try to interpret nor
assume, and that is where it stops.

[*Reverse of tape:*]

Through the years Indian people have learned to give just the
right information to researchers, and keep out the rest, because of
the approaches used. They say, "I'm here to find out about this and
that, can you tell me about it"—questions. They get in there and
open a tape-recorder, and sometimes Indian people will not give
the complete information. I knew a psychiatrist once named
Wolfgang Jellick who could treat all races: Chinese, white people,
Hungarians and what have you—but he could not treat Indians.
This was a challenge to him so he went to live with the Sallish on
the coast. Eventually he was accepted into some of the clans and
healing ceremonies. After seven years he came back, very
successful, with a culturally-based therapy for Indian people. The
Sallish taught him because he convinced them of his honest desire

to learn. The other question here, "Are there details left out or changed?" O.K., if Joe Poor Eagle and I were to sit in on another medicine pipe ceremony, we would not have the right to interfere. Joe Poor Eagle would say, "Oh! They do it a little differently, but that's how they do it." There are additions, things left out, because of their locality, and because of the people involved. "When would such a story be told?" These stories would be told to anyone who asked for one—he might pay for it—or when the elders gather to have the winter counts, and evaluate what has happened in the year. All the elders exchange stories that go as far back as when they used to record the winter counts on Buffalo hides. "Who would tell it?" It depends on what a person wants, or the proper time, the proper setting, the proper approach. There is no specific person who tells you everything. "How would he gain the right to tell it?" Well, as soon as it is told to him it becomes his property. He is responsible for it. "Would there be an exchange of goods for the privilege of hearing a story?" Yes. "What gifts would be given, and who would give?" It depends on who is doing the giving and receiving. A child, for instance, will receive, from the stories about Nabi, all the cunning and intelligence of the animal, and his other attitudes and characteristics brought out in the legend. Everything that Nabi did in these legends explain to a child why these things are there, but as he grows he keeps thinking about them, and he comes up with his own decisions why that thing is there. O.K., why is the crow all black? There's a story on that.

How come there's a lot of rocks coming down from the north right down to near High River? There's a story about that. Why is it there is one lone pine near Indian Creek? There's a story about that. "Can you tell us what these problems were and how one could overcome the bad by violating the rule?" A person is responsible for the stories he hears, and if he abuses them, people are reluctant to tell him more. He creates a negative image of himself in the eyes of the people who gave him this information. The same thing as when I gave him this tape-recorder, the next thing I know when I meet him it's all cut up, and there's no cord, and I ask him why? Well, we had a party and somebody threw it out the window. There's an image right there, so next time he comes to me for something, I have to think, next to my heart, and find an excuse not to give him what he would ask. These are some of the questions that were asked.

Even though the Indian people are changing with the times, making the transition, we retain that base we have always had. This stays the same, except for slight differences of locality. If a Blackfoot child grows up outside of his environment, deep inside him there will be an urge pushing him for the rest of his life, and if he does not find out what it is, this urge will trigger certain attitudes that we can see. We wanted to point this out. Also, people who have been raised outside of their localities are not good informants, even though they might study like hell to find out about themselves— and there is nothing wrong with that. Also, there are some things which are very sacred, or very personal, and you cannot give them away, or let anybody see them. What would happen if I walked into an old Catholic Church and told the priest that I would give him 50 bucks for his crucifix, because I was setting up a white museum?

Now when you put it down, you re-arrange it in your mind, it's called in your language editing, you edit it, the whole thing, or you would dramatise it so it would appeal to scholars, or appeal to people that publish these books, or appeal to a trend, or appeal to a set of rules that are set. Likewise, you take an Indian standing here and apply to him a set of rules that are already existing. If you change the format you're going to get one set of friends, scholars and such, who accept or touch it up. But this isn't right, doesn't sound good, because attitudes are already set here, and it's frustrating to get this information and then apply it in some other setting. And how you present it is the next question, how do you present it? If you say that Indian traditions are like furniture in a house, these people here, Joe Poor Eagle and Lewis Running Rabbit, can tell you how the furniture fits, in our house, what it is all about, how the furniture came into being, and who the people were who made it. So, I'll open the floor to your questions now.

[*Allan Wolf Leg translates for the elders*]

Is there anyone in here who feels offended, or is it good the way we have spoken?

Q.   — Maybe we feel a little guilty sometimes.

(J.P.E. and L.R.R. in Blackfoot)

[Allan Wolf Leg translates for the elders]

When we are talking about the Indian way of life and religion we put our hearts into it, and tell it as it is, because this is how we were told to tell it and show it. What was told by our forefathers is how we tell it now. The telling is intriguing, interesting and mysterious to the teller as he orders it in his mind. It is information that is not written down, but is fed to the child to grow up with.

A.W.L. — I would add to this that Indian songs must be memorized not only because they have to be preserved, but because they have an important place in the ceremonies. Take pow-wows for example—there's another English term!—Indian dancing, we might do a chicken dance, Frogs dance, a crowhawk, and so on. There is a different song for every dance, and every drummer has memorized the songs. Joe here has thousands of songs in his head. Ceremonial songs, and all the ceremonies he knows right through, from the first thunderings of springtime, when they open the medicine pipe, on through the Beaver bundle, tobacco ceremony, and sun dance. The sun dance is composed of many societies, all of whom have a place in the sun dance. At the sun dance there is only one place where I may put my tipi up, because my family belongs to a certain clan. There is only one place where the Horn Society may put up theirs, and only one time at which it may be done. There are many societies, one of which is the sponsor of the dance, and nobody says: "Hey! What do we do now?" Everybody knows what to do and when. All the songs are in their right place—the Horn Society sing theirs four times, every one of them. For nights they sit in their tipis before they come out to dance and they sing their songs, and sing for hours. Everybody goes to their tipis to sleep but lies awake listening to these songs. And if they make one mistake, everybody packs up and goes home. So these songs are memorized by all, and have a place.

If I ask Joe Poor Eagle to sing me the long knife song, or the wood song, the bell song, the rhine pipe song, or any portion of a by-gone ceremony, he would sing it. Joe here knows a thousand ceremonial and ritual songs besides chicken and grass dances. All this is memorized and passed on and on, and every year, every day, even this hour somebody is composing a song. So when you see an Indian dancing, listen carefully to the tunes, because some of them all look alike, but there is quite a difference in all of the songs.

(J.P.E. in Blackfoot)

A.W.L. — What you are looking at here is the future white man. The white man has our artifacts, our traditions, and in the next 50, 60, 70 years you will be Indians, and we will be white and start to go researching. (applause).

I didn't hesitate to come to this conference, but I asked if when it was my turn to ask questions, I could have information too. Are there any questions?

A.W.L. — I would like to elaborate on Poor Eagle. The Blackfoot are the only band within the Blackfoot nation who still have the tradition of the holy couple. Also, the Blackfoot retain complete knowledge of all their ceremonies, because they have been very cautious. They've given away only about 15-20%. The holy couple is the key to the start of a sun dance. Other reserves who have lost a partner, or do not have a sponsor, or someone to officiate at the ceremonials, go and try to find couples, go after them, and once you have asked them they cannot refuse. If they do not want to do it, they must hide. This summer the Blood Indians wanted a sun dance, and they were after Joe Poor Eagle and his wife all winter, spring and summer. Joe was watching the hill and took off to the bush when he saw them coming. (Laughter). The Peigans have not had a sun dance for the last 50 years, and all of a sudden they too were looking for Joe Poor Eagle and his wife. So all summer they were running around hiding in a bush. That is how it is done. It is not that Joe did not want to do it—it's tradition, and a challenge, like a game.

Some of the rituals, I heard somebody say, are very serious, but often in the ceremonies someone will crack a joke, and everyone will laugh. However, it always happens at the right time, the right thing is always said.

If I was about to enter a Society, I would approach a member of that Society, and by transfer I become his equivalent in one of the highest orders or richest societies of the Blackfoot, and he would give me his membership. This would make me a new member, but as long as I have this membership I may not see him, nor cross paths, share the same room, nor speak to him. Should this happen, it would be announced immediately and both parties of the family must exchange gifts. Then vows are sworn again, and the whole thing starts over. This was called the Peace Treaty and was the concept Indians shared when they signed the Treaty of 1877. However, when a person has membership in a Society, he can become a grandfather in that Society, and thus a valuable resource person. If he's asked to go help them out he would go. If the ceremonies went down, because those who were members died, and nothing was transferred, we had to abide by the rule. If the transfer ceremony had lapsed in that Society, there would be no safeguard against doing the traditions wrong, and someone who said he knew, but never received membership, would be a false informant. So the bond that such gift-exchanges form between the families of members of Societies safeguards against outside influence.

What you experienced today, you saw that man pray in the
theatre there, this person prayed with a pipe. What happened
actually, to his belief, or to the Blackfoot is, once a person does
that, the smoking of the pipe has given him the permission to share
some of the information with you people, but without that he
would keep most of the information and give you other less
important information, but because of that being performed this
morning, he is obliged to give you a lot more information than
what he intended. In the future if you want some old person to
look at the whole thing, just like this person is taping it, or if you to
tell somebody, please tell me about that and make sure somebody,
an elder Blackfoot, smokes a pipe to re-open it. It's like re-opening
a book, because if you don't do that, another elder will interpret it
a different way, and will not give you what is actually on the tape.
What he has shared with you today are like confessions, rather than
information. He is confessing some of his knowledge, some of his
experiences, things which were given to him and which took 30 to
40 years to accumulate, since he was a boy, so he has shared with
you because of that pipe.

Q.   — I have read quite a lot that has been written about
Blackfoot religion, Wissler, Duval, Grenel, but no writers have
anything to say about the supreme being. They speak of Nabi but
never of a supreme being. As a consequence of this white men
does not know what a Blackfoot means by this.

A.W.L. — Yes,Nabi ... It all depends on how you use the
phrase—we give the name Nabiquan to the white man when we
saw the way he acts—when the Mounties came out in 1874 we gave
them the name of Nabi—the trickster Nabiquan. When they came
close to the lakes near Winnipeg, and on the other side we had
many scouts, the Crees, Crows and even some Blackfoot. We
watched them run around each morning setting up their cannons,
pointing their rifles at nothing, blowing the horn, getting on their
horses, roaming the hills laughing their heads off. What word did
we give them? Nabine Nakiqua—it all depends on how you use it. If
you are praying, he-wo-si-quan nakiqua—there is god. Our God is
the same you people have recorded, and pray to, except you have
Jesus Christ and his disciples; but to us God has agents in Nature,
spiritual powers given to these people, like the Beaver from which
we get the Beaver bundle, or the Buffalo, the Horn Society, the
Pigeon Society, the Old Woman Society, the Brave Dog Society, and
so on, originated from something and everything has a meaning. In

the Horn Society each member wears something that means something, that came from some place. The things they use, the dance they do, all these originate from some place, or from some one of God's agents. This is Nature, but old anthropologists and Ministers call it devil-worship, paganism, where it's really the same thing.

My mother was a Catholic, but after my father came back from the war alive—he was wounded in the Sicily invasion—he vowed to commit himself to the Horn Society. He dedicated himself to this commitment, and as a result my mother was excommunicated. She went then to the Protestant Church, and a few years back my father was asked to come to the Roman Catholic Church to preach in Blackfoot. So, you see, times are changing and attitudes are changing. But harsh interpretations were given, harsh judgments all for reason of love, but not respect. When a person is trying to understand, he interprets, so a lot of white people see an Indian and say, "There's a damn drunken Indian," even though we only have a small percentage on skidrow in Canada. Also, they see something they can generalize because they are interpreting all the time.

I was once told by an elder that we are not made to understand. If the eagle and the gopher understood each other, the bear and the fish, man and the deer, everybody would starve, die off. But the key is respect. From the Blackfoot point of view, kids are taught respect. As a child, I look at that Bundle that's hanging in the house and I'm not supposed to cry there. I'm not supposed to run around, I'm not supposed to misbehave, I'm not supposed to swear as long as it's in the house. I didn't know anything about it, but I respected it. When our people go through a dance or a song they do not have to understand it, so long as they respect it. As a result, they don't go through the ceremony with someone standing over them checking them. If a discrepancy should come up it would be mentioned at the proper time and three or four elders would gather and talk about the bundle, the whole of it, and if they come to a story that one fellow tells differently, he says, "That's how I heard it." They would check each other that way.

Any more questions? Did I answer your question?

Q. — Thank you, yes.

Q. — As you can see I am a Cree. I think many people wonder about Wisakaychak and Nabi—what's the relationship between Wisakaychak or Nabi and God. This is very difficult.

A.W.L. — From the Blackfoot point of view, Nabi is never told, is never referred to as doing his deeds for God or for creation.

Q.   — He never prayed?

A.W.L. — No.

Q.   — He wasn't a religious man?

A.W.L. — He went out and did things. Nabi told his little friend the kit fox to give a big rock Nabi's shawl, because Nabi pitied the rock. Just then there was thunder, so Nabi told the fox to tell the rock to return the shawl after the rain stopped, but the rock refused. Nabi went up and took the shawl and put it on. Then Nabi and the fox started walking but the rock followed them, so they began to run like hell, and the little fox dove into a hole and covered up. This is why foxes live in holes. But Nabi kept on running and called to some sparrows to help him, which they did. They flew up and down taking chips off of the rock until the rock was too small to move, and Nabi was safe. He went up to the birds to thank them. They opened their beaks and Nabi fed them, but he was a little put off because the more he fed them the more they wanted, so he split their beaks. This is why the beaks of young birds look like they have been split. Nabi did all these things: he used Nature and altered Nature. He challenged it but he never prayed.

Any more questions?

(J.P.E. In Blackfoot)

A.W.L. — There are a lot of similarities between Indian tribes, but where they live makes some difference, their language, and other things. Cuthand mentioned this figure who is identical to our Nabi, he did other things, whereas in our legends he did these things, but they are similar. Ceremonies too are similar, yet with little differences. I have been to ceremonies, and have been the main person for five Blackfoot sun dances plus numerous other ceremonies, openings of bundles, and other things, but I have no right to tell the Bloods how to do these things, nor the Blackfoot in Brownie, Montana, nor the Crees. One time I experienced during a smoke ceremony on the Blackfoot Reserve a while back, with some Bloods participating, a Blood Indian who suddenly started telling us how to do the ceremony. But we ignored him and I continued to do it like I was taught to do it, the whole ceremony.

Q.   — I'm not familiar with the religious traditions of the natives. I am wondering whether you might give us a sample of one of the dances and its purpose, the differences due to locality.

A.W.L. — When the Prairie Chicken Society dance they lie on the ground, as prairie chickens lie on the grass. Once the music starts they start to go around, and as they pass each other they get up and dance. One will start first, then all of a sudden they all will be dancing. They form a queue of four or five, and make zigzag lines. They will circle and land, dance on their knees and take off again. When the drum stops they go back to their places and lie down again. They repeat this four times. I won't go into detail, because these things are the property of the Prairie Chicken Society, and I must respect this.

Blackfoot Seminar

September 17

This is Lewis Running Rabbit and this Joe Poor Eagle. I am Allan Wolf Leg, and we are all from the Blackfoot Reserve. These two have been involved with various social and ritual activities since childhood. They have both belonged to societies. They have experienced the transition of the Indian people, and yet they are both Catholics: they believe in their native religion but they are both Catholics. This is the situation of the Indian people across North America. The Government needs something to put down. They do not put down the white religions; they put you down if you are pagan. Yet there is no difference. It is the same God. Are there any questions?

A.W.L. — It is difficult to talk against any religion. If someone talks against his religion, does he talk against God? If there are bad feelings for a Minister because of his interpretation of the Bible, or his treatment of the people, the people will go against him. But this does not mean they talk against God. This is the very attitude that was present at the Conference of the Stoney. The other thing that you mentioned, about young people "going back" to the native religion, this is not actually the way it is, though you hear this phrase used all the time. You see, if they are born into it, that religion is never separated from their way of life. Also, the Indian way of life and religion are one and the same, and this is a day to day process, which is what culture means. The heritage, the philosophies, the message that came from God through Nature to the Indian people, these are the same as what Jesus Christ means to Christians. God came through Jesus Christ and his disciples to the people just as He came through His agents in Nature to the Indian people. The latter is called paganism. Carl here, myself, and these two, and those two ladies over there live in between two attitudes, and we see this truth plain as the day coming. You live on the other side but do not try to dislocate yourselves from what is part of you, and even if you are not actively practising some discrimination, it's always there.

Q.   — I have been talking with some of you beautiful people, and my friends all have rather large families. Several of those with whom I am travelling have said that their children or their parents have not carried on traditions from their parents or grandfathers, or aunts and uncles. This seems very sad to me. What is eventually going to happen? Speaking as a white person, I would like to know what may be done to preserve these beautiful traditions. Let's face it, we are all getting older and the elders will not be around forever.

A.W.L. — It is unfortunate. You have asked me two questions. Firstly, I might say that in the 1800's the Catholic faith and the Protestant faith came to our reserve. Lacombe set up his headquarters on the east end of the reserve, and Tibbs set his up on the west end, dividing the reserve in half. They built schools which still stand today—the Crowfoot and the Old Sun schools. The life was harsh. You go to school at the Indian school and you do not go home for ten months, and you pray 12 to 18 times a day. For discipline you would have to kneel for hours in the church. Religion, as a disciplinary weapon, was forced upon you, and your language, your language was all of a sudden called evil, and you were dissuaded from speaking it. If you used it, you were punished. Any child in school who had parents taking part in Indian ritual, well, the parents never got it, but the kids got punished.

Lines are given in school for throwing spitballs or something. In the Indian schools, lines were given not to believe in your own way of life. Most churches were like that. When I was a child I spent only one night a week at home, though later on, in the fifties, this was increased to two nights. Ten years of our lives, ten months of the year. All there is to hope for is to reach the age of 16 when you can quit school. When you leave school all of a sudden you are exposed to the white world. Suddenly you begin to realize that Jesus Christ wasn't an Englishman, or an Italian, but a Hebrew with dark skin, and you react against them, and your language is important to you—all these things. As a result you turn inwards and grow a shell. If you are called a drunk, because you yield to the whole situation, you shake your head and agree, because you have accepted life on the skids. If you get a chance to work on the oil rigs, you do that, but you will always live the life of the reservation. Your parents lived this life, and they did not know how to break the shell, or did not know how to cope with things, or did not want to trouble other people with their problems. Their children follow suit. However, there are some, like Joe Poor Eagle here, or like those over there, or those, who, later in their years, manage to break out of that shell, and their children change too. It moves back and forth like this. That's your first question.

How does one help preserve the traditions? It starts in the home, your home. It starts with you and your children, your relatives, neighbors, friends, the people you work with; your community, your province, your country. Show positive and sincere feelings towards Indian children, or even a person on skid row. Do not say: "Oh that man, he's dirty!" Those people whom one might hold one's breath until he has walked past them—these people are my greatest teachers. They ask me for 25 cents and I ask them where they come from, and what they are doing in that place, and I give them 25 cents. I encourage them. All it costs is 25 cents, but that is the way of it. By ignoring, avoiding, hating, you multiply one person into a thousand such people, and you multiply yourself a thousand times. It is no use giving money—say, donating 100 bucks to the Blackfoot Reserve—because it all goes into the books controlled by Indian Affairs, or into certain Indian Affairs sevices. You don't know where your money goes, maybe to a local politician for one good happy trip. It's no use that way.

I have seen people who tried to help an Indian family who got into a situation with which they could not cope, and everybody got hurt in the end. I have seen this a lot. So it is best to start at home by taking a good look at yourself, evaluate yourself, and whatever history you can find, and so on. I once said this same thing on a panel in Calgary, and a Sociology professor who had worked with the Indians for 30 or 40 years took what I said to heart and went home and wrote down, as truthfully as he knew how, all of his feelings. He did this to test himself. He found that he was actually very prejudiced.

This is related to the presentations we heard today. These presentations, I know, are made with good intentions, but the researchers do not feel the language, and they do not know themselves. I could never agree that papers in university courses help a student understand. But take Carl here. Carl couldn't be working in a university unless he knew himself. At least I know that Carl knows himself. If you ask him who he is, he will tell you, and if you ask him what the rituals are, he will tell you. "What is an Indian"? He will tell you, though there are personal things he will not tell you. You would not get that far with some scholars and professors. Somebody asked Carl to react to an Ojibwa paper, but even if Carl knows that there is something wrong with it, he cannot interfere. People like Wissler had no right to interfere with the Blackfoot dances, because he was not invited by those people. So there is this. In the English language schools some people feel that

we are withholding information, and they are automatically on the
defensive, and scholars begin interpreting, without ever doing a
dance.

Have I answered your question?

Q.   — My son is sixteen, and in the classroom he has good
friends among the native kids. My feeling is—being a white person
who must interpret at second hand, of course—that the average
teenager does not have the knowledge to preserve the traditions.
But—they have persisted despite those religious schools you spoke
of! On the other hand I am afraid that we are losing it now.

[*Carl addresses the audience*]

Indian people have been doing these things for hundreds of
years, knowing that it is right in our sixth sense, that feeling sense.
We feel our children learning, we feel their responses to the elders;
we feel the relations we have with natives of our own clans and of
other tribes. Also, you could call the next native experience a
period of white/native relationship. The pilgrims who landed on
the rock came to practice their religion in freedom, but they
denied the Indian that same freedom. They fell down on their
knees to give thanks to the Great Spirit for giving them this great
free land to live in, and then they fell upon the aborigines. Maybe
Helen will try to explain the next aspect, the missionary period, and
how it was an attempt to convert the Indian to Christianity. I would
only like to say that to me our religious ceremonies are more
spiritual than the other. I am a Christian too; I am happy to be able
to say that I have two religions.

The next period was an extermination period. I am sure you
have all heard the old saying, "The only good Indian is a dead
Indian." The pilgrims wanted more and more of the Indian's
land—pushed farther and farther into Indian territory. They found
out that the Indian was hard to get rid of, and so they put us on
reserves. They wanted us out of the way so they could practise their
"progressive" way of life. In the name of progress we were isolated
instead of having been included in the whole.

Then came a period in which the Federal Governments both
above and below the border determined that the Indian should
have the same housing, the same life-style, as the town people.
Many treaties were drawn up and signed which guaranteed certain
rights and privileges to the Indians; then the Government hoped to
do away with these treaties and forget about us all together. That
period is finally coming to an end. We are going to see that the

treaties are enforced—for another 100, or 200, or 500 years—whatever.

Today is an era of participation. Elders everywhere are being included in the education of the children, whether in an all day school in Old Sun, or Cluny or the Blood reserve. The Federal Government likes the elders to participate in the activities that it funds. However, the Government has not yet agreed to fund the native/English language program for the Reservation Schools. But we do get a little, a little at a time, with which to preserve our language and obtain some of the good things of life that are enjoyed in the towns. We hope that the general public will participate with us, instead of standing aside, aloof, waiting to see which way we will go. If they do that they will not see those things that are going to happen, and things are going to happen because we have leaders like Allan here.

There is something happening in our society that has never happened before. There are some good things that the Indian people have which are being included in our society. The town society—superficially at least—are trying to grab hold of our way of life, that is arm and arm in nature. Indian life-styles are included in your educational systems, but you seem unwilling to give us the credit of having made a genuine contribution. You want to think you thought of it yourselves. For hundreds of years the Indian people have longed to communicate to the white society a respect for the land and its resources. Today finally you have seen what we have been saying about living in harmony with nature. So, thanks to these elders and people like Allan Wolf Leg—who are promoting businesses on the reserve—the general public and the Government can no longer take advantage of the poor natives, who only want to sit down and enjoy the reserve and feel at home, in a way of life that Indians have created.

We will make it as long as we are given the opportunity to participate, and everybody keeps an open mind, and everybody works together.

A.W.L. — In fact, an Indian warned one of the big oil companies near Calgary of the problems of oil there in 1921, to be exact. I have seen the letter.

Q. — Was the vision quest an important part of the Blackfoot culture? I would just like to hear whatever the elder wishes to say about the vision. I do not want to ask him any specific questions.

A.W.L. — No. When I'm talking to you I feel your head is upside down, the hair should be on the other side. No offence. (He translates this question into Blackfoot). In Blackfoot your question doesn't mean anything. Vision only means something to those people who dream, in Blackfoot.

Q.   — That's why I asked the question. Yet how vision affects a person's life—or, particularly, I'm interested in the contemporary culture as compared to the traditional culture—if there has been a change. There hasn't?

A.W.L.   — No, once two fellows, one this man beside me, and another from the Glenbow Museum were fishing on the Bow River, in 1948, standing on the river in bright daylight. All of a sudden one saw a tipi directly across from where they were standing, and the one called to the other: "What do you see, what do you see?" And the other said, "Yes, I see it," they both saw it, but they saw totally different designs on the tipi, and it was in plain sight. Now this was a vision, when they were fully conscious. They checked each other out, in fact, for 29 years. Today we can see the one tipi up in the reservation with the visionary design on it, but his friend has not put his up yet. One saw a yellow tipi with a rainbow design, the other saw a snake design.

That is one vision. In olden times visions—either conscious or dreaming—would be taken to the elders to be interpreted. Not after the first time, but after several—four times. These visions had to be recurring, and sometimes it took 20 years till a fourth dream came. Most of the societies in this area were begun by a dream given, or powers given. These days it is rare to receive a power from Nature, though it happens. This is as you might expect it to be, since modern Albertan society has driven the animals far away from man. Also, many people at one time can be affected by a vision.

The elders are able to interpret visions because they have a right to. They have a right to interpret and develop them, and if they did not have this right and this capability, people would fear dreams and visions. In our language the word for fear is respect, a very high respect for what is on the borderline. You fear all the possible consequences.

O.K., the artifacts used in ritual ceremonies, the ones in the Museum, have never changed. They are the same as they were when they were first created, and nobody has the right to change them. If a bundle has all these animals, nobody has the right to add another animal, or change a story. They are very real. For example, scholars call all the stories we use to explain the contents of the Beaver bundle myths. But I could say that the stories in the Bible are myths if I did not understand what they meant. However, I have no right to call them myths. Take the crucifix. It is real. O.K., the artifacts in the Beaver bundle are very real. These things are there and I would respect them for what they are.

Q. — "Myth" in academic jargon refers to what has a real meaning, real words behind real action. The Christian explanation of man is myth, by myth we mean it is true, not like science.

A.W.L. — Well, what I mean by not real is that you cannot touch it. It is not there, but it is in your mind.

Q. — It is the same with reality.

A.W.L. — Yes, and even though it is in your head it is passed down whenever it is given to somebody.

Q. — I was told the use of the word "myth" that I am using. We understand what we are talking about, but the dictionary definition is what most people use: something that is not true.

Q. — Oh, we have the same problem in our classroom, we use the word "myth"and I still think it means something different from what he means.

Q. — I have seen one Blackfoot ceremony, and I kept thinking how little was the information I was given about sweat lodges among the Cree. There women are never allowed.

A.W.L. — That's Cree. The same thing happens with the Blackfoot though. There is a women's Society completely composed of women. They have a lodge and their own rituals. It was not formed because someone noticed that women did not have one, it was created with a woman in it. The Horn Society did not exclude women because women had a place in the original story. They follow these stories, and they take materials from Nature to act. It would be the same thing if you take the story of Jesus and orient it to what he did, and act it out.

Q. . — This morning the speaker mentioned that women who were at the end of their menstral cycle could not take part. You interpreted to me that this was because it was unclean, and I bothered you when I thought that this did not seem fit, since at this time of the month women are much more powerful because of the life presence in her.

A.W.L. — But you are interpreting this. To us this is how it was told to us. This is how they are doing it; it is the same with the white women. Don't question faith, but believe. So if it says that in the original story, that's how it is.

(J.P.E. in Blackfoot)
A.W.L. — You have seen a sun dance, you have heard about them, and you want to know how a woman fits in. If you draw a pyramid

of a sun dance, marking off the place of each society, each person right up to the overall leader, the leader will be a woman. If no woman wants to sponsor a sun dance there would be no sun dance. If Joe Poor Eagle's wife does not want to sponsor a sun dance, it does not take place. She has sponsored five sun dances.

Q.   — Thank you. Why did you say yesterday that it was part of the ritual for the sponsor of a sun dance to try to avoid being asked to be a sponsor, or does that refer to the singers.

A.W.L. — It is not that it is a burden to be avoided. It is more like a game, but those people I spoke of yesterday were called to sing the sun dance songs for the sponsor, they were not being called to be sponsors. Then again, we would never hesitate—to respond to such a religious commitment, it is part of trying to avoid it for the sake of the ritual itself. When I talk about the sun dance you have to remember that each tribe is different. You cannot generalize and say: "This is how the Plains Indians do it." The Crees will demand that a certain one be the sponsor. With the Blackfoot the holy woman is the sponsor. Besides there is only one person who can dedicate himself to the centre pole in our sense of the sun dance. So the person who is tied to the pole has dedicated himself to that pole, and when it goes up to God his commitment is to God. Today anthropologists include this ceremony with the sun dance, though it is not really a part of it.

(J.P.E. in Blackfoot)

A.W.L. — You see when they look at that bundle, that Beaver bundle, well—the paper was good the way it was written but from Joe's point of view there were three mistakes in the whole thing, but he won't say—you made a mistake here.

Q.   — What about the term "medicine man?"

A.W.L. — I do not want to say that anyone has made a mistake here, but some terminologies do not fit. You take a dictionary word and try to make it express Indian activities. Take the phrase "medicine man", which to some means witchcraft or whatever. A person in that field is born into it, and stays in it all through life. As he grows, and as he grows old, always things are happening, things related to you. All of a sudden you have got a baby name, and as you grow you belong to different societies, you earn this or that, always getting new names, maybe six, eight names on your way up. Crowfoot when he died had two names, all related to deeds, but he actually had three titles ...

(Tape Change)

A.W.L. — Actually the term "medicine man" corresponds to "doctor" in your language, Doctor of Science, Doctor of Medicine, Doctor of Music, a foot-doctor...it is the same thing. They are professional people, specialists. As they grow, they acquire more and more knowledge, and they make it to the level of medicine man because they have acquired knowledge—they've made it. You could compare with the tree trunk, here's the bark, very fragile on the outside, and you can do the tree a lot of harm, but in the centre, the heart, that feeds the tree, that's these people. They are the teachers, the ones that cure. Did I answer your question?

Q.   — So there are different levels, steps of medicine man?

A.W.L. — No, not steps, it's a development. They can only help based on their experience, in their areas of experience.

Q.   — How many people within the Blackfoot today have become medicine men?

A.W.L. — Joe here and his wife are examples. Joe has a specialty. I am not, I am a student just like any other anthropologist.

Q.   — Are there many left in this Province?

A.W.L. — These are old fellows here, trying to understand what is round them. They are willing to share the things they know and they are tired after three days. We have been here since Wednesday, and they have not moved. They sat, they spoke, gave, yet in this room there are many impatient people, not ready to commit themselves. They just come in, pick and go back, just like a bird, take something back to their nest each time. Any more questions?

Q.   — Are you beginning to become a medicine man?

A.W.L. — Not necessarily. It is a profession, not likely a career. They are born into it, grow into it, grow old with it. They when they grow old they are going to have responsibility, so as they go in their lives they learn as much as they can because when they get old, they will have something to give back to people, and not just because they're Indians, it's human nature. What would happen if a coyote is born in a cave, doesn't want to leave for five-nine years and all of a sudden he should be leader of the pack. But the young will attack him because he's weak, not experienced, and by the time he's twelve, all of a sudden he's all by himself. It's only human nature, but it's the way to share and survive in a society. Another thing is, not everyone can be a medicine man, so some become consultants, advising and being resource people. Even though they do not have a specialty, they do have knowledge. But you can't compare that to a career.

Q.   — But the way you assist, the people give it a role in the society ...

A.W.L. — Well, maybe way back somebody got a vision, got the power with certain herbs to cure certain things, and along the way he passed it by transfer to another person. This person doesn't have to see the vision, but you transfer the whole power, he's taught the ritual. Sometimes the medicine man decides there's nobody around him or it's getting too late to teach somebody and he takes the alternative of getting it recorded in a white man's way, a film, or white man's words, even though there's hundreds of native people around him, it's his decision.

[*Moderator*]
   Our appreciation for all your help. Thank you.

Cree Seminar

September 17

I am chairing this meeting, this symposium. My name is Stan Cuthand. I was born in 1889 on the little Pon reserve on the South Battle River. I am a Cree, and I will translate for these fellows here (Emil Piapot and Marius Nanipowisk).

First of all he wants to say something about offerings. He says his grandchild gave him offerings this morning at the pipe ceremony. These offerings are often given to elders, sometimes they are given tobacco. I will take these offerings home, and then will take and hang them in a clean place among the trees. That is the usual custom.

He says he has spoken to the Almighty about what he has been doing here. When he goes back he will do the same things with his son (i.e., the other elder). He is always searching for work in terms of native religion, and when his children have seen what he has done, they will know and follow what he is trying to do. He says he is always thinking about his children and grandchildren, because his days are getting shorter. He says he wants to make things easier for them, and he speaks for them. He says his father told him many years ago that he would see many changes, and that times would be very difficult.

Many times he has given thanks for life and knowledge gained in the past. Elders have told him many things when he was a young man, such that whenever you are offered a pipe, never refuse it, learn all you can about it, learn how to use it. He has always obeyed these instructions. Once an old man named Strong Eagle told him that, if he would see changes in this life, he should use the pipe and all the other instructions the elders would give to him, and he has tried to do this. He says that when he feels weak, he often feels that the Almighty supports him, but he does not want to boast about this. He just feels that the Almighty does help him and support him in his experience. Just before he left home, he went to a clean place and had a pipe ceremony with sweet grass and prayed to the Almighty for support and guidance on the journey, and at this conference. He says he knows nothing but what the elders have passed down to him, though there was a Roman Catholic Church at home, and the priest spoke Cree. This priest taught him many things and tried to convert him—but he stuck to the elders' teachings. He says, "I'm not against the white man's religion, I think of my grandchildren and my children, and to tell them what has been taught me through the elders, he says these things were given to us, the pipe, the sweet grass, tobacco, and offerings, the elders' teachings, and I try to do the same. Now we have two Churches at home, and sometimes worry that my grandchildren will be converted. If I were a Chief on the reserve perhaps I would tell them to leave the reserve."

Now there are not many elders left, but whenever he meets someone older than him, he tries to learn as much as he can from their words. He says that people come to him from as far away as the United States to ask him to pray for them with the pipe and the sweet grass. "They say speak for me grandfather, so I speak for them. He says he is very happy that there are some young people here who come to him and they call me grandfather, he says I am very proud of that, he says I'm not afraid of being called grandfather. Some of this tobacco here, he said, was given to him by a friend in this conference who was not well. This friend wants prayer for her, he says I am very happy to be able to do that, and I am really glad to see all of you.

I see a lot of white people in this group, and some of them I feel as if I had known them before, there is a tremendous fellowship in this group, and I am glad to have that kind of fellowship with all of you. I think of my grandchildren I'm glad to see them, and they come to me and they want me to pray for them, so I pray for them. You hear me talk about the elders and you hear me talk about many things, but these things have been passed on to me from the elders."

Q.   — I'd like to ask a question, or even make a comment on what happened yesterday. Through that whole session I could not figure out just what was happening, something, most people were unhappy, and there was something that went wrong, and then on the way home I thought, and I hope I'm right, that what had happened was when Mr. Piapot talked to us we weren't ready to listen, we were trying to talk about whether the legend of Wisakaychak were accurate, whether Wisakaychak was a small or a great spirit and so on, and it occurred to me afterwards that perhaps you can tell us Mr. Piapot. You told the story about your father being baptised by the rain and telling the Priest that he had been baptised by God, and you asked us to say what we felt about this, but we didn't, something happened, and we talked about other things.

Now it seems to me that the whole purpose of the meeting was to find out more about native religion, about the basis, the belief in God and so on, and we missed that point, I think we should have known that elders speak by illustration, stories or parables, the elders are teachers, some of the great teachers in history started perhaps with Christ and the Greeks, and some of the Wisakaychak stories are parables and so on. Now what I got from your statement afterwards, finally, was that to the Indian, God is the Universe, God of the Universe or Nature if you want, or the Universe is God, and that when your father stood and made an act of will to be baptised by the clouds or by God he was getting a better baptism than otherwise. I think Professor Hultkrantz told us yesterday morning of the idea of the relationship between nature and God, God being the true being, almost, in that sense and I felt sorry that we missed that yesterday. Is that right Mr. Piapot?

S.C. — What was it that you did not like yesterday?

Q. — NO! It wasn't that I didn't like it, it's just that I couldn't understand why there didn't seem to be any communication!

S.C. — You weren't listening?

Q. — Well, we were listening, but not hearing right.

S.C. — You misunderstood?

Q. — Well . . . yes. Let's not get involved with words.

S.C. — Yes. But do we need to harp on it?

Q. — No, I don't want to harp on it, but I want to say that I learned from here the basic thing that we are trying to get in this conference is to try to understand the native's attitude towards God, and I missed it yesterday, and I'm saying that I caught on finally.

S.C. — We tell stories, but you people write it, and very often the written form doesn't come out the way it should be. That's the only thing that he doesn't agree with. Sometimes when you write a legend it's through interpretation, that's where the gap is, that is my own comment.

Q. — I was here yesterday, and what came through to me was this. To the Indian there is a Great Spirit, a supernatural being, which he called God. But this God is not Nature, as such. The spirit of God is in Nature but God is over and above it. Is this not what you were saying yesterday?

S.C. — That and other things.

(Tape Change)

[*The interpreter speaks*]
S.C.   — Any one else?
S.C.   — He is going to tell a story. (E.P. in Cree)
S.C.   — Once, when he was feeling ill, his wife told him to see what he could do for himself. You must have knowledge, knowledge of medicine, knowledge of spirit. You must have a totem to help you. "Do something for yourself," she said. "No! I just want to sleep," he said. So he went to sleep and he had a dream in which he saw an old man sitting down, facing the setting sun. The old man was whittling away at something with a knife. The grandfather turned around and said to him: "Do you know what this is?" And when he said he did not, the old man said: "It is a herb—medicine." And he said, "You people are making a mistake, not using the herbs. The Almighty gave herbs for you to use, and you are not using them." That was the first part of the dream. In the second part when he opened his eyes, he saw a woman standing before, him, dressed in the old style, with very long braids, but she did not speak to him, and he did not speak to her. She just stood there like a vision in the room. The next morning, when he woke up, he felt much better, he recovered.
        — And that's all from me, he says . . . .

(E.P. in Cree)
S.C.   — You know, when an old man talks as he's sitting, give him the Bible, give him a little tea, it makes the old man feel happy, and if you want an old man to tell a story O.K., (says something in Cree) here's the Bible, tell us a story, and you sit close to him (says something in Cree) he starts telling a story, that's the style, but he's so far away from everyone in this room.

    He says that he has had all his experiences in his life in the form of visions, seeing things. He has tried to do his best, doing what the elders told him to do, trying to live right. He says he is not boasting—this is his experience. Any questions?
Q.   — Would he be what they used to call a medicine man?
S.C.   — No, he would not call himself a medicine man. They existed a long time ago but not any more.
Q.   — Are there any left?
S.C.   — No,

[*The interpretor converses with another Cree, in Cree*]. When you speak of medicine men, you might say there are some, though they are rare. Those who sponsor sun dances and other rituals are not called medicine men, but they perform the ritual dances. They are rare now, too. Another thing is that the rituals are sometimes interpreted differently these days. He says that some of the other elders will use alcohol, which is not good.

Q.   — Is there a difference between holy men and medicine men?

S.C.   — I do not think the word "holy" applies. It is hard to translate the term. Perhaps, when one speaks of priestly funtions. Does a priest consider himself holy?

Q.   — Yes, at least as far as I know.

S.C.   — I do not think a priest who is humble would call himself holy. He is a person who sets himself apart to perform certain rituals, because he has to experience and dream in order to be given the authority to do this. I think that would be more to the point. No, there is nobody who should be called holy, because that holy person would be a very whole person, clean. We're attended by original sin, imported from the Church. (Laughter).

[*Dr. Hultkrantz from floor*]

May I say just a few words in connection with this. I think it is in a quotation of Dr. Huldram because really we use the words Holy Man for certain (Lakato) Medicine Men who have just these priestly functions, for instance, Black Elk was one of them; and then you have the gentleman who mentioned that, but the term in the Lakato language is Wakan and that means supernatural power, and not holy, so this is not correct.

S.C.   — Yes, a person endowed with supernatural powers. However, some people misinterpret this, saying that we must be superstitious—but let's not get into that. Any other questions or comments?

Q.   — You mentioned that medicine men are scarcer nowadays, men who have supernatural powers are scarcer. Is this because conditions have changed?

S.C.   — Yes, they have. Well there is a renewal within the Indian society, it's a resurgence, it's just like the resurgence of the charismatic movement, they believe in miracles and in healing, and I think this is happening to the Indian people.

Q.   — We do not have enough details on the different rituals, and how they came to be, and so on. Could you elaborate on this problem of rituals?

S.C.   — There are many rituals. The ways the elders explained this was in story form, a very long story, and so he is reluctant to start on rituals. It is much the same thing as the Bible—many facets of ideas—and the Bible is pretty big. "As the old people used to say," he says, "it's a long trip." You can keep on telling stories forever, there are so many stories about rituals. You could never finish, it is never-ending. Tell a story about how rituals came into being, and you have got a *long* story.

Q.   — Mr. Chairman, yesterday a man from C.B.C. mentioned that he felt there was a revival going on, an increase of interest in the Indian religion. I wonder if Mr. Piapot could tell us whether there is such a revival today, or not, and what the native point of view might be.

(E.P. in Cree)
S.C.   — His daughter, Buffy Ste. Marie, was away from home a long time, in the United States. When she did come home, she said there was a resurgence there in native religion. The idiom is: "The native religion is coming back home." She wrote a song about the sweet grass, the drumstick and the drum for us, and she sang it last summer on July 1st. He says it is coming home, and that is the way he feels about it. It is getting stronger, he says.

Q.   — And does he feel that it was dying out, at one time?

(E.P. in Cree)
S.C.   — Last fall the Mormons showed a film of a sun dance in which the commentator, a young man, said that the custom was dying out. They seemed to be laughing at it, and he told them that they did not know much about it, and that they should not laugh at it. It was not dying out, but coming back. The sun dance was outlawed by the Indian Act of the 1920's, and it went underground. It survived that way, because, instead of having it eight consecutive days as it was supposed to be, they chopped it up. In the midst of a potlatch, when the mounties showed up, we put everything away, pretended nothing was happening. When he left, we started up again.

(E.P. in Cree)
S.C.   — He says that his mother taught him that the Almighty is always watching us, always knowing what we do. He was taught by his mother. The elders taught this too. They would gather in a circle very often, and select an old man to speak. He would speak, and this is the way he was taught. Elders were not taught to read and write, they were taught by tradition. When he was selected he

would say a prayer and worship, then he would speak, that was the style.

S.C. — Now he says it is your turn to talk.

Q. — I would like to make a comment or observation. It seems to me, as he mentioned earlier, that white man's mind is longing and longing to go analytic. They seem to have different perceptions. Their world is different because of this, and I was just wondering what the feeling is? Can a non-Indian understand an experience, the tradition and the beliefs? Like the attitude seems to be that the non-Indians can't really understand, it seems to be the reaction to the papers presented, they don't really understand what we are talking about. Can they understand, I mean can they be shown? Can there really be meaningful communication at the educational level?

S.C. — Yes, they have to change gears, though. The Indian goes 30 mph, the white man goes 80. An Indian will go into the forest and not eat or drink for four days. He is not in a hurry to get back. His mind is totally immersed in what he is experiencing, the spiritual world. Of course many white men go on retreat now, and they go into a room and stay the week-end. They want to be absolutely alone, but the door never gets locked. They can go outside any time they want to.

Q. — I do not think that the word "retreat" actually translates the Indian experience. The white man closes himself off. The Indian is seeing the creation of God. The white man shuts out nature. The Indian experience seems much greater.

S.C. — We are wasting time here because we are not getting a response from the learners and the observers. Are we supposed to stay here until four o'clock?

Q. — I believe most of us would like to stay for ten minutes or so. Would you like to ask for people's opinions?

S.C. — I keep asking them to ask but it is hard to get them to talk. He says he is going to go outside first—an idiom—he is going to the toilet. (Laughter).

Q. — A few times he has spoken of going to a clean place. What does that mean?

S.C. — Oh! What he means is that he goes to a place where nobody lives, a place in the wilds. An uninhabited place that is not polluted. That is what he means.

S.C. — I'll be the elder for a while, O.K.?

You want to hear a story? Here's a story:

Long ago a small band of Crees were crossing the prairie. An old lady was with them, and with her there was a small child, a boy. She was leading a big dog on a leash, and the dog was pulling the child in a travois. All of a sudden the old lady lost her hold on the leash, and the dog ran off to chase the Buffalo. The Buffalo stampeded. She lost the child. The dog went for miles and miles chasing the Buffalo until he stopped to drink from a water hole. There were no wheels on the travois, just two sticks. These got stuck and the dog crawled out of his harness, leaving the child behind in the carryall. The dog came home but the child was never found.

In the meadow there were two bachelors, an old bull and a young bull—we speak of Buffalo as if they were people—and as they grazed around they heard the child crying. The old Buffalo said, "You know, I feel sorry for this child. Let's raise him up as our own." The young bull said, "No, let's kill him because the human beings are always after us, they always kill us. If I get there first I will kill him." So *M'qsayno Kumais*, the smarter of the two, said, "Alright, let's have a race. If I get there first, we will raise him, if you get there first you can do whatever you like." They raced and the old bull got there first because he tricked the other, he made him stumble. He pushed him into a gopher hole and got there first. The young bull was very angry.

— You made me stumble. That's why I came here last.

— No. That's not the agreement, the agreement was whoever got here first would win. Now we will raise the child.

So reluctantly the other agreed and they took the child and carried him on their backs. They went and got berries from trees and they raised him. He became very handsome and tall—heroes are always very handsome and tall. One day old *M'qsayno Kumais* said, "Now we are going to the setting sun. You will see many of us coming together as we always do, but mind your P's and Q's, because you are not one of us. And do not look at the women. Buffaloes are very jealous of their women."

After four days they got there, and there was a tremendous number. The young man was told to stay and wait on a rock while the bulls enjoyed themselves fighting over the women. It was a huge happy festival. Early one morning he became very thirsty, and when he looked down into a pool beside the rock he saw a beautiful woman coming down to fetch water. He ran down to her, but he remembered what the old bull had said. So he always kept his head low, he never looked at her. She was very beautiful, you know. He asked for some water and she gave him some, but he always looked at her feet. As soon as she had filled her bag she went up the hill and started yelling: "That young man *M'qsayno*

Kumais is raising was flirting with me!" She happened to be the wife of the white bull, the chief's wife, and the mighty bull was angry when he heard this. She was a trouble maker (women are often pictured as troublemakers). *M'qsayno Kumais* came running down and chided the young man severely. "He will challenge you to a duel, and you will have to fight him to the death, for he will try to kill you." So the next day the two bulls took him into a clearing. "This is where he will meet you," said the old bull. "Now you will have to become one of us. Do as I say. Roll towards the high noon." The young man rolled towards the high noon four times. "Now roll four times towards the setting sun." When he had done this he was told to roll four times towards the south, and four times towards Venus, the morning star. Then the young man got up and he was a Buffalo, a beautiful animal and very strong. "Now you are one of us. See the big crowd piling in, and there is the white bull." The old bull told the young man where the white bull's weakness was, right behind the front legs. "If you can catch him there, you can kill him. You are young, he is older, but he is very strong, very powerful." So he came closer and closer with his head down and his horns are just sparkling in the sun, and he says, "You will challenge me, you spoke to my wife. I'm going to walk around you four times, and then I'm going to fight." The old bull yelled at his son, he says, "Watch him, he's tricky, keep pacing him." So the mighty white bull walked around four times, and finally he charged, and they locked horns, and the white bull pushed him back, and then all of a sudden he pushed him back and they pushed back and forth, and sometimes their front legs would lift up like this, and this is where you have to watch if you were a Buffalo. Apparently, when they do that if someone loses balance the other one will just hit him. Anyway, they fought all day towards about four fingers high, the sun was coming down, about four inches from the horizon, they were just panting, sometimes they stopped and they faced each other. The old bull says, "Now remember what I told you, son, try your best." So again they locked horns, and they raised them up and he thrust his head, knocked him off balance, and he hit him right behind the front feet, and the white bull says, "Oh! you got me, you got me," he says, "Which way will I fall," and the young man says, "I don't give a damn which way you fall, fall whichever way you want to," he says, "I'll fall towards the setting sun," and he fell over and died. It's just like an opera, you know. Then the whole community was for attacking the young man for killing their chief, but old *M'qsayno Kumais* said, "No. We will take him away so that you will never have to see him again."

The three went west towards the South Saskatchewan River, but not before the young man was turned back into a man by repeating the rolling in the grass. When they came to the flat prairie the old bull made him roll for a third time, four times towards the high noon, four times towards the setting sun, four times towards the south, and four times towards the morning star, at which he was once more a mighty Buffalo. Then the old bull said, "Sit down. You cannot go back to your people. We raised you but you are not one of us, so you will have to be something else. But you will always be remembered. Your people will find you, and they will always come back to you." Then he prayed and blessed the young man, and waved his leg over him and he became a great rock.

In the meantime, the old lady had asked the medicine man to ask the spirits what happened to the boy. So they built a lodge, they had the shaking of the tent ceremony, and then the spirits came and said they knew the whole story. They said that they could find him in the setting sun along the South Saskatchewan River. So a small band of Cree went and travelled for many days. Their leader said, "We will find him because he is a spirit, he is drawing us." "We will find him," they all said. All of a sudden they came upon a great rock shaped like a bull Buffalo. "That's the one! That's the one!" they all shouted, and they camped there. And every year after that they camped there, having the pipe ceremony and leaving gifts and offerings to the spirit of the lodge.

In the late fifties Prime Minister Baker fulfilled his promise to have the river dammed. The C.F.C.Q. station in Saskatoon raised money and public support to have the sacred rock excavated and moved to higher ground. However, it was much bigger under ground—about 60 tons—so the engineers drilled holes in it and blew it up. They took the broken pieces and set them up where it was safe. I still have a piece of that rock, given to me in 1969, when I became Superintendant of Community Affairs with the Department of Community Affairs.

Mohawk Seminar

September 17

[Mr.Tom Porter, a young Mohawk, speaks]
Well I guess I should start by letting you all know that about a
month ago I received papers in English on native religion. I went
through them at the last minute—we do our best at the last minute,
and that's characteristic—but I still have trouble with the big words.
One page told of the creation in small words and I went through
that pretty fast. I thought it was quite close to the way I heard those
stories, except that there were a lot of omissions. Basically it was
pretty close to the way I understand them. The thing I want to
emphasize at this time is that many of the legends or stories retold
in those papers were reserved among my people for telling at
home at wintertime, when the snow is high. This is what we call
story-telling.

We don't tell stories of the bear and so on in summer because
they have certain powers, and we don't know whether or not we
may be offending them. We wait until they are sleeping. If there
are any questions, or certain things you wanted to discuss?

Q.   — I am interested in Handsome Lake. Could you say a few
words about this tradition.

T.P.   — Oh, yes, the Handsome Lake code. First of all, for those
of you who are not familiar with it, these traditions are a recent
addition to the Six Nations—I myself am not troubled by them, but
it is a source of problems amongst my people as a whole. In the
time of Handsome Lake the Six Nations were going through a
period of transition, so to speak. Many people felt the tribes were
disunited, whiskey was being introduced in a heavy way at this
time. Its consumption was very bad for our people, and when
Handsome Lake got into the drinking, he became alcoholic, and all
this was due to the whiteman and his whiskey. Handsome Lake fell
very sick. He was so sick that some say that he died, but others say
that he was just unconscious. In this unconscious or dead
state—whatever you want to call it—Handsome Lake had an
experience.

Handsome Lake's nephew—I believe it was a nephew—had
been taken to Pennsylvania, and he was being educated there by

the Quaker people. Handsome Lake visited several times with his nephew who had learned how to read the Bible, how to read English. Handsome Lake didn't know much about Christians at all, but he journeyed to the Pennsylvania mountains and spoke to his nephew. Senakolyetis, his nephew, read the Bible to him, translating it into Seneca. Now, of course, the Bible would have been very different in Seneca, or in Mohawk language. In our language it would have become like a 3-D movie. Our language is very physical, the descriptions would have been much more physical or vivid, and Handsome Lake was amazed when he heard these stories, the teachings of the Bible, being translated. And it was just shocking, you know, in many ways. I guess Handsome Lake thought they were just stories, and he didn't know just what to think about it and ignored it and so on. But he remembered, he remembered.

So as Handsome Lake lay unconscious there was a fight within him. In his unconscious or dead state the Indian customs and ways of doing things, and the things that his nephew must have been telling him were going through his mind. Somehow in his mind those two things, the Quakers' Christianity and the Indian beliefs found a place—a sort of unifying factor. This message is called *guy wheeo* in my language and it means 'righteousness', or right things. So Handsome Lake came up with a code for preaching, and it was very much like the Baptist talk—the devil, what happens after death, and so on. If a woman was unfaithful to her husband so that she would just go with any man, then in the afterlife she would go to a place or spirit world where she would have intercourse with men, but that intercourse would be like red-hot iron. If a man sells land—our land—in this life so that he would be piling up a wheel-barrow with money, then he would go to the afterlife with a wheel-barrow and pile it up, dump it over there, put it back in—for eternity I guess. Stuff like that, and it goes on and on. It takes four days to recite the Handsome Lake code: they start in the morning and talk until midday, and in the afternoon they have repentance, for four days.

What they call repentance is a new thing to us. My own family are not strict adherents to the Handsome Lake code. We feel the new Indian ways aren't like the old Indian ways. Some call it the New Testament, the Handsome Lake. My grandmother, who will be ninety soon, is a very strict adherent of the older teachings, and she doesn't favour this other thing, the Handsome Lake. But many of the Six Nation people do. I myself, being a young person, am not as critical of it as my grandmother is, though I still follow her thinking.

This fall when our longhouse is scheduled to have the *guy wheeo* I will go there and I will listen. I will help them. I'll help them cook, I'll help them do whatever must be done, but I won't repent of the old ways. The way I understand it—like the way my grandmother talks about it—the Handsome Lake has saved our people, but it has also pacified us, as a baby is pacified with a bottle. In other words it has become a religion. Now we have religion whereas before we had a way of life. With the introduction of Handsome Lake our way of life became like the whiteman's, where there is a separation between state and religion. So now we have two of what you call wampums. In my language these are called *gogista*; 'sacred fire' is only an example of *gogists*, the English words are only examples. Now we have two capitals, or two main fire places—sacred fire places—one religious and one political. The *Onondaga*, the political fire, is near Syracuse, New York, and here the grand councils take place. On the other hand, the religious fire is held on the Tonanwanda Reservation in the Seneca country. Some young people like myself resent a little this turning of the Indian ways into European ways. We resent the separation of religion from our lives. So that's one thing I have trouble with. My grandmother doesn't go for the idea of repentance, where all you need to do is repent and the slate is wiped clean, but then you can do wrong over and over and keep repenting. My grandmother said that in the old days things were strict, you had three chances and that was it. After the third chance you had to straighten out. There was no such thing as repentance and forgiveness. What was weak was weeded out in the old days. We were a very strong people. And we are a very strong nation today, I feel. I can see that the Handsome Lake code saved us, but at the same time it has made us jellyfish, took the backbone out of us. As far as the nation goes.

Q.　　— Was there never anything like repentance in the old days?

T.P.　　— Yes, but it was different. My grandmother told me that one would go off by oneself and make a little fire, early in the morning, when the sun is just rising. At that moment you are alone with the creator, who is all creation. According to the old ways you had to present yourself to the creator: if you are going to impress anyone, it has to be the creator. You had to be alone and apart from other people, but today they go into the middle of a floor amongst many people who listen to them, and my grandmother says that at that time the creator goes way back in the back-row.

She said that then you are trying to please the people, and not to be alone with the creator.

Q.   — Is there still religious feeling in the way politics is conducted?

T.P.   — Yes, even though, as I said, there is a political fire and a religious fire, whenever the chiefs go to the grand council, or whenever the Mohawk nation has a national council, it has to be done in a religious way. There has to be an opening prayer, or thanksgiving address, to say that the creator is before us. It is still this way in longhouses clear from Seneca to Mohawk country. Even the small meetings are done in this way. So there is still a lot of that way of life there. What bothers me is that there isn't just one fire. You find that most of the Six Nation people accept the Handsome Lake, but most often among the Mohawk there are those who do not accept it. We're noted to go the other way in the canoe, when the others are all paddling one way. We are noted to be sort of trouble-like.

Q.   — Are you at liberty to say anything about the midewiwin ceremonies?

T.P.   — I suppose I could. It is one of the biggest ceremonies that we have, I would say, almost equivalent to the sun dances of the Dakotas and the plains Indian people. In fact we have our sun dance on one of the days of the midewiwin ceremonies.

In the Mohawk country it takes five and sometimes six days to complete the midewiwin. The Onondagas, Senecas or Cuyahogas sometimes take a month. The midewiwin is a bit different for each nation, but everyone within the Iroquois nation shares four main things. The differences are partly due to the fact that in the Mohawk there are only three main clans, and the Onondagas and the Senecas have as many as nine, so theirs are longer.

We go by the stars. At a certain time when the stars are directly above and the moon is new, we sleep five times and then it is time for the big midewiwin to start. It begins our new year, the yearly cycle—completely. Sometimes it goes in the middle of January, sometimes in February, it depends. Thanksgiving ceremonies are performed that go over the past year since the last midewiwin, giving thanks. Thanksgiving is put through to the forces of nature, towards the end of each cycle, a ceremony for each force. There's a ceremony of appeal for good fortune in the new year. We must eat a certain kind of food during the sun dance, and the sun dance goes together with the moon and the stars. And it all goes around the sun. We make big bread—something like 'ghost bread' in our language—and a little bit smaller bread, or the grandmother bread. The grandmother bread means the moon in our language, moon's bread. The big bread is sun's bread. We call the moon grandmother. Then we make lots of little breads, and these belong to the stars. Every family fixes these breads so that there are baskets full on the floor. There are also songs and different things for the sun, for the grandmother and for the stars. When all the songs and dances have been put through, everybody feasts with those things that were presented. In a way, I guess, we become a part of the sun and the stars and the grandmother when we feast on those things.

My people believe that the creator ordered, I guess "ordered" is a good word, the grandmother to be head of our women, and that's why we rejoice, because children are still being born. My own grandmother told me that the moon is the head lady of all women, not only of human beings, but all other animals and birds too. She is the head. When I asked my grandmother to tell me more about this, she said that the moon goes round once a month in so many days to make a new moon, and when the moon is full the god gives her the power to be the head of the women, and to touch the business of life. In other words she determines when the babies will be born, and when people will die. She determines how the fish will swim in the world, how the river will flow. Grandmother moon is given that duty by the creator of creation. She has the power to lift the oceans up and down, the big waters of the Pacific or Atlantic or whatever ocean are in her power every day—the tides I think you call it in English. The biggest thing my grandmother said to me was that the moon doesn't care, she doesn't care if it's a white woman or an Indian woman, a millionaire or the poorest woman in the world. She doesn't care if she is the most educated or the most uneducated woman. She says, "O.K. you women, you must bleed every month to purify the blood. It doesn't matter how rich you are, you have got to do it." She says: "You must bleed every month to make the body new so that a new human being can get ready to nest." Grandma moon is the boss-lady, she touches peoples heads, and that's why in our ways in the midewiwin they are fixed that way for those reasons. As I said, children are being born, and that's why we still do it.

The midewiwin lasts four days among the Mohawk, largely because of the number of clans we have. I don't know if you will understand what they call 'clans.' A person's clan is determined through the female line. My mother was of the bird clan, and her mother was bird clan, so I am too. My wife is of the turtle clan, so my children are turtle clan. Our whole life, our medicine, is determined by what clan we belong to. Where did you come from when you entered the world, and who led you here, you see. As for me, the bear led me here, so this is why we have two houses. Anthropologists call this *moitie*, I think. The midewiwin is divided between clan and house. In our ceremony, it is divided by two, by the moitie; even when people die the different house determines which one would initiate the starting to do the ceremonies that's supposed to be done, the work that's supposed to be done, the cooking, whatever, the songs to be sung, the many dances to be done. It is all decided by the big peach stone game, the big dice game, we call it.

It is held in the new years, because this is the right time to play the dice to divide the two moitie. The clan structure is different in each nation, but I am only going to talk about the Mohawk. I'm not sure what the Seneca do. In my longhouse the turtle clan and the wolf clan sit on one side. On the other side, my side, the bear clan, we always take the small clans, the other Indians who come to visit and live with us. When we are ready to make the decisions, we say we are going to play the dice for the gods, we say we are playing to amuse the world, to make the world laugh, the creator laugh, the trees, the sun, the water, the animals laugh—that's why we play this game. The oldest people and the smallest kids all play. Only two years old and he knows how to shake the bowl. He can play too. We play the game all day long, and we say that the winner is in the hands of the creator. We all bring our best gifts. If someone is a singer, he pledges his lungs as a prize, and so on. If one is a good dancer, he brings his best moccasins. If one is a lacross player, he brings his lacross stick, the best he has. You give of yourself to the other clans, and this promotes oneness among the Mohawk people. You might lose, you know, but . . . . Both sides bring the gift baskets and they collect it from the people and tie it together—each moitie with the other. This represents the oneness of the Mohawk nation.

You sit there on the floor with your gift ready and then you get the bowl, a hand-carved bowl, and they have all the counters there, and the score-keepers—so many men and women. They all got duties. One can only hold the beans that we use as counters, another one is selected only to pay the other side and there is one guy and one woman and they are the only ones that can call the next player, and they make sure that everyone gets a turn. You have to wait till they call your name then you can throw. It goes on like that all day.

After the game, they distribute the stuff. You don't offer anything that you don't value very much. We believe that after death we join our grandfathers again, over there, and we want them to see the honour we have won in this life. This is why whoever wins gains the honour of initiating the ceremonies for the rest of the year. The winners tell us who will be doing what chores and so on. You are not supposed to say no, so you play all the harder to win.

In the springtime we have another game, in which the men play against the women. This has to do with who will be working the garden, the man or woman. Springtime calls for thanksgiving to mother earth, to the seeds and to medicine. This is another big dice game, and we have lots of fun. The game divides the house. There's an imaginary line down the middle of the house, and if you cross it they will beat you back with sticks—they do it too. Even the little ones get hit—that's how they learn where they belong, I guess.

So those are some of the things the midewiwin games are about. Oh, I forgot a big thing. At the midewiwin everything is made new, you are like a new-born baby when the midewiwin takes place. So it is a time when everybody cleans their house, and those who still believe strongly make new clothes, new moccasins. You make new friends, and if there has been a quarrel in your family, you patch things up. Wherever there is trouble they have what they call dream guessing so that instead of apologising directly to somebody there is supernatural medicine, so those families that have had disputes, so it's not exactly like you having to go directly to somebody and say "I'm sorry," you know, it is done by spiritual means through what they call dreams. And then the different ones get the dreams and then they will start talking about them. Sometimes it's right in dreams and they all bring up to the surface why there was a dispute and then that's washed away too. The year starts new again. This is what midewiwin does, and this is our equivalent of the sun dance of the plains.

Q.   — Are there ceremonies which commemorate the ending of the year as well?

T.P.   — Yes, towards the end of the year's cycle, in October or November, we have the last ceremony of the year. After that we get together again and we say that we have finished this year, so it is time to decide whether we want to continue to live in this world, see the sun and the moon rise for another year. Then we decide at what time to start the new year again, and at this time we have to have lots of meat to make feast with. We need the deer, the beaver and different kinds of game. So at that time we'll have another ceremony of which we will ask for luck so that warriors can go to the north, hunters can go to the north and get the beaver or the deer or whatever kind of meat they are going to have for these feasts that are coming for the next year. There is a special ceremony for this. There are other ceremonies that take place at night, different kinds of society medicine, and these determine what kind of medicine you have. The medicine is usually in a bundle or bag. Some medicine is for the fish. If you have this you will have good luck with the fish, catch lots of fish. Some medicine is for the deer, and so on. Each medicine is owned by an individual, it's not something on a national scale. These ceremonies are done at night, in a secretive fashion. No one is supposed to see who has what medicine, and if one finds out, he's not supposed to tell anybody about it. If you do, your family will get sick, or you will get sick, or misfortune will come to you.

Q.　— Are you describing secret societies here, or do you mean something else?

T.P.　— When I say secret—uh, I mean that they are not really 'secret,' we don't go around telling our people "Hey, you're secret now!" But somehow you just don't tell. You do your duties, and that's it. You don't say, "Well, we didn't do that right," or something like that. None of these things are rehearsed or anything people just do their thing. Some people will have to have a certain kind of medicine man or society attend to them. Since there's no way to know when we are going to need it and so it's got to be done whenever it's called for. And so we set it that way. And also these things are usually found out through what you might call, I don't know what the English word is, people who look into the future, fortune teller or something like that. We have those so anybody is sick or something wrong they can go to those people and those people look at their blood or look at their medicine or look at them somehow and they can tell what's wrong with them and what needs to be done. That's how they find out what kind of society has to do their medicine for them.

Q.　— Could you tell us if your grandmother used to diagnose and treat people with physical or spiritual ailments?

T.P.　— She was in her nineties, pretty near to 100 years old she might have been. Not last summer, but the summer before, she passed on. She was the head; everybody went to her. She would look at the blood or the medicine and somehow she could tell what the trouble was.

Q.　— Would she have instructed someone to be her follower when she was gone?

T.P.   — She could have. She had helpers but none could take over in her place. That's because one cannot select such a person, you have to be born to that sort of thing. Even as much as my grandmother wanted her knowledge to go on, she really couldn't do anthing about it. All she did was to water it, as when you water a small plant.

Q.   — Do the older people like your grandmother have a special way of knowing who is best suited to learn this knowledge?

T.P.   — Oh, yes. It's not unusual to see older people going around and touching the little kids, little girls and boys. They're always shaking hands with them, and they claim that certain kids can given them a shock right up to the elbow, and that's how they know if one is born to be able to look into the future and that sort of thing. If they get a big shock, they know a strong medicine was born.

Q.   — Your other grandmother sounds so vigorous. Could you tell us about her. I mean, does she have some special knowledge or gift as well?

T.P.   — Well, she . . . she will be ninety soon. Her biggest gift, I guess, is that she is tuned in to the people and the family at home. At home she sits like a monument and you can never change her mind. She makes her mind up about things and you cannot change it. Her name is Bwanadaha in my language, and it means: 'one who carries the village, the village carrier.' When she has made up her mind she makes people go the right way, she carries them. She knows some of the things my other grandmother knew, and her best thing is that she looks into the future, though she doesn't do that much anymore.

Q.   — Are the seers always women?

T.P.   — No, The only reason I talk about the women is that in my family the women are those who have the knowledge. In other families, it is the men. I am allowed to talk about women's business only because I'm married.

In the Mohawk nation there are three main clans, the bear clan, the turtle and the wolf clan. Each of these clans is also divided because there are more than one kind of bear, turtle and wolf. Each of these smaller divisions is further divided into the men and the women. In our ways it is largely the women who initiate the ceremonies: they are the ones with the big say as to which men will conduct the procedures. The clan mothers are really like women chiefs. When there is a vacancy, 300 people might be eligible. The head woman can call a council fire with or without the men—it's her choice. She will call all her aunts and nieces and cousins, all her clan, and they will find a new candidate for chief. They will talk about their sons, and each others' sons. A chief must be married and have children. He must have kindness in him, he must have seven hand-spans thick skin, he must be ambitious. He must be spiritual, knowledgeable, and much more. These are the kinds of things the women are looking for.

My grandmother said that women make the human being, guide him, teach him. When the baby is first kicking, when a man's voice is changing, when a woman's first period comes, the mothers and the aunts are right there teaching the language, how to live the ways. That's why in our councils the women choose the leaders. No matter what kind of a woman it is, animal woman or human woman, the woman is the one who have the babies in the stomach, they know as soon as the baby moves already she starts to know him, how that baby kicks, how that baby moves inside for nine months when she is carrying that baby, also tell when that baby come out how he is going to be too. See they study that too. When that baby is born and woman she had a lot of pain for that baby, not me, or not my brother never would know nothing about that, so that woman after the baby is born feeds that baby right here and so I can't do that too and so that's why the woman she knows that baby. If you want to know about somebody, ask his mother. It's the mothers who give birth to the nation, and it's the mothers who will lead the nations. After they have made several nominations and a selection of the best choice, then they will submit this to the men's council of that clan, to have it confirmed or reaffirmed, to agree with the women. The reason for that is because I said a long time ago the men go way out hunting for weeks at times, and go to another Indian's territory, those women don't know if when we went hunting, maybe that man fooled around with another woman or did something he shouldn't. That's why in the old days, they have to ask the other men "Is he fulfilled, is he all complete, in his body and in his mind." They ask the other men for their confirmation of these nominations and to make sure that when he was in the Ojibway country he is not messing around. And if he is over there he does right when he hunts, you know, does not waste stuff, and just kill to kill and all that. It's very seldom that they don't, because the mothers know. That's why.

Q.   — They vote on several nominees do they?
T.P.   — They don't raise hands or make up ballots or anything

like that. If anyone sees something wrong, they talk about it. They don't just say: "I don't like him!" They have to tell the history and the reasons. That's how they come to a conclusion.

Q.　— I would think that it would be difficult for the mothers not to say that their own sons are the best. How do they decide? Is there only one nominee, or several?

T.P.　— Well, they nominate several. You see it's not an easy thing to be a clan leader. It is understood among my people that you don't campaign for such a thing. Although it is one of the greatest honours, it is also very much dreaded, if that's the right word for it. Once you are a leader you don't belong to yourself anymore, you don't belong to your wife anymore. You belong to the entire clan, the entire nation, the entire Six Nations people. You belong to all of the people in the world. Whenever there's a meeting you have to go there, drop whatever work you're doing right there, no matter what. If somebody is hungry you have to give him food from your home place—that's why in our community the leaders are still the poorest ones. And the women know that. They know who has these characteristics. And they don't usually want their sons to do this thing because it's rough.

My grandfather once told me about what they call a pine-tree chief, how he was selected. It's like walking into a field. You see a rose growing there, in bloom, the brightest rose you have ever seen, just standing there with dew on it. You smell it, you see it right there. That's how the leaders are chosen. You know the rose is beautiful, nobody has to tell you or instruct you—you just know. And that's the same way with these leaders; they're watched from birth until they are adult and that's why, like that rose, nobody has to say anything much, they know from the birth to that decision. It's a little more involved than that, I'm just generalizing. The men are not usually told that they are being considered. Some excuse is made for them to be called off to another reservation or somewhere, while the talks are going on. In the old days these talks were called condolences, because a new chief is only selected when the old chief dies. We Mohawks had a big one. The other united the Cayahoga and the Tuskaroara. Part of the condolence is a very beautiful song. The other nations have theirs as well, and every time a new chief is raised up—the condolence is like a dead feast in which the spirit of the dead chief is also raised up—there is a roll call of all the fifty leaders of the Iroquois nation. When this happens the women make a hat, what in my language is called a 'stoah hat.' I don't know if you know what a stoah hat is, so I should say that it has little split feathers all over it. It's our kind of head-dress, you see. The Mohawk wear three eagle's feathers straight up, and to this particular head-dress the women will attach deer's antler, and this hat is a symbol of chieftainship of the clan. So when all the people are assembled at the condolence the woman goes up to the man and grabs his hand, and that's the first he knows about it. Then she brings him before the Cuyahogas and Unitas, who will question the man, and puts him to a test right there, in front of all the people. If he passes, she puts the hat on his head, and he no longer belongs to himself. I'll tell you there are many nights that he will get no sleep, because people always have troubles.

Now, the council sits, three to the east, three to the north, three to the south, and to the west the woman sits. The north council of three chiefs of the turtle clan—well, that's where the law starts. Then it is reviewed and it crosses the sacred fire to the women's clan, where it is considered. You only listen to the turtle clan when there is some sort of trouble. When the clans are of one mind, the wampum goes to the fire-keepers. The people don't participate, we just watch and listen while all this is going on. The leaders of the turtle clan are asked for their confirmation. When it is confirmed, it becomes law of the Mohawk nation. The supreme law of the Mohawks.

The same thing happens at the grand councils of the Six Nations. There the Mohawks and the Senecas sit together on one side of the house, and on the other side the Cuyahogas and Unitas and Tuskaroaras sit. The Onodagas sit at the head of the council, and they are the fire-keepers. The Onodagas do what my clan does in the Mohawk ceremony. All the mothers are there, because they want to make sure that their sons, the councils, follow their spiritual guidelines in the correct manner. They are concerned that the generations of the people are led into the future in the right way. Before each council the women open the proceedings with a ceremony. The laws are made on the basis of a foundation: seven generations from today, the laws must not be harmful to the children. That's how strict the councils are, and that's why the women are there to watch. Now if that man did wrong, or he did wrong in council or did not compromise—you see there's no majority or minority in this council. It's got to be consensus, and everyone has to agree to the law, the ancient law amongst the Iroquois and you've got to compromise to get one mind of all nine leaders. If one chief is hanging his feet, and tries to be funny and doesn't want to get one mind he'd better not because the woman is watching. We have a man called the war eater, the war chief of the Mohawk nation. She'll call him over and then he'll go over to that man, her chief, the one who is not trying to make a compromise, and the war eater will say: "I got orders from your mother to tell you to straighten up!" If he persists his grandmother will go to the war chief—"Come here!" she will say—"Go tell him again!" Sometimes she will herself go and call him outside the council, and she'll say: "We need you, that's why we selected you. All of our family is in your voice, the smallest baby, the eldest grandma. That's why we put you here. So think about it, my son. Go back to the council now." Then she goes back and sits down, and the war chief sits down. But if he persists on holding up the compromise—that's how the laws are made, when all the chiefs agree to compromise— then the women call the war chief over a third time, or she will pick her biggest nephew, and send him over: "Now go over there, take his horns off his head and bring them back to me. This is our third time." This time she won't go with him. You see, usually the women don't cross the floor of the council. The chief starts to whine and plead and asks forgiveness. They say that when the women take off his horns the blood will flow down forevermore, forevermore he will bleed, and the blood will not let him see his people ever again. This is what we call dehorning. It means a man is no longer a chief, and he is just like a dead man. Then the women call together their clan and select another, and that's the women's role in the Mohawk country.

Q.   — I would like to ask you about marriage customs among the Mohawk. Did a girl have to be chosen from another *moitie*, for example?

T.P.   — Yes, in the old days, but nowadays it is less strict, and she must only come from a different clan. About two generations ago you couldn't marry even into another clan, if that clan was in your *moitie*. In those days it had to be a girl from the other side of the house altogether. I guess it's changed because the reservation isn't so big anymore.

Q.   — How about marriage itself? Does it come at any special time of year, or does it take place at anytime? And could you tell us what the ceremony is like?

T.P.   — It is hard for me to answer that. It has changed now due to Handsome Lake, so I don't know how much of it is Christian. I have never seen the old style of marriage.

But I can tell you how we get married now. The women—the mothers, aunts and especially the grandmother will go out looking for a man, a match in another village, another clan. Either the boy's or girl's parents can initiate a match, or even from the boy or girl. My grandmother said that in her time the kids had no choice. They were told they were getting married, and they did. But she said that that wasn't really our way either—I don't know where that came from. A long time ago, before this world came, the Mohawk mother worked closely with the children because she wanted them to have good luck. When the child had a dream of somebody in a village, and they told the mother, the mother would go and find the village of the dream. They got married like that. Later, during my grandmother's time, the mothers just chose. It must have had something to do with the Catholic Church, but I don't know.

Q.   — I wonder if these different ways cause problems among the young people?

T.P.   — Especially amongst our young people. In our area the Handsome Lake code causes a lot of frustration. And It's very hard to separate the two. Many of our young are wondering whether they want the pure way or the mixture. I'm not as strict about this as my grandmother, because I try to play both sides. I try to anyway. When they ask me which I think is right, I say you have to believe what you want to believe.

Q.   — The word *horenda* interests me, but I've never heard it used much. Is it a name, or something someone has invented?

T.P.   — It could be like our word, *oulonta*, which means 'soul', and only applies to one person. But it also means something that makes a person whole. This other word seems to refer to the whole nation, the ulunda of the whole nation, the sphere. This is a good way of looking at it. I had not thought of it that way.

Q.   — Getting back to marriage, is there divorce among the Mohawk? And do some young people simply say, "Well, we love each other and that is enough for us." No ceremony, and so on. Or are your traditions too strict for that?

T.P.   — Well, let me put it this way. When you have a wife, you always have that same wife, and you cannot be a playboy. We have to do it the way the golden eagle does it. That's the bird that watches over my home from the top of the tree. But there doesn't have to be a big ceremony. That's a matter of choice between the families. Often a big ceremony just brings people together to share a feast. They have to make promises to each other, and to ask the creator for good luck. When I got married we exchanged baskets, and we made pledges to each other for as long as we are living, and I didn't like that.

Q.   — You want to be a playboy?

T.P.   — No, I didn't want to be a playboy exactly. But I didn't like making that sort of pledge. What if I live to be 200 years old! I cannot see two or three years into the future like my grandmother. I want to be with my wife the way I know how to be with my power I have. I have seen the movies on the television already, the stories about cloud-number-nine love, and I don't know how much I am influenced by this. I don't know just what that is, or even if I could get on one. But if this idea of cloud-number-nine is true . . . .

Q.   — Is there no recognized divorce, then?

T.P.   — No formal divorce, no. But a long time ago a woman could take all her man's clothes and leave them outside the longhouse, if she didn't like him. That meant: "Go on, go back to your mother!" But it doesn't work the other way around, because the house doesn't belong to the man. It's the woman's house.

Q.   — Then I suppose the women don't walk ten paces behind the men!

T.P.   — Nowadays this would be funny, even though the women in my nation doesn't know much about women's liberation and that sort of thing! In our way of life, it seems to me, there is already equality between the men and the women, because there are certain things that women do that we cannot do. And we have certain ceremonies that the women cannot participate in either. So it works out equal as far as I can see. I feel satisfied with the way it is. When I tried to talk to my grandmother and explain it to her I don't think she understood, because even when I talk Mohawk to her the concepts of United States Union just can't find foundation in my grandmother's thinking. So that's why I think she can't understand. She said the main thing is that if the white brother is going to switch parts of the males, both men and women will go crazy. This was foretold in the prophecies, that the white brother would do that, but we don't have to do that. She said that if you are going to talk about women's liberation at the university, remember that if one takes the clothes off of the men and the women, they will all look the same. "Only when a baby is born will a woman know the pain," she said, "All I ask is that the fathers appreciate that." She told me to tell the liberationists that, as long as they stay within the natural function, the way it was meant to be on the earth: "I guess it's alright."

Q.   — May I ask how the school system works?

T.P.   — We do not have any control over education in the Mohawk language. We only have what I would call a token gesture in this direction. The way I feel about school, the way my wife feels

about it, our experiences of it and so on, we have no desire to send
our children to school in the United States, or Canada, or
anywhere. In my mind, I wouldn't feel that not sending my children
to school would deprive them of anything. There is so much that
our people have lost, that time is needed to teach them Mohawk
ways. I wouldn't encourage my children to learn the American or
Canadian ways until they are 12 or 13 years old. Then English would
be a second language, and white man's culture would be a second
everthing. First will be Mohawk. It doesn't bother my conscience,
not sending them to school. I feel very good about it.

Q.   — What was your experience of school?

T.P.   — My experience was very, very bad. Neither my
grandmother nor my grandfather had good opinions about school.
My grandfather, my grandmother's uncle that is, went to Carlyle
school in Pennsylvania. He ran away from there, and he used to tell
me stories of the bad things that happened to him there. My
mother's mother, my grandmother—the one I'm talking about all
the time—she knew the United States when the cavalry was still
fighting out west, and she had a very great distrust of the American
people. So I never wanted to go to school there.

I was seven or so when boarding kids out at schools stopped.
Then a Mohawk lady who was working for the government—I don't
know if she was a social worker or something—but she came up to
my mother and my grandmother and said that she had records
which showed that I hadn't been to school. She said that I had to be
in school, and my grandmother said, "No. We don't want him in
school. I have already sent a lot of my grandchildren to your school,
and now they are no good. They don't even know how to speak
Mohawk anymore. They've gone off to the cities by themselves.
And they're nothing but alcoholics now. There's no use for me in
talking to my children now, and that's why I don't like your
school." In my grandma's time the boarding schools were run by
Catholics and Methodists, and to become educated you had to
become Christian as well. My grandma's own boy—he's in his 50's
now—he yells at her when she refuses to be baptized. He starts
drinking and he yells at her. Then she comes to me crying and says:
"Why does my son do this to me?" It was because of the school.

So the lady from the government said that if I didn't go to
school, the government would take my grandmother and my
mother—all the elders in my home—to Franklin county court,
where they would be declared unfit parents. Then I would be sent
away not to the Mohawk school only six miles away from my

grandmother's house, but to foster home. So I decided to go, but my grandmother was very upset, and I made her a promise. I said: "Now I will go to school, and I will try to learn. But I will also promise you that for sure, for sure, when I finish with the school, when I get out, I will still talk to you as I do now, in Mohawk. I won't forget how to talk to you!" She said that she was worried I would never return home again, and I said: "When I get out I'll come back to you, I'll come right back here, to your cows and hay fields." And she didn't say anything.

When I got to school the lady spoke to us in Mohawk: "You are here to get an education, so you won't have to dig ditches, so you don't have to do the white man's shit." That's what she said—if you translate it into English, that's what it means. "You're here to get an education," she said, "and that's what you're going to do. If you don't, you will be in a lot of trouble. If you learn really well, every time you stand up to drink your coffee, you are going to hear the big noise inside your pocket." She discouraged us from using our own language. "Even out in the school-yard, when you're playing on the chin-up bar, don't talk Mohawk, because the other kids will get mad at you. You must learn English, pay attention and copy us." So we sat down and I was scared to death, scared to death, scared even by the stink of that building. It smelled different than my home altogether, you know; kind of a mossy smell, like a stone, you know, smells . . . and my heart was just going about 200 miles an hour I was so scared, and I don't know how to talk English.

Mohawk, they didn't know either. Mrs. Crifty was the teacher, there were two teachers, I remember her well because she had a long neck, and she was a sexy old woman. She'd sit down and she'd pull up her dress and you could see her underclothes, and she would never sit like a moral lady. A moral lady has a long dress and she keeps her legs together but not her. Oh gosh, we Indian people never saw that before, and she was the talk of the whole reservation. We'd catch her too, and she liked the men more than the other teacher. She was the principal's wife (the principal of the school), so she could do almost anything she wanted. She would stand up there talking and talking and talking, and we're sitting back here, my cousins and I and we don't know what she's talking about. So all of a sudden I ask my cousin in the next row what that means, and I wonder what we're doing here anyway. Right away, as soon as I said that, she—knock, knock, knock, knock, just like a rabbit. She walked up to the front, and I got the chance to put my hand out. Anyway, she had two kind of things that she used, one that big ruler with the iron on it inside the edge and the other the same thing that Mohawk people have and that was a stick, called grey willow or snake bush. She used one of those two things every time she hit the kids, and I was the first one of the whole class, of the whole first of that year to get hit. I really got hit. It stung me you know. You see my mother never beat me up, my grandma she never beat me up, never, because that's part of the thing you don't do to kids, and that woman hit me, and it just went all over in my whole body, not just here, but through the whole body, right to my heart. I got so mad that everything seemed to be flying; I could even see the air flying, it looks like little drops of something. From that time I know that what my grandfather was telling me about was true, I never believed it. I used to say that it might be just a story. I know now that it's a fact. My grandmother used to tell me about school and the United States people, and I know I now have no use for it in my own heart.

So I failed kindergarten, and so did half of the class. We failed three times. Then we go on to first grade. I failed again, and so did half the class. We went on higher and higher until we got those Canadian pictures—what do you call those pictures?—Canadian Games Book, and Spotty Dog and all those. That's how we learned to read. We'd look at the picture of how they were kicking the ball, chasing the ball, the dog chasing the ball, and we learned how to read that way. It took us a long time, but you know I hated school all that time. I really hated that school and I never gave up hating that school, except once in my life I did. When I first learned how to recite the ABC,—I was way in the sixth grade when I first learned why I should know that, and that's when I come to try to learn it, in sixth grade. Can you imagine that? That's how much I hated school. I always felt very embarrassed about myself because I was still beginning, and I really felt apart because that's the first time that somebody told me what it's for, or made me understand the reason. At that time all Indians go to one school, and no white man goes to school with Indians because they were just Indian schools, for all Indians.

In 1956 onwards they start to talk about centralization. The first time that we heard of it, not as integration, but centralization. They do away with the little old farm schools and make a big central school in a big district where everybody gets bussed. This is not the bussing they're arguing about in the States now, but the centralization that was going on at that time. At that time I never went to school with white folks, and my grandmother was worried

because there was talk that all Indians after sixth grade were going
to go to a centralization school. So I got scared too and so I failed
the sixth grade. I was going to fail anyway, but I made doubly sure
that I failed so I wouldn't have to go to school with the white man.
And so, the next year I go to school and I go to sixth grade again. I
did everything to fail that grade so I didn't have to go. So I tried
three years to fail, and finally after the third year the teacher
wouldn't let me stay because of my age. Then I went to Salmon
River School. It was the first time I ever got to go with the white
people in the white people's school. It was a big school with
corridors in the hallways like this kind of floor, shiney as can be,
and lockers on each side. I remember that as if it was yesterday
because we were scared, we were scared of it. Then they took four
or five kids, Indian kids to a room, to each room to separate us. We
always sit in the back of the room together, just united. Out there
this white man said,—This can't happen like that so they'd have
alphabetical order and place us all over and they separated us.
Every time the teacher turned around we'd run back and sit in the
back of the room, chasing the white man out of his seat and we'd
sit together. For two weeks we did that. We didn't talk to the kids,
those white kids, not a one, because I'm afraid of them you see. So
after two weeks we started to make friends a little bit,—there's Irish
people and English people, and different kind of people, at first, so
we made friends, we started to talk, and we started to know a little
bit. But, of course, there were some of those kids who would call us
names too. They said,—"Indians, you Indians didn't have to come
to this school. This is a nice school, why don't you go back to your
own school where you used to belong." They made comments like
that and they didn't want us to talk. But most of the kids didn't say
that and they talked to us saying,—"I'm afraid to ask about your
Chief" and other things.

That year we had a teacher named Mrs. Brockerly, and she was
wide and short. I remember her because she wore a lot of make-up
on her face, thick, and red lipstick. She stinked so good because
she used a lot of perfume, and she was a history teacher. She was
brought up about four miles from my home, just off the
reservation. And she passed out these books, history books, and
told each and every one of us to familiarize ourselves with its
contents, because it was the book we were going to use all winter
long. So we looked at it, turned the pages, and I could hear
everybody doing the same thing. In the middle of the book, I saw a
picture of our grandfather; he had long hair, wrapped around his

head under the fur, a nicely shaped feather on his head. It looked perfect you know, and it just made me feel so good. I just can't describe to you what I felt when I saw that picture, and something went through my mind right away. I said to myself, I must be the dumbest Mohawk in the whole world that I would hate this school as much as I hated this school, yet here is one of my grandfather's pictures right here in my school. If it's good enough for my grandfather's picture then it must be alright for me.

I just hated myself for fighting the teachers as I did all those years, and I knew that some time in this year that that teacher was going to read that book, and that chapter, and everyone of the Irishmen and Englishmen and Frenchmen in this room, including my own people, were going to look at that picture. When the whiteman looked at that picture he would talk about my grandfather and the teacher would talk about him. I'm going to be so glad, I'm just going to be so glad because all the whitemen are going to know about my people, and they're going to know my grandfather was the best grandfather in the world, and I'm going to feel so good. That's how good I felt you know,—Gosh!

All the years from kindergarten, I would have an ear ache, or a stomach ache, or sore eyes, or sore ears, so I wouldn't have to go to school. It ended up I wouldn't even go half of the year almost, and my grandma and my mother backed me up all the time. Any time I wanted to get an ear ache, I got it, so I didn't have to go to school. But that year when I saw the picture, I didn't miss one day, I didn't miss one day of school. You know why? Because I was afraid that if I missed school that teacher might skip the talk about my grandfather, or I would miss it, and I didn't want to do that, so I went to school and I wasn't even late, not once. That year was the first time I made the honour role even though I lacked one point or something but they put me on the honour role. All the teachers looked at me and said, "What happened to you, how come before you received red marks all the time and yet now you make the honour role." The teacher couldn't figure it, and I used to say—there's nothing to it. But you know why, because every night I took my book home and sometime even though I'd finish work at school and I would take it home. I'd read that book, whether it was spelling, or English, or Science, or whatever, I took it home. I want to read now, because to me that picture of my grandfather endorsed those books at the school and everything was related. Now I could be like them.

So, I went to school, and I was doing good and I even wanted to be a doctor, a white man's doctor, or a lawyer—I wanted to be a lawyer. I had my friends and we'd talk about going to college, about being doctors, lawyers, whatever, and then one time said, "You be the lawyer, I'll be the doctor, if you don't like it, I'll be the doctor, you be the lawyer," we'd talk that way. So finally about December we came close to the middle of the book. I know we finished that chapter, the one next to the chapter our grandfather's picture was on, and I just waited, waited, and I waited. Then the teacher said "Everybody turn the page." I knew at the same minute that every page was making a noise, and the same minute the eyes of everybody at their desks were going to see that picture, and as soon as I heard that page turning I turned it and I looked at it. Again, my blood went really fast, and I could have been just so strong, even I could pick up a tractor just like this, no sweat, that's how good I felt.

So Mrs. Brockerly stood up there looking at the book, and everybody's looking at it, Mrs. Brockerly she said this to me, not to me to everybody, but me because I felt it the most. Mrs. Brockerly said, "Now children, this year we're running behind schedule, we don't have as much time as we thought. We are going to skip this chapter on the Indian people because we have little time left in the year, and we have more important things to do and to cover." And I didn't understand exactly that right away, so I raised my hand. Mrs. Brockerly she says, "What do you want," and I says, "Are we going to read about my grandfather today?" I didn't understand what she said. She says, "No, we're not going to read about it, we don't have enough time." I raised my hand again, I said, "Do I hear right?" I say, "Are we going to read about my grandfather today?" You know what she did—she says, "No." She came over where I'm sitting way in the back there. "The sooner you Indian people realize that that's water over the dam. The sooner you Indian people realize that, the sooner you're going to get better, you're going to be better off, the sooner you Indians get educated the modern ways—there's not going to be so much alcoholism among these children and all your children. The white man provides everything for you Indian people, and you Indian people haven't got sense enough to get away from it. You live in tipis so small that each one of you is nearly on top of each other."

At that point I took the book and I shoved it, and I couldn't do anything, all the power went out of my body. That black came back again, the bluish-black. In my heart it started to look like it was the foggiest day that you ever could see, the black was smokey like. I found out it wasn't water—I was crying. I sat at that desk and I couldn't hear what's going on. I can't hear anything and I got so mad. I noticed I was starting to cry, and don't want any white man to see me cry, so I go like this (put his head down). For about fifteen minutes I think about this: I'd like to jump in the St. Lawrence River where it's the most deep spot and where it's the swiftest, or maybe that teacher's going to get a shotgun, I'll even count with her to three and let her pull both triggers, shoot me right here. I don't even want to go home any more, I don't want to go nowhere any more, just shoot me that's all. If that teacher had shot me I would've been so glad.

Fifteen minutes, and twenty minutes went past and then my tears dried up and my hearing came back. I could see right again, everything wasn't blurred any more and I was sitting there, near the big window. Something came in that window, at the top, it looked like maybe lightning or something and it hit me on the side of the head, right here, and it went in and shook me and gave me such a shock, like—just like when you jump in an ice cold river in the winter. That's what it did to me, and my heart went fast, very fast again, and that's when I heard and was real strong again.

(Tape Change)

[*Person who is taping speaks*]

There's a portion of tape missing here, so I'll fill in.

What Tom heard was some of the children in the classroom speaking, reading about Abraham Lincoln, and they would take turns, go around each one—read a couple of paragraphs, and they were reading all about how Abraham Lincoln lived in a little log cabin and he lived in this state of poverty, and he used to read every day at home and walk so many miles in the snow just to get to school, and now this was all a very important man because after doing all this, and even out of this state of poverty he becomes the President of the United States and frees all the slaves and all of that. And Tom said, while he's listening to this going on he started feeling real good, he didn't really know why, but he just started feeling real good again, he could see now, he could see very clear, and he could hear, and he could see the sunshine, and all the kids sitting around, and the teacher there, and they were reading this book, and he started feeling real good.

T.P.   — . . . stallion horse, young stallion horse, something like that, that's how I felt strong, I know what I want now, and I raise my hand up again, even though they were still reading. The teacher yelled at me, "Don't you know somebody's reading?" I raised my hand, she says, "You can wait till after them." I stood up right away, I like the girl that's reading. The teacher yelled at me, "Sit down." I says, "Mrs. Brockerly, I want to ask you a question, a very important question now." She said, "I told you to sit down," and I say, "Mrs. Brockerly," I say, "I got a question about education for me, and I want you to answer it right away," and I say, "I'm not going to sit down, and if you want me to sit down, I'd like to see you come and try to put me down, I want you to answer a question." She says, "Sit yourself down," and I say, "No, Mrs. Brockerly, this Mohawk's not sitting down no more," I said, "Mrs. Brockerly, those Indians,"— there was four Indians of us you see, three younger than I was egging me on— and so I say, "Mrs. Brockerly, I want to know was that Abraham Lincoln and that George Washingon, and that other man you're talking about, were they born yesterday or last week, or was that Abraham Lincoln and that George Washington, because I want to know if that's water over the dam too, I want to know now?" She said, "You shut your mouth, nobody makes a fool out of me. March yourself right down to the office." I says, "Mrs. Brockerly, I want an education, were they born yesterday? Tell me now." She said, "You get your whatd'callit right down this hall and go to the office." I did, I walked in front of that room and I feel just like the rooster partridge, I could just see all my feathers go out, and I walked up there, and my people are looking at me, just smile at me, and I'm walking up front, and I stop to go out the door, big door, and I could see a long hallway, a shiney floor, all your lockers on each side, and I can remember grandpa and grandma talking about the United States Army killing my people when I go out the door, and I just thought maybe somebody's going to stop me going to that office, a big-shot guy, and I thought about this Army Grandpa used to tell me about killing Indians, and I walked down that hall. I didn't walk really, I went sideways because to my mind I was going to see the King of the world. If the Army comes and tries to stop me I'm going to be ready, that's why I walked sideways down that hall. I could see the President of the United States Army just scolding me like that after I'd hit him, just a feeling like that is so nice I almost just feel like I was owning the world. Finally, I got to the office, the Superintendent is Mr. Cavanagh, and they say what can I do for you—Gosh that feels good. "I don't think you can do nothing." They said, "well, what do you mean," I said, "I came here just to tell you guys that you see where it says exit on that door in the red writing, this Mohawk Indian's going out of there pretty soon, and I'm never coming back to your school, your no good school, your rotten school, I'm never coming back here again as long as I'm going to live, and I said some day I may be lucky by God, he will give me a wife and I might have children if I'm lucky, and I'm going to make one thing, I guarantee it, if God ever give me children I'll never put them in your school, I'd rather kill them than put them in your school, so I'm leaving. This is my independence day, I'm going." He said, "What in the world ever made you come to that kind of a conclusion?" I thought he was a pretty dumb man, but he says he needs to know, so I tell him. "Every since we came to this school you've been telling us the Mohawk language is no good. We come here for an education. I didn't want an education and you won't teach us Mohawk language. You teach us about music, but you don't teach us Mohawk songs—you teach us how to sing Yankee Doodle and Ring Around The Roses, and that means that Mohawk songs are no good. You don't teach us about the water drum and the rattle, and that means our water drum's no good. And now, now in that history class down there, that what you call history, you won't teach us about my grandfather, and that means my grandfather's no good, now I know that it's your school that's no good. My people's been told they're worth nothing, day after day, year after year, that's why I'm going out of the door, and that's why my kids would never come here either if I had them."

That's the way I went to school. I'm only 33 years old, that's why when my people talk about death, they only try to stand back up on their foot. Then they say in the United States and in Canada too, that my people have the highest suicide rate and killings. Killers start as a young boy or a young girl. When they said about my own people nationally that our life expectancy is only 45-50 years. They say we went crazy, and that we shoot ourselves, and we're drunks, and we're lazy—I would say that's true, the statistic is true, I'm not proud about it either, but it's true. One white lady asked me one time, she wished she was in Indian shoes because the Government pays our education right to the University if we want it, she said I wish I was in Indian shoes. I would not wish that on her at all.

Like human beings, we like to do something, clap our hands and say—My! What a nice artist you are. My! What a good singer you are. My! You know how to make a nice selection of colour of clothes to wear, it looks good. All human beings want to be wanted, to be needed, to be appreciated, that's the thing that makes most human beings click, a great bit is to be wanted by each other. So that is why, it must be easy to see why my young people shoot themselves, and my own people don't give a damn, and they are the biggest skunks, not all of them, but some of them. So that's the way I went to school.

Slavey Seminar

September 16

(Moderator)

I would like to introduce to you Julian Hardisty, who comes from Fort Simpson, and who has agreed to tell us something of his traditions. Hopefully he will tell us some stories. Generally speaking, we hope that you might tell us anything about the Slavey culture, religion and traditions. Perhaps you could begin with some of the things that happened to you when you were a boy, some of those things which may not happen again. Then we can open the floor to questions.

J.H.　— What do they want to know?

Q.　— Well, we are not here to perform any definite task, we want to learn about the traditions. For instance, do the Slavey people have a story about the creation of the world?

J.H.　— Well, yes, but I never understood it all. This morning one professor talked about a story in which a beaver burrowed down to the bottom of the sea to get some mud for the start of creation. There was a rat and a muskrat in it. There is the same sort of story among my people, or it was told many years ago, but I cannot remember it anymore.

Q.　— Well, when did they tell these stories, these people, the old people?

J.H.　— Back when I was ten years of age I heard many stories. I remember another story about how the McKenzie River was made, and it is a story which is close to me. It is an old legend about a guy we called a medicine man—though whether or not this term is right is hard to say, depending on the time it was recorded and so on.

This guy started down the McKenzie after three beavers he was trying to catch. He caught up to them at what today we call Mills Lake, but the beaver splashed their tails and made the river widen there. They got away, but after that the river narrowed down and he caught up to them again just by Fort Norman. It was right there that he got them and roasted them—in the same old way they roasted the beaver. Now, when you are just coming up the hill into Fort Norman you see what the Indians call the smoke. It is like that coal that has been burning there for centuries, and it is still burning because I have seen it, fifty years ago. That is where he roasted the beaver. Then on down you get to Bear River, and you see Bear Rock, a great big rock, a thousand feet high up to the tip of that rock. If you had ever been up that way you would have noticed that rock. There are three round circles of spruce, a big one, a smaller one, and a smaller one. Well, that spot the Indians would tell you about, that it has been there for ages. That is where the beaver spirits hide.

Now, while this guy was there, a terrible commotion started. He drew out his bow and arrows. While he was shooting his aim went wrong and the arrows went into Bear River. When I was a kid down there, 15 or so, they used to claim that two drift-logs that were still sticking out of the river were those arrows. They used to tie a tow rope to them and pull them way down river, and the next morning they would be back again. Well, I have seen it myself. I do not know why, but finally, aften ten years or so of doing this, they disappeared. So that is how the story goes: these darned things would come back upstream. And if you ever go down Bear River you will see those three spruce circles, and the smoking hole. The medicine man dragged the beaver in there, and you will see the smoke.

Q.   — Tell me, do you know a character, like the Cree have, a kind of fellow who does all sorts of miraculous and marvelous things?

J.H.   — I have heard of him, but that was before my time. I don't even know his name.

Q.   — The Slavey have a character in their stories like that?

J.H.   — They did have, but I was so young then, I do not know the stories much.

Q.   — Do you have any stories about where your people come from?

J.H.   — Yes. Actually the people from my area used to be around Fort Lehoot, and the people from that area are in my area now. According to the stories there was a lot of fighting between the Chipewyans and the Slavey Indians. It was not the Slavey who started the fighting, it was the Chipewyans. About 400 miles up north from where I am now is where the people who were called the Hare Indians were. They were pushed south, and their camping ground is where we are now, Fort Simpson. They were all Hare Indians before. I think we came down from Slave Lake. I'm just gathering up my old stuff here, I have heard many different things, like the Chipewyans pushing out the Hares. It was hundreds of years ago, I guess.

Q.   — Are these stories about the old wars still remembered
and told?

J.H.   — Right now there is nobody left in my area to tell them. All
the old people are gone. Our sons have become Christians and
there's nobody to share tucker with kids (laughter).

Q.   — When you were young, were there special occasions at
which the old people trotted out these stories—special
get-togethers?

J.H.   — Not in my time. The only way to hear the stories was to
be a good boy and get into bed with the old timers. I did not have
much of an opportunity to hear them. I was sent to school when I
was barely ten years old, and I spent five years there before I came
home. After that times were rough. My father-in-law was hard on
me—that is why I went to school. When I came back things were
the same. The only way to make a living was to trap. I didn't know
anything, but I took off to the bush. I have been a lonely man since.

Q.   — Is your experience a common one?

J.H.   — Yes, it is. I never had anybody to be with, so I don't know
the ways of a lot of other people, for which I am sorry now.

Q.   — Did they have medicine men when you were young?

J.H.   — They are talked about, though I have never been around
with one. A lot of them are supposed to be true.

I know of one guy who was supposed to be a crack medicine
man, a peace man from Fort Lehoot. They claimed that he was shot
in the head—snipers—but they never killed him. He talked with the
old people and they said he had that chip out of his skull where the
bullet hit. He is dead now, but they claimed that the wound would
have killed him if he was not a medicine man.

I don't know. It's hard for me. I can't believe it, but I can't say
it's not true, because that is how I feel about miracles.

I heard about another old-timer by the name of Squirrel. He
borrowed one of those muzzle-loading shot-guns, he got his gun
and was going across the river when he dropped his gun in the
middle of the river. He dropped the gun, and he went back and
told the person he borrowed it from that he dropped it, and this
guy was ready to kill him. So he went back to where he figured was
the right spot and jumped in, overboard. They said he was not
found until a long ways downstream, but he came up with the gun,
the same gun. I don't think a white man could do that. There must
be some spiritual power they have . . . but I don't know anything
about that.

Q.   — This spiritual way, that enables them to do these things, have you ever heard of how a person becomes spiritual in this way?
J.H.   — Animals, mostly animals, and the thunderstorm. The Indians believe that thunder is a bird that travels around in the sky. I was talking to one old-timer—I think he is alive still, though I have not seen him for a while—up in the high mountains. He told me about a place in the high mountains where these birds, these thunder-birds he told me about, nested and everything. There are trees up there all burned up on the top of the mountains—that is where they have nested. It's hard to believe, until you see it.
Q.   — Yes, but how do you fit together the belief in the story of the thunder bird, and the white man's explanation of thunder?
J.H.   — I wouldn't know. I wouldn't know. If you want to know anything you have got to figure it out for yourself, that's what I think. I never had the opportunity to get people to tell me things, and that's the best way. As I said I was a lonely guy, make my own life, never mix with anybody. That's why I'm so dumb right now.
Q.   — Were there any animals you could not kill because they were of a sacred nature?
J.H.   — No, not according to the Indians. Well, some people say this about a certain animal—like an old tiger—or a certain waterfall. To them these things are God. You can't touch a cat if he's black. I have seen one guy who would not eat a bear, and one day he ate some and he got sick and almost died. I am an Indian, but I can eat anything. A lot of these things are still going on in the north. Some guys will eat only certain types of food. Maybe that is what they call their medicine.
Q.   — When you were young were there certain things that young people did when they passed from childhood to adulthood, certain rituals they followed?
J.H.   — Well, no, not in my time anyway. Us kids were taught to work. You either had to work or starve or freeze. Nowadays, the kids are . . . well, it's a funny thing. Many a time I had to sleep under a spruce tree without a blanket, with nothing much on, which was foolish but . . . .
Q.   — It was the tough that survived, I guess.
J.H.   — Oh, yes, for people all over the Northwest Territories. They are losing their culture. I have children, now I have lots of grandchildren, and I see this. What will happen now? There are not many old-timers left in our town. I saw in the paper where one old guy—he must have been a good hunter—took some young guys into the bush with him. They got lots of muskrats, lots of beavers. In the evening he told them to go skin them. They did not know how

to use the knife, they did not even know how to skin a muskrat—things like that. What are these school kids going to do: no jobs in the north. They cannot go out into the bush. They do not even know how to set a rabbit snare. One old lady told a 28 year old girl to skin a rabbit and here she was plucking it. When you come to think of it, it's pretty sad.

Q. — What are some of the things that should be passed on?

J.H. — I guess there are a lot of old-timers trying to help the young people. Trapping is still open. Further north there are lots of hunting, good hunting out there. We tried to get help from the Government, because you cannot buy traps for 50 cents anymore—the biggest ones are $12.50 in the hardware stores. So they were trying to get the Government to start a trapping program, bush camps for the younger generation. Take the young people out there in the summer and keep them out there. But now—I can't make head nor tail of it—they are giving it up.

So what are we going to do now?

Q. — How did you learn—your family?

J.H. — We went out in the bush. I spent five years in school, dressed up at school. In those days school was different. We only had one teacher for over 125 students. She taught all the classes. Then they had to split the classes in half, half in the morning, half in the afternoon. We had dog teams—Headmistress' permission of course—soon we had three dog teams. Sometimes they tired of us and gave us a couple of dog teams and told us to get the heck out in the bush. We would spend the whole week out there you know, and that is how I learned. I never lost my culture, I never lost the feel for animals. When I got back I was 15 but I had learned how to hunt, how to kill—I've done a lot of it in my days. I have done some pretty good trapping, for the last 30 years now.

I did not lose my language or anything. I was a Protestant at that time, now I am a Catholic through marriage. My grandfather was a Protestant Minister, he had his teaching. I don't know how in the heck he ever got his training at McGill's University, it was way before my time. Then, you see, I married a Catholic woman in the 1930's, and my mother before she died wanted my wife to become Protestant. But I became a Catholic when she was about ready to die anyway, because Catholic and Protestant in our vicinity are about the same anyway. I have seen priests in the Protestant Church and Protestant Ministers in Catholic Churches. It is a little crazy. If there is such a thing as God, you only pray to that one God, so why have a bunch of Churches?

Q.   — Were any of the other children that ran away to residential school still studied in Indian religion?

J.H.   — Some of them, yes. Many of them came to our school from the north coast, and some were Eskimos. It was the only residential school in Inuvik. I have met some Eskimos in Winnipeg; they are from a different kind of family. Actually I have met some of the guys I went to school with around the coast. They are, nearly all of them still trapping to make a living. They did not lose their culture at all.

In my time, after I got back from school, we were as crazy as kids are today, always crazy with dances and stuff like that. We would come in for Christmas, stay over till New Year, then you couldn't find a young guy in town after that. These days it is different. You cannot get a young person into the bush.What is it? We don't know. It's a civilization more or less—more or less getting caught up in it.

Q.   — You mentioned dancers, was this traditional dancing?

J.H.   — No, not rock and roll that's for sure (laughter). Old time barn dances, tea dances. You will find that there are lots of drum dances, lots of them. The Dogrib tribes that's all they do for about two months of the year. None of what the Dogrib tribe calls spiritual dances, drum dances at our dances. What you would call spiritual dancing—there is none of that.

In the summertime there is one outfit up there run by Nicola Black. You might have seen him in your courses here. He has his own drummers, five drummers who travel along with him. For the last three years now he has come over from Fort Raven down to Fort Robinson. He takes a boat from there down to Fort Norman, and performs the drum dances as he goes. This is more or less a spiritual dance—that is what he calls it. I have seen them do one or two dances at Fort Simpson, at a pow-pow we had there. The stories he told then were mostly religious. I do not think it is the same religion the Churches go in for. He is like . . . like some sort of Prophet. He can foresee things ahead and he sees that somebody is taking a drink. If somebody drinks and goes to his dances, he just quits drinking right there. I saw it happen once in Yellowknife. There was a dancing ceremony and everybody was sober, and the dancing was really good. It was right in the community hall there. Then around midnight some drunks came and they just dropped everything (all drinking). So I guess it is some sort of religious ceremony he was giving up and down the river.

Q.   — Does Nicola Black try to help people get in touch with their spiritual life?

J.H.　　— Yes, that's what, I think that is what it is all about. There is only one kind of guy he could be, and that is a Prophet, lots of luck and spirit. I have seen this. Also the dancers, they can see things ahead too. But there are those we call false Prophets, and at their dances there is more drinking going on, and everything, and it can be very dangerous.

Q.　　— They are a little more authentic if they outlaw drinking?

J.H.　　— Yes, I guess so. There are a lot of people—dreamers—who live by dreams. I believe that dreams are very true. When I was about 17 I was up at Bear Lake, and there were not many boats there. I used to swim here. There was an old man there who was supposed to be some sort of Prophet. I asked him how the boat would make it going across the lake, the crossing takes about 2 days—around 200 miles. He said he saw a boat crossing the lake, and catching on fire just before it reached the shore, and one man badly burned. We waited for word, and sure enough it happened. Before the schooner got into Fort Raven it caught on fire, and one man was badly burned. Things like that, he could see. It was the first time that I had seem him. He was a very old guy.

I went out again, a year later, to a small Indian village on the edge of a big bay. One day there was a young chap paddling a boat across the bay, and an old man was sitting in it. When they landed we got the old man out. He was partly blind at the time. I went over and shook hands with him, and he said, "I knew you were in town." But I don't know him because I don't know anybody in town. He could not see me anyway. Then he was telling me about the time he knew my grandfather. He was very old, my grandfather died way back in the 1800's sometime. He told me stories about the people in Fort Rigley, Fort Simpson, about how much booze there was going around.

One old-timer I knew used to be a drummer, and he called himself a Prophet—a spiritual or something like that. He was telling me once about this old man, how he calls himself a medicine man or spiritual man, how anytime you go into the dances there are always drunks in there. He helps them lots. I hope nobody tells anybody about this, but I guess he must be dreaming. It is very very hard for me to understand stuff like that, but what he told me was exactly true.

Q.　　— Have you ever had experiences like this yourself?

J.H.　　— No, I am too wild for that.

Q.   — Did any of the old-timers teach special things which you
should do like when you kill a moose, or bear?
J.H.   — No, well the only thing I can think of that everybody did,
if we got a pregnant moose, the calf would be hung up. And then
how to cache the meat so the dog would not get at it. I found it out
myself, the hard way. I was a bear hunter in my young days, but I
was never as good as the old-timers. I mean the native population
will kill the bear. I used to kill a bear with two others, and there
were always people who wanted to eat it. There is no use in wasting
food. Then again, I used to watch some when it was there—lots—
on the stove, some did not eat it.
Q.   — At home when we made a shot, we put the bones on a
tree, all of them. Isn't it bad not to recognize the animals that way?
J.H.   — Well, not in our manner. We would put the skull of a
moose, for example, up in a tree so the dogs would not get at it.
That's the only thing that was taught in the Indian traditions. But we
have a penchant that if we go out for food, and can't use it all,
there's no use wasting it, because if you do not eat it, the gulls can
have it.
Q.   — Do any animals bring bad luck?
J.H.   — Not according to my knowledge. I was told that if a man
shoots a porcupine when his eyes are open, he would have a hard
time getting a moose but I've shot a porcupine and it didn't seem
to hurt my moose hunting.
Q.   — Did you ever get bothered by wolf rings on your trap
line?
J.H.   — Oh yes, lots of times, they were a pest. There was one
year I'd lost about $300-400 worth of fur before those guys and the
price was not good at that time. Now that they are worth over $100
I can't get any (laughter).
Q.   — Do you own a pipe?
J.H.   — No. Never smoked a pipe. You will not see much of that
in the north. In all the huts there, people on the reservation call it
the peace pipe, but we haven't got that in our band. I've seen
one—one fellow from the reservation is the head of the tree of
peace in Yellowknife. He came to a ceremony in Fort Simpson. He's
quite a talker, you know, and he had his pipe, his peace pipe. It was
the first time that I had ever seen one. He started to talk of the
stories of creation, like the muskrat story, that's all.
Q.   — Do you remember if the world, you know in the stories,
was the world created only once, or was it a thing that happens
over again?
J.H.   — Well this, not according to our Indian legend. It would

be better if you got the right people, the right old timers will tell
you about those stories. In my time I haven't heard anything.

Q.   — Do you and the Slavey practise sweat lodge?

J.H.   — No, we do not know of this. But we are starting to . . .
yes, one fellow by the name of Dan Green . . . I remember that at
the end my mother was talking about the sweat lodge. People on
the reservations in the south practise a lot of things we don't know
anything about in the north.

Q.   — What part did the Church play in the loss of traditions in
the north?

J.H.   — Well, not much. I blame it all on the Government.

Q.   — You are very generous.

J.H.   — I thing that if the Government would just let the people
alone the way they used to live, they would be a lot better off.
Instead of enforcing laws on the people, they should stick to the
treaties, like treaty 7 and 8. According to the old timers, as long as
the sun rises and sets the kids will not run out of clothes as long as
the treaties are not broken. At that time the land was used for
hunting and fishing, and we could live off the land. When the
Government restricted the killing of moose to one per each family
per year, it caused a lot of problems. I know one old-timer, a good
moose hunter. He would hardly ever come into town. He was hard
of hearing, you had to shout at him before he heard you. In the
spring, after the winter they passed that law, he came into town
with a moose, and the Game Warden came up and took it away
from him. No one had told him anything about it. He was fined 15
bucks, but I was not in town then.

   You must have heard about Dick Turner, who writes books
about the north. He was from Calgary, and he knew this old-timer
pretty well, and he just picked up the fine for the old man and they
just told the old man to get out. Things like that. That's how the
people have lost their culture. Trapping was good, then you were
only allowed five martins—and now there are hundreds, of martins.
Another time they closed the beaver off altogether, then there
were hundreds of beaver, and you have to have a special permit to
kill ten beaver, for I don't know how many years. Things like that.
These fine people lost all their faith in trapping, their culture and
everything. This is what the Government did. When the beaver as
closed off, I was out of a job. It was through the Anglican Bishop
and all the Indians banded together and sent a nasty letter to
Ottawa. So, the Church has nothing really to do with it, the culture,
how we lost it, and I blame the Government, and always will.

Q.　　— To what extent do you think that Government regulation of hunting has affected native well-being and other things?

J.H.　　— Well, I don't know. The old timers who lived most of the time in the bush hardly ever got sick, though there is a lot of disease. I think the reason is this canned food they have introduced up there. A few years ago, you would never hear of cancer in the north, it was all east. I travelled down to the coast this summer. I talked to many different people. There are many cancer cases out there. The old people say it's the chemicals and stuff in the food. A lot of these things could be right, you know. You never can tell.

Q.　　— How many children do you have? How many are still alive?

J.H.　　— I had six, no—I had eight. Two died.

Q.　　— Did you lose them when they were small children?

J.H.　　— No. One—he had four kids—was electrocuted on a job. He broke both his ankles and gradually developed cancer. The family had a hard time. I lost my other boy, and I have six alive. One has given me grandchildren, and I have another boy who works in the grocery store across the road. I am a widower for five year.

Q.　　— You say some of your family are at home. What do they do at home?

J.H.　　— I have two girls. They are both married, they are both cooking.

Q.　　— You must be retired now?

J.H.　　— No, I have a year and a half to go, if I live that long.

Q.　　— Do the young people still learn the Slavey language?

J.H.　　— Yes, most do. I trust my grandchildren will. They understand it, but they do not speak it. Only one does—she has a lisp. She has an education but she can still speak the language. It is what I want for the kids. There are about ten of them and if you say anything in Slavey they go the other way. I guess there are a lot of others who are losing their culture. It is no use worrying about what you cannot change. I cannot help. I'm having a rest.

My sister-in-law and her sister do a lot of moose hair handicrafts. I guess you have seen some of that Slavey embroidery. They do handicrafts that went to Toronto last year. Have you seen it? Quill work, moose hair.

Q.　　— Oh, yes! It's very good!

J.H.　　— They really make good money on it. They use little pictures. They sold some in Toronto, when they came to see me in the hospital, for $200.00. There is a market for the handicrafts right in the town there, too.

Q.   — Are there any of the young people wearing it, as well as selling it?

J.H.   — Oh yes, there is a little settlement in the village, about 70 people. They do all their work there, in Jean-Marie. There is some going on in Fort Simpson too, the hard work—basket making and things like that. They have a team. They are doing very well, leather jackets, beaded leather jackets. My sister-in-law sold one of those in Toronto for $400.00. The pictures are very pretty.

Q.   — Do they make their own dyes, their own colours?

J.H.   — No, they buy that stuff.

Q.   — Do they use traditional designs and colours?

J.H.   — Oh yes, yes, lots of that stuff. I have not seen a great deal of them, but I have seen much of my sister's things. It's moccasins and mukkluks—they sell a lot of that in Yellowknife—there are about 400 people there.

Q.   — If we could back-track a minute, when you were first married, were marriages arranged between families?

J.H.   — Well yes, you go around and find a wife. You fall in love and then you arrange to get married. I was only 19 when I got married. It was up to me to ask her father.

Q.   — You asked the father, and then what?

J.H.   — He, they agreed to it.

Q.   — Was there any opposition because you were a Protestant?

J.H.   — No. Well, we married in a Catholic Church. I still kept my religion, though. If we had had kids, they would have been baptized in the Catholic Church. Years later I became a Catholic, even though I was going to remain a Protestant yet. It was my mother—you would not believe it, she was a Minister's daughter—she told me to do it. She was 82 years of age when she died. At that time there was hardly any difference between the Catholic and the Protestant. All I had to do was show baptism papers. That was all there was to it, there was no fuss over anything.

Q.   — Were there more arranged marriages when you were young?

J.H.   — Well, I have heard about it yes, I have heard about it, I knew one old-timer . . .

(End of Tape)

Moderator – Thank you.

The Tale of the Making of Maple Sugar

by

Marius Nanipowisk

Nanipowisk, a member of the band, still living in the Piapot reserve,
tells a story that concerns the making of maple sugar. It may be a
surprise to a lot of people to know that Crees still make
maple sugar, tapping it from the dwarf mountain maple or the
mountain maple. But in this case, a Cree named Flying Ice and his
wife had settled near the sight of the present town of Craven and
had tapped a number of trees. Each morning Flying Ice would make
the rounds of the sap pails, but he was annoyed and puzzled to
discover that the sap pails would be empty even though the sap was
running. First he thought someone was stealing sap but then he
noticed that the pails did not appear to be disturbed. At this point
he decided to go shooting for prairie chickens. He knew a place
where they gathered to perform their mating ceremonies. He took
his muzzle-loading gun and went to the spot where he lay on his
stomach and waited for the birds to appear. Presently several came
and for a while he watched them. The ceremony was most
interesting. Then he fired and with one shot he got two birds. With
them he started home and went by way of the trees he had tapped
to have another look at them. In the trees he saw what he took to
be two small boys, though they did not seem to be more than knee
high and their clothes were not those usually worn by white boys.
They had knee pants and swallow-tail coats. But Flying Ice decided
to run after them and as fast as he knew how, he pursued them
through the woods. He could not gain on them and presently they
disappeared. He ran on looking for their footprints but he could
find none. Very annoyed he went home to his wife and told her
what had happened. And when he was through, she said,
maimaykwaiswaq; we must move away. This is their country no
matter how long we stay, we will never have any maple sugar.
Wherever there are cut-banks and sandy pits there you may come
upon these little people.

Mythological Section

Myths in Native North American Religions

by

Åke Hultkrantz

Any effort to dissect and classify the myths of the North American Indians in a short presentation must necessarily be selective and superficial. Not only is the concept of myth as such highly controversial and therefore difficult to handle, North American tales which may pass as myths are extremely numerous. Some of them have been dealt with in detailed, bulky monographs, but most of them have either been published in collections of tales or have not been published at all: they exist as manuscripts in the files of the Smithsonian Institution or other public or private archives. Many mythological tales are still part of the traditional store of narratives told on Indian reservations.

It is not my intention to try to embrace all this material here, to account for scholarly achievements and the range and dimensions of North American Indian myths. My object is more specific, as the title of my paper reveals. In my consideration these myths have not received in all respects the scholarly treatment they deserve. My aim is therefore to outline the religious import of North American myths. In contradistinction to most colleagues in anthropology and folklore I consider "myth" to be primarily a religious concept. Consequently, its place in religion and its meaning should be sought for first of all. To my understanding this analysis has been used very sparingly, whereas historical, formal and psychological investigations have been performed quite frequently.[1] In proceeding from a religio-scientific point of view we may arrive at important conclusions as to the types of myths, the role played by myths, their relations to the ritual and to belief systems. Moreover, it can be shown that each cultural area of North America has a myth system that corresponds to historical and ecological factors.

The reader should be aware of the fact, already made clear, that in the face of an enormously abundant material the following account can only be very selective. First of all I have used material with which I am well acquainted and which has been discussed earlier in my literary production. If this means a slight predilection for myths from the Plains and Basin areas it cannot be helped.

Mythological research in North America

Myth is, as I said, primarily a religious concept. This statement will no doubt be questioned by opponents: why should a tale, a myth, be analyzed solely from the viewpoint of its religious contents when there are so many other aspects that could be applied? "Myth" is a *terminus technicus* in many disciplines (cf. e.g. Chase 1949). Literature, history, folklore, anthropology all contend that the subject of myth properly belongs within their own domain. Myth is oral "literature", or folk tales, or speculation about natural occurrences, or untrue statements about the world around us. With the exception of the latter category all the others are products of scholarly thinking over a long time.

It may be advantageous here to look back upon the approaches to North American myths and tales that have been in current use up until now (cf. Dundes 1967, pp. 61 ff., and Hultkrantz 1967, pp. 21 ff.). Disregarding euhemerism and other early western ways of understanding the myth it was the symbolism of O.T. Müller and the *Naturmythologie* of Max Müller and others that constituted the prevailing myth interpretation when the scientific study of myth began. As far as I can tell it left few traces in North American Indian mythography except for Brinton's obsession with solar and Kunike's with lunar mythology (Brinton 1882, Kunike 1926). The historico-geographical schools started by Boas in anthropology and Krohn in folklore have far more important repercussions. Most myths and tales were analyzed according to the diffusionistic key provided by Boas. The latter's *Tsimshian Mythology* and Reichard's study of Plateau Indian myths are good examples of the method (Boas 1916, Reichard 1947), while Krohn's influence may be traced in Thompson's famous study of the Star Husband tale, for example (Thompson 1953). As Dundes has shown, the preoccupation of the same Finnish school with tale types and motif indexes had a precursor in Swanton's call for a concordance of North American myths and Kroeber's and Lowie's listing of mythological catchwords (Dundes 1967: 63). This was a line that Thompson took up later on; his survey of North American Indian tales from 1929 remains a source of comparative information (Thompson 1929). Tale type and motif index mean to a historical interpretation what genre analysis means to a religio-scientific interpretation: they are both necessary methodological tools.

In the time between the two world wars Malinowski's functionalism had a great following among students of myths. Its impact on North American scholars was less remarkable, however, due to the predomination of the Boas school and its, as it were, submerged functionalism. (As Kroeber has demonstrated, Boas was more interested in function and process than in history.) Malinowski's genre analysis of Trobriand tales is well known; it had apparently little effect on American anthropologists and folkorists. This was unfortunate, for in this way the religious factor in mythology continued to be bypassed. Indeed, Waterman's analysis of explanatory tales had demonstrated the nonessential import of religious *aitia* in such tales (Waterman 1914).

Another trend from the same time, the psychoanalytic approach (also present in Malinowski's writings), had a stronger and more lasting impact on the interpretation of North American myths. A mythical key-figure like the culture hero (or, as American students of myth prefer to see him, the trickster) attracted, because of its Janus-character, the attention of both professional psychoanalysts (Róheim, Jung) and anthropologists (Radin, La Barre) (Róheim 1952, Radin 1956, La Barre 1970). The center of the interest was and is irrational man, in particular his *id* and its sublimations. Religion comes in as an illustration of the sway of the subconscious forces. This reductionistic attitude, clearly demonstrated in La Barre's work, has unfortuantely meant that, for instance, the solutions to the trickster problem residing in the religious context have been overlooked.

A most important way of understanding myth was introduced by sociological students. Two main approaches may be distinguished, originating with Robertson Smith and Durkheim, respectively. The former stated that mythology on the whole constituted a description of ritual. He is therefore held as the progenitor of the British myth-and-ritual school, later called the Cambridge school (after Jane Harrison and others). The Near Eastern mythology investigated by this group (and like-minded Scandinavian historians of religions) yielded a good harvest of confirmations of the theory. However, the close-knit societies in the Near East have few counterparts in North America, and although a case might have been made for Zuni and Winnebago myths, North American Indian myths were not investigated from this perspective.[2] Here, again, the lack of concern for religion among most American anthropologists may have played a role.

Durkheim's position, subsequently heralded by a majority of French sociologists and, in Britain, by Radcliffe-Brown and his pupils, was simple enough: religion, including myth, is modelled on and integrated with society. It will remain a problem whether the American studies of cultural reflections in mythology, initiated by Boas (on the Tsimshian and Kwakiutl) and followed up by, for instance, Ehrlich (on the Crow), Spencer (on the Navajo) and Stern (on the Klamath), were stimulated by the sociological school (cf. Hultkrantz 1956:24, Dundes 1967:66 f.). In any case, these studies are the closest counterparts from the North American field to this kind of mythological research. Common to both approaches was a deficient interest in religious aspects of myth and, in the French-British social anthropology, a tendency towards reductionism in dealing with religion and myth. These reservations on my part should not conceal the fact, however, that the sociological school has contributed greatly to our understanding of religious oral traditions in their socio-cultural setting. Likewise, the students of this school have shown in what important ways a myth can serve as a *charta*, or sanction, of both ritual and profane institutions.

The latest fashion in mythological research is, as we know, structuralism. It has greatly affected North American Indian mythology. The culture hero behind this approach, Lévi-Strauss, used Tsimshian materials from Boas' already mentioned monograph in his classic essay on *Asdiwal*, and North American myths have been used extensively in his later volumes, known under the collective name *Mythologiques* (Lévi-Strauss 1958, 1967). There is no need to recapitulate more closely the French scholar's ideas here. His main target is the operations of the human mind, not the myth as such. By structural analysis he finds that all myths aim at resolving conflicts that haunt human existence. In coded messages the myths hide their ulterior meanings, which may be found out through dialectic logic and different kinds of transformal procedures. The manifest, religious contents of myths are never discussed. Such questions have to give in to the deeper problem of the structure of the human mind. Indeed, Lévi-Strauss confesses that he does not understand what religion is (Lévi-Strauss 1969:43).

This is not the place to launch a full-scale criticism of this scholar's program. Some scholars are satisfied with it, while others, like myself, are not. His analysis is both arbitrary and, with respect to the results, monotonous; that it evinces the brilliancy of a creative thinker is another matter. What cannot be disputed is that this structuralism reveals the inherent logic of a myth, its rhythm, its style. Questions of style have been an enduring theme in studies of

American tales (cf. Reichard, Jacobs), and no doubt Lévi-Strauss has contributed to the genre.

Nevertheless, some students of religion have approached the structuralism of Lévi-Strauss in a positive way. There is thus an analysis of the Sedna myth among the Central Eskimo in which the author, J.F. Fisher, finds "that Sedna mediates between several sets of oppositions in Eskimo culture". He also concludes that Sedna provides a means of dealing with oppositions that are inherent in the Eskimo world view (Fisher 1975:36 f., 38). This is a trivial conclusion. The main fact is that Sedna, mistress of the sea animals, is such a central person in the Eskimo world that she has attracted a set of myths, well analyzed by Fisher. As we shall see, it is dangerous to infer from myth what belongs to religion.

A structural approach also underlies Dundes' analysis of North American folk tales. However, it concerns the narrative rather than its contents. It is in many respects a scholarly work. Unfortunately the author commits the sin of identifying tales on the basis of their structures as outlined by him. The outcome is that, for example, the North American Orpheus tradition is identified with a completely different abduction tale (Dundes 1964:77). This example shows that formal structures are too general to define a tale. Only analyses of contents can lead to constructive definitions. If we are dealing with religious tales—and the Orpheus tradition belongs to this category—the functional setting of the tale is also important.

This short review of research on North American myths and tales shows that scholars have avoided denoting myth as a religious category. Only one American, the philosopher Alexander, endeavoured to identify the religious contents of American Indian myths after Brinton (Alexander 1916). It is remarkable that the editors of the series *Mythology of All Races* designated a philosopher, not an anthropologist or folklorist, to compose the North American volume of the set. Scholars like Lowie, Radin and Speck occasionally subjected myths to religious analysis, but halfheartedly (cf. Hultkrantz 1967: 192, 194 f.). European Americanists with their background in comparative religion did more, but they were few, and their ideas were ruled by fashionable theories of perishable nature.

This is no condemnation of the approaches and methods that have been used so far in studies of North American myths. The field of mythic creations is a wide one, in which many disciplines are involved, and many facets are explored. However, myth is more than just a tale. It is a myth because it has religious relevance. As myth it should therefore be primarily investigated with an eye to its religious value. Thus the necessity to perform such research seems urgent, indeed, compelling here.

The definition of myth

This approach presupposes, of course, that we know what a myth is. Here again there is much confusion, not least in the ranks of North American mythologists.

Let us return to the source of our systematization, Jacob Grimm himself. In his *Teutonic Mythology*, first published in 1835, Grimm laid down the essential differences between myth, legend and fictional folktale, or fairy-tale (*Märchen*). He observed that the folktale is flighty, fantastic, migratory, and the legend local-bound, close to history, whereas the myth portrays gods and supernatural animals and all kinds of metamorphoses (Grimm 1966 III: XV ff.). This scheme, admittedly inspired by the specific conditions in continental Europe, was widely accepted in its general outlines (whereas the criteria for the respective categories were soon refined). For instance, it was adopted by British folklorists and students of comparative religion (Hartland 1914, Harrison 1912: 330). When, at the turn of the century, American anthropologists published collections of epical narratives under the heading "myths and folktales" this was an echo of Grimm's classification (see e.g. Boas 1915). At the same time American folktales were never systematized in a rigorous way; anthropologists speak indifferently about myths and folktales even today. Indeed, Boas was opposed to a classification if it was not supported by native terms (Boas 1915: 310). It is true that few American Indian collections of traditions can be categorized according to Grimm's system; Bascom lists a few, however (Bascom 1965: 9 f.).

This is scarcely surprising. The Oriental "wonder tale" that invaded Europe in the eighteenth century gave rise to fictional tales. Among American Indians this type of tale is not unknown, but there is no doubt that it was introduced at a rather late date by Europeans (cf. Thompson 1919). The original situation in both Europe and North America was, then, that two types of narrative could be distinguished, both of them objects of belief: myths and legends (traditions). It is necessary to stress the word "could" here. If we go back in European cultural history we find that the Greek word *mythos* originally meant tale in a very general sense. Since most of these tales concerned the gods the genre was soon settled (cf. Kirk 1970). Similarly, many American Indian tribes know only one word, tale. There are, however, quite a few tribes that distinguish between two categories which we could label "myths" and "legends" (cf. Beckwith 1938: XVI f.). As Boas has pointed out, the two classes refer mostly to a distance in time. Among the Winnebago, for instance, the *waika* refer to divine actors in a distant mythical era, while the *worak* refer to human actors within the memory of man (Boas 1915: 310 f.; Radin 1948: 11 f.).[3]

Even in those cases where only one native (linguistic) category can be identified an analysis may show a covert categorization. Thus, in my interpretation of Shoshoni religious narratives I found the term for narrative stands for two man types of religious epic accounts, myths and legends. Not only the distance in time but also the attitude of veneration and sacredness were criteria for my judgment. A third category, fictional tales, has apparently developed in more recent times but plays a minor role (Hultkrantz 1960). Some may object, as Boas did once, that an analysis which is not supported by the overt categorization of the aborigines themselves should not be permissible. My answer is that modern cultural research is acknowledged to operate on two levels: we may see things as the natives see them, or we may systematize them according to guiding principles which we perceive to be basic. Anthropologists talk about emic and etic units (Pike), or unconscious and conscious models (Lévi-Strauss). Certainly, Bascom is in agreement with my views when he says,

> Despite the incompleteness of the evidence, and despite these variations in native categories, the definitions of myth, legend and folktale offered here are analytically useful. They can be meaningfully applied even to societies in which somewhat different distinctions between prose narratives are recognized (Bascom 1965: 15).

With his article on the genres of folk narratives Bascom has reintroduced the Grimm classification as a legitimate tool in American folkloristics. It would be advantageous if also American Indian traditions could be subjected to the same kind of analysis. In that way we would arrive at a clearer understanding of the religious contents of North American tales, and could compare them with Old World myths in a more relevant way.

With this discussion in mind the genres should be defined. A thorough definition should contain all those criteria which have been laid down as essential by Honko in an important paper in 1968. However, most of our North American materials were collected during the first fifty years of this century, without the collectors transmitting to us information on all the circumstances that we need to know for a classification in Honko's spirit. If we use a few basic criteria it should be possible to identify, as I have tried to demonstrate in my book on the North American Orpheus tale, a good number of texts in archives and printed publications as myths, legends and fictions (Hultkrantz 1957: 274 ff.).[4] I suggest that our criteria will include the time and scene for the action, the character of the personages, and, as far as it goes, the form of tradition. We arrive then at the following classification:

(1) The myth. It takes place at the beginning of time, its acting personages are gods and mythic beings like the culture hero, primeval man and the prototypes of animals, and the scene for action is the supernatural world. The myth has a fixed pattern of events, and actions are often repeated four times in North American texts.

(2) The legend. It takes place in historical and recent times, its acting personages are human beings in their encounters with representatives of a supernatural world—spirits, ghosts, monsters—, and the scene for action is this world or the supernatural world.

Both these categories are considered to be true. The myth depicts events in a far off time "when animals were human beings", as it is often said in North American myths. Furthermore, the myth has been passed down through the generations as a sacred tale, or as a contribution to knowledge about the world. The legend, again, with its supposed roots in a later, historical reality can often be traced back to a memorate, that is, a narrative of a certain person's meeting with a supernatural in a version or a dream. It stands to reason that North American Indians with their vision-quest pattern have a rich store of such legends.

(3) The fictional tale. It belongs to any time and any place, but it is always framed in a world of wonder. Its characters are fictive persons, in North America mostly supernaturals from European tales. The form of the tale may reveal the same European provenience.

Strictly speaking, the fictional tale is not at home in North America. Hallowell mentions that the Saulteaux of Manitoba believe all their tales to be true (Hallowell 1947: 547). It seems the same rule prevailed all over North America. Only where a disintegration of old cultures has taken place, or where European fairy-tales have been accepted, the genre of fictional narratives for entertainment has spread. Many would perhaps refer the adventures of the trickster to the fictional tales, but they are indeed basically myths (see below).

The sanctioning power of myths and legends

Our genre classification means, of course, that the range of folktales that may pass as myths becomes much more narrow than it generally is in the opinion of most of my American colleagues. It becomes even smaller if we separate sacred myths from other, less functional myths. On the other hand, there is an affinity between sacred foundation myths and certain legends having the same general function. This complicates our picture. However, in the interest of comparative research the line we have drawn between myth and legend ought to be upheld.

In principle every bonafide myth serves as a model, a *charta*, of the world and of human institutions. As I have expressed it in another connection, "the myth gives instruction concerning the world of the gods, and therewith concerning the cosmic order; it confirms the social order and the cultural values obtaining and it is in itself sacred" (Hultkrantz 1957: 13). Modern scholars of religion, in particular Eliade, have emphatically asserted that this is the real importance of myth; they have thus expanded the view put forth by Malinowski that the myth "expresses, enhances, and codifies belief" (cf. e.g. Eliade 1949). (The latter statement is, as we shall see, not entirely acceptable regarding North American material.) If the myth allows us to experience a drama *in illo tempore* (Eliade), in a "dream-time", to quote Australian aborigines, which is present even today, this mystery is facilitated by the tense constructions of Indian verbs (Brown 1976: 28). At the same time there is the deep meaning behind it all that the mythical events form the prototype for things today: not only the world-view but also the daily occupations and events have their model—and of course, their origins—in the mythical world. In a way the perspective is aetiological, but this concept does not include the model and sanction functions of the myth and is therefore insufficient.

This is the ideal myth, as we meet it in Eliade's writings. I suppose it is the same type of myth Kluckhohn seeks when he points at "the connotation of the sacred as that which differentiates 'myth' from the rest of folklore" (Kluckhohn 1942: 47). However, North American myths are not always sacred, as will soon be demonstrated. Furthermore, there are legends that have mythical functions; we are here reminded of Boas' general view that in North America myths may turn into legends and vice versa (cf. Boas 1915: 310 f.). These reservations are justified, if we proceed from a general idea that myths and legends always keep clear of each other. But in fact, all I want to do here is to insist upon a correct *classification*. Myths, or at least mythical patterns, may be integrated with legends, just as legends may be reinterpreted into myths. Both processes may be illustrated with the North American Orpheus tradition. As I have tried to show, it is basically a tale of a shaman bringing back a sick person's free-soul from the realm of the dead, a soul-loss cure through the shaman's soul-flight (Hultkrantz 1957: 259, 261). In most North American cases it appears as a legend, but in a few societies it is told as a myth. It is a real myth among the Modoc, Nisenan, Navajo and Taos Indians in California and the Southwest, and among the Cherokee of the Southeast (Hultkrantz 1957: 279). The actors are here exalted supernatural beings. Among the Winnebago the legend has been endowed with mythic details so that Radin classifies it as a "myth tale": it includes "motifs and incidents from the mythological background" (Radin 1926: 22). Surely, the demarcation line between myth and legend is not absolute in this material.

Whether the same situation obtains or not in other areas of the world, there is no doubt that the importance of the vision quest in North America has determined the ease with which genres overlap. The vision paves the way for the mythical integration of the legend or the legend's transformation into a myth. Indeed, the vision is so powerful that it even creates myths. This is the situation among the Mohave Indians of California. Their medicine-men receive whole myths in their dreams (see on this matter e.g. Kroeber 1948: 1 ff.). In practice it means of course that dream-contents are worked into a prefigured mythic pattern. Above all, visions have produced many legends which have the same sanctioning power as sacred myths.

Some examples. The Orpheus tradition in North America which is mostly a legend reinforces and gives authority to beliefs in the afterworld (Gayton 1935: 285, Hultkrantz 1957: 290). There is positive information that it even forms eschatological ideas (Hultkrantz 1957: 282). In the last century the Orpheus tradition, probably on account of its shamanistic background, functioned as an "institution legend" for the Ghost Dance (Hultkrantz 1957: 145 f., 263, 307, 311 f.). Another legend with similar functions tells of a warrior who, resting on a hill distant from his camp, received a vision. A buffalo spirit appeared to him, gave him instructions on how to set up and perform a Sun Dance, and ordered him back to his camp to realize the vision. The Indian did so, and that was the beginning of the Sun Dance. This tale is told by Shoshoni and Ute.[5]

Finally there is the well-known legend of the two Dakota men who met a buffalo maiden out on the Plains. One of them wanted to seduce the beautiful girl, and turned into a skeleton; the other had decent thoughts and was endowed with the sacred pipe by the buffalo maiden. This is the origin legend of the sacred pipe and the ceremonies surrounding it.[6]

These legends all show that supernatural actions in legends in which humans take part may receive the same binding force as such actions in myths on two counts, namely (a) if the course of events is supposed to have happened long ago, and (b) if the events have proved to have importance for a whole group of human beings.

Classification of Myths in North America

The North American Indian myths may conveniently be divided into sacred myths and myths of entertainment or—if that term is preferred—mythological tales. By the latter term I do not mean what Boas had in mind (or Radin, when speaking of myth-tales), but tales which have the status of myths but have no serious function. The sacred myths, which all have a sanctioning purpose, may be divided into cosmological myths, institutional myths and ritual myths.

We arrive at the following four groupings:

(1) Cosmological myths are sacred myths that describe the cosmos and the interrelations of its phenomena by anchoring them in a series of supernatural events in primordial time. The cosmic phenomena are thus seen as products of an *Urdrama*, a cosmogony. Cosmological myths may be connected with a ritual, but this is not always the case, particularly not among the hunting and gathering peoples. Cosmological myths procure for man a world-view, but not necessarily a religion (cf. below). The people that appear in these myths are not necessarily the deities and spirits of practical religion.

Among cosmological myths proper we may primarily count the creation myths and the astral myths. The former exist in many different types (Rooth 1957). There is the North Central Californian myth according to which the world came about through the power of the Creator's word (cf. e.g. de Angulo and Benson 1932). There is the South Californian myth that describes the emanation of the world as a result of the cohabitation between the sky god and Mother Earth. As Kroeber remarked it recalls Polynesian creation myths (Kroeber 1925: 677). And there is, last but not least, the myth of the Earth-diver, in which the Creator orders animals to dive for mud in the primeval sea, or dives himself; out of the mud he creates the earth. This myth is associated with a wide-spread mythological theme, the rival twins (Count 1952). This is not the place to discuss this interesting relationship. However, there is clear evidence that both the myth and the idea of dual creators have disseminated from the Old World (Hultkrantz 1963: 33 f., 44 f.).

The position of astral myths is somewhat enigmatic in North America. Usually a myth is not astral all through, but it ends with an astral motif, or the final episode in the narrative has astral symbolism. Among the Wind River Shoshoni, for instance, many tales of Coyote's adventures have astral motifs appended at the end. When Coyote tries to seduce his daughters they flee to the sky where they become a star constellation, or three mountain bucks pursued by hunters finally flee up to the sky and turn into stars (cf. Hultkrantz 1960: 567). These endings remind us of Waterman's discussion of explanatory tales. It is difficult to judge how they once came about. However, knowing the development of the trickster tales (cf. below) it is possible to see them as remnants of old myths, perhaps attached to other tales (cf. Hultkrantz 1972: 348).

There are, namely, astral myths in a true sense, myths that connect the star-spangled sky with primordial times. The Pawnee and Blackfoot possess such myths. Indeed, the former identify their gods with stars (cf. Dorsey 1904, 1906b). Many tribes in the Southwest, Southeast and on the Plains connect the Supreme Being with the sun. Among them, the sun figures in a few myths, but shows little of the religious dignity and kindness that is the stamp of the Supreme Being. Most wide-spread is the myth of the cottontail and the sun. In some versions we are told that the sun burned the earth, killing people, because she (observe the sex) was not as much loved by them as her sister, the moon. The tension between stars is a dominant theme in many star-myths. The San Juan tale of two stars, man and wife, who follow each other through the skies, is an example of the genre (Parsons 1926: 22 ff.).

To the cosmological myths we may also refer the transformer myths and the myths about human origins. The former are associated with the assistant creator, who is often also the culture hero. Raven of the Northwest Coast Indians and Glooscap of the Northeastern Algonkin belong to this category of divine beings, vigorous in primordial times, but not active in the present. The myths of Raven, for instance, describe how, among other things, he stole the fire (or the sun) and the salmon from the mysterious beings who kept these treasures, and delivered them to mankind.

Among the myths about human origins the emergence myth deserves particular mention (Wheeler-Voegelin and Moore 1957). This myth that is disseminated in the southern parts of the continent (and quite clearly related to agricultural ideology) tells us how the first human beings ascended from the underworlds where they have lived before. Most Navajo regard this myth as their most sacred, but, if we may believe Kluckhohn, it is not held by them to be the basis for any single ceremony (Kluckhohn 1942: 60 n. 61; cf. however Haile 1942).

There are many other myths associated with the beginning of times which could be mentioned here, for instance myths about the origin of night and day, the change of the first beings into animals, and the dispersion of the animals, etc. Of particular interest are the myths of the origin of death. They tell how the human fate was determined by two divine beings through an agreement or by divination (Boas 1917).

(2) Institutional myths relate how cultural and religious institutions were established in primordial times. The way the mythic beings arranged it has to be followed today by the people. The ancients gave the pattern, the people repeat it, but there is no ritual identification. All those myths belong here in which the culture hero instructed the ancestors how to make houses, canoes, how to regulate the laws, how to deal with menstruation and death—although these myths may often also be catalogued as myths of entertainment.

As we have observed, many of the institutional myths tend to merge with sacred legends. We have seen how the Shoshoni and Ute had their Sun Dance presented to them by a buffalo spirit that appeared to one of their warriors. In the Cheyenne origin myth of the Sun Dance the warrior has turned into the culture hero Erect Horns who, with his woman, receives the ritual in the mythical mountain of Roaring Thunder (Dorsey 1905: 46 ff., Powell 1969 II: 467 ff.).

Very prominent is the place taken by institutional myths in the celebration of sacred bundles. For instance, the opening of the Arapaho flatpipe bundle is accompanied by four nights of telling the myth that belongs to it (Carter 1938).

(3) Ritual myths are cosmological myths which serve as "texts" for ritual performances. The ritual procedure is identified with the incidents of the myth, the officiants of the ritual represent the mythic personages. Not all cosmological myths are, or are used as, ritual myths. Students of religion who deal with Near Eastern

mythology tend to consider all myths as ritual myths, and they consequently conclude that every myth has taken form in a ritual setting (cf. Widengren 1968: 130). The North American materials show that such ideas are unwarranted (cf. in particular Kluckhohn 1942: 61). Although no exhaustive investigation of the occurrence of ritual myths in North America has been done it is my impression, from my own reading, that cosmological myths occasionally are integrated with rituals, particularly in more complex and agricultural native societies. (This statement needs, of course, empirical corroboration.)

Let us adduce an example. The Sun Dance is, at least among the Plains Algonkian tribes (Cheyenne, Arapaho above all), a reproduction of the primeval creation. It is a dramatization of the myth of the Earth-diver: pieces of mud that are placed on the ground of the Medicine Lodge should represent the solid ground that grew from the sods picked up out of the primeval sea. Furthermore, the Sun Dance pole is held to be a ritual replica of the cottonwood tree on which the woman of the Star Husband myth climbed to heaven (Hultkrantz 1973: 10, 15). Thus, two migratory myths, one of them—the Earth-diver—of Asiatic provenience, have in this instance become ritual myths. It would not be possible to prove the other way round.

The impersonation of mythic beings (not necessarily divinities in religion) may be illustrated with details from the Great Medicine Society (*midewiwin*) among the Ojibway. The person to be initiated into the society is identified with the culture hero, Minabozho, and his actions in the sacred lodge imitate, for example, the journey of the culture hero to the realm of the dead as described in the foundation myth of the ceremony (see Hoffman 1891: 280).

Ritual myths, as I said, seem primarily at home in the fertility rituals of agrarian societies. This does not imply that all myths from these societies are ritual myths, particularly not in the east. In a Seneca myth the corn goddess, who is the daughter of the earth goddess (cf. Demeter—Kore in Greece), becomes a captive of the bad twin under the earth. However, she is found by a sunbeam and returns to her fields (Converse 1908: 64). This is an accurate description of the life of the grain during the agrarian year, and a close counterpart to a well-known theme in Near Eastern and Mediterranean mythology connected with a ritual. However, we do not know if the American myth was part of a ritual. There is greater probability that the Pawnee sacrifice of a captive girl to the Morning Star was connected with the so-called immolation myth.

The latter (which has a wide diffusion in eastern North America, Mexico and South America) describes how the corn mother is killed and her body dragged around on the ground, thus giving rise to corn and other crops (Hatt 1951: 854 ff.). In the Pawnee ritual drama the body of the sacrificed girl was cut in pieces the blood of which was poured over the soil to enhance fertility (cf. Dorsey 1907).

The evidence from the Southwest is less controversial, and less spectacular. Zuni creation myths are recited during ritual performances (cf. Bunzel 1930), and the Flute Ceremony of the Hopi may be seen as a dramatization of their emergence myth (Parsons 1939 II: 1042).

(4) Myths of entertainment, or mythological tales, are myths that have been elaborated by the raconteur and thus lost their sacredness, but are nevertheless considered as basically true. Their counterparts in literate cultures are the literary myths (Homer's books, Snorri's Edda). The whole series of so-called trickster tales belong here. However, the trickster is just one side of a mythic being that also appears in the sacred myths, the culture hero. What seems to have happened is that this ambiguous personality, at once both adversary and helper of the Creator, because of his ludicrous shortcomings has become a favourite object of the raconteur's imagination (Hultkrantz 1963: 35 ff.). In particular his sexual appetite, his greediness and anal capacity have been embroidered upon in these myths, but also his buffoonery, stupidity and treachery. On the Plains this category of myths is the most beloved, the most told, and the most wide-spread.

Two questions naturally arise here: why do we call such stories "myths", and why did not the raconteur also manipulate other myths?

A perusal of all these tales (as far as they have been available to me) has convinced me that they are basically sacred myths that have developed into plain folktales. They have lost their sacred cosmological character, but have kept two original qualities: they are considered true (at least by old-timers), and their main character is a true mythic being (cf. Hultkrantz 1960: 559 ff.). They are consequently not fictional tales, even if the listeners know that some episodes have been added to the general pattern. "Truth" is of course a relative concept here. What is true to some is not true to others, and the degree of truth can vary in one and the same individual. But the tendency is clear enough.

The role of the raconteur has been particularly stressed by Radin (Radin 1926). There is certainly always a raconteur's talent at work in oral tradition. However, its influence is restricted in the recounting of a sacred myth,[7] unless the actions and character of one outstanding personage invites to diffusive narration—and the Coyote of the western Plains and Basin folktales is such a personage. The composition of an original sacred myth has a firm structure, whereas Coyote myths offer a chain of unrelated incidents that betray their origins in the raconteur's art.

Myth and Religion

Myth has thus a religious value, but is myth religion, as many anthropologists and historians of religions tend to think? The foregoing account, with its differentiation between cosmogonic and religious figures, between gods and mythic personages, should have given the answer. Myth deals with primordial times, religion with the present day; myth is epic, religion symbolic. There is thus a natural separation between myth and religion. However, ritual myths create a link between myth and ritual, and thereby afford an identification between mythic beings and the gods of religion.[8]

The situation is different in different places. In the Pueblo area myth and religion go together to some extent. In the Great Basin the reverse rule holds (Hultkrantz Ms). The Wind River Shoshoni believe in different sets of supernatural beings, one belonging to mythology, the other to religion. There is almost a wall between these "configurations of religious belief" (Hultkrantz 1972). The Winnebago clans have each one a separate creation myth. Nobody finds this peculiar: the recitation of the origin myth is a kind of clan identification (Radin 1923: 207 ff.). Also subdivisions of the Cheyenne tribe have different creation myths that legitimized the political existence of these divisions. The consequence is, however, that group conflicts arise (Moore 1974: 355).

The religious import of myths is thus highly variable. It is to be hoped that more research will be done on this interesting but much neglected subject which, in my estimation, is the most important aspect of myth.

Notes

1. It is however possible that the "new ethnography" will mean a turning point. Scholars working in this vein attempt to place ethnographical traits in their proper setting, the cognitive world of the peoples concerned. Religion is part of that world.

2. American scholars have not been immune to such studies in other fields, cf. Hyman 1955. The intimate relation between myth and rite in North America was observed by Matthews, but he meant that myth had priority over ritual. See Matthews 1902.

3. Like Bascom I am inclined to identify the second category with legends.

4. I am aware that misjudgments may be caused since we do not know one of the most essential details, the attitude of the listeners, the situation of story-telling.

5. The version given here was told me by the Wind River Shoshoni. For a Southern Ute variant, see Jorgensen 1972: 26.

6. There are many versions of this legend. See, for instance, Brown 1953: 3 ff., Dorsey 1906 a, and compare the ritual in Flectcher 1883.

7. Informants are particularly keen to point out that they have memorized the right words of the sacred myth.

8. Some Papago rites have a vague connection with myths which, according to Ruth Underhill, is "a rationalization made for the sake of unity" (Kluckhohn 1942: 49).

Bibliography

Alexander, H. B.
>1916. *North American Mythology: Mythology of All Races*, vol. 10. Boston.

de Angulo, J. and Benson, W. R.
>1932. 'The Creation Myth of the Pomo Indians', *Anthropos* 27: 261-274, 779-796.

Bascom, W.
>1965. 'The Forms of Folklore: Prose Narratives', *Journal of American Folklore* 78: 3-20.

Beckwith, M. W.
>1938. 'Mandan-Hidatsa Myths and Ceremonies', *Memoirs of the American Folklore Society*, vol. 32, Boston.

Boas, F.
>1915. 'Mythology and Folk-tales of the North American Indians', pp. 306-349 in F. Boas et al., *Anthropology in North America*. New York.
>1916. 'Tsimshian Mythology', *31st Annual Report of the Bureau of American Ethnology*, Washington.
>1917. 'The Origin of Death', *Journal of American Folklore* 30: 486-491.

Brinton, D. G.
>1882. *American Hero-Myths*, Philadelphia.

Brown, J. E.
>1953. *The Sacred Pipe*, Norman: University of Oklahoma Press.
>1976. 'The Roots of Renewal', pp. 25-34 in *Seeing with a Native Eye*, ed. W. H. Capps, New York: Harper and Row.

Bunzel, R. L.
>1930. 'Zuni Origin Myths, and Zuni Ritual Poetry', *47th Annual Report of the Bureau of American Ethnology*, pp. 545-609, 611-835, Washington.

Carter, J. G.
>1938. 'The Northern Arapaho Flat Pipe and the Ceremony of Covering the Pipe', *Bureau of American Ethnology Bulletin* 119: 69-102, Washington.

Chase, R.
>1949. *Quest for Myth*, Baton Rouge, La.

Converse, H. M.
   1908. 'Myths and Legends of the New York State Iroquois', *New York State Museum, Bulletin* 125, Albany.
Count, E. W.
   1952. 'The Earth-Diver and the Rival Twins', pp. 55-62 in *Indian Tribes of Aboriginal America*, ed. S. Tax, Chicago.
Dorsey, G. A.
   1904. 'Traditions of the Skidi Pawnee', *Memoirs of the American Folklore Society*, vol. 8, Boston.
   1905. 'The Cheyenne, I: Ceremonial Organization', *Field Columbian Museum, Publication* 99, Chicago.
   1906 a. 'Legend of the Teton Sioux Medicine Pipe', *Journal of American Folklore* 19: 326-329.
   1906 b. *The Pawnee: Mythology*, Washington.
   1907. 'The Skidi Rite of Human Sacrifice', *Proceedings of the 15th International Congress of Americanists*, vol. II, pp. 65-70.
Dundes, A.
   1964. *The Morphology of North American Indian Folktales*, FF Comunications 195. Helsinki.
   1967. 'North American Indian Folklore Studies', *Journal de la Societe des americanistes* 56: 53-79.
Eliade, M.
   1949. *Le Mythe de l'eternel retour*, Paris.
Fisher, J. F.
   1975. 'An Analysis of the Central Eskimo Sedna Myth', *Temenos* 11: 27-42.
Fletcher, A. C.
   1883. 'The White Buffalo Festival of the Uncpapas', *Reports of the Peabody Museum of American Archaelogy and Ethnology*, Harvard University, 16-17: 260-275.
Gayton, A. H.
   1935. 'The Orpheus Myth in North America', *Journal of American Folklore* 48: 263-293.
Grimm, J.
   1966. *Teutonic Mythology*, 4 vols. Dover Publications.
Hiale, B.
   1942. 'Navajo Upward-reaching Way and Emergence Place', *American Anthropologist* 44 (3): 407-420.
Hallowell, A. I.
   1974. 'Myth, Culture and Personality', *American Anthropologist* 49 (4): 544-556.
Harrison, J. E.
   1912. *Themis*, Cambridge.
Hartland, E. S.
   1914. 'Mythology and Folktales: Their Relation and Interpretation', *Popular Studies in Mythology*, Romance, & Folklore, no. 7, 2nd ed., London.

Hatt, G.
    1951. 'The Corn Mother in America and in Indonesia', *Anthropos* 46: 853-914.
Hoffman, W. J.
    1891. 'The Mide'wiwin or "Grand Medicine Society" of the Ojibwa', *7th Annual Report of the Bureau of Ethnology*, Washington.
Honko, L.
    1968. 'Genre Analysis in Folkloristics and Comparative Religion', *Temenos* 3: 48-64.
Hultkrantz, A.
    1956. 'Religious Tradition, Comparative Religion and Folklore', *Ethnos* 21 (1-2): 11-29.
    1957. *The North American Indian Orpheus Tradition*, Statens Etnografiska Museum, Monograph Series, vol. 2, Stockholm.
    1960. 'Religious Aspects of the Wind River Shoshoni Folk Literature', *Culture in History: Essays in Honor of Paul Radin*, ed. S. Diamond, pp. 552-569, New York: University of Columbia Press.
    1963. *Les religions des Indiens primitifs de l'Amerique*, Stockholm Studies in Comparative Religion, vol. 4.
    1967. 'North American Indian Religion in the History of Research, Parts II and III'. *History of Religions* 6 (3): 183-207, 7 (1): 13-34.
    1972. 'An Ideological Dichotomy: Myths and Folk Beliefs among the Shoshoni Indians of Wyoming', *History of Religions* 11 (4): 339-353.
    1973. 'Prairie and Plains Indians', *Iconography of Religions* 10 (3). Leiden: E. J. Brill.
Hyman, S. E.
    1955. 'The Ritual View of Myth and the Mythic', *Journal of American Folklore* 68: 462-472.
Jorgensen, J. G.
    1972. *The Sun Dance Religion*, Chicago and London: University of Chicago Press.
Kirk, G. S.
    1970. *Myth: Its Meaning and Function in Ancient and Other Cultures*, Berkeley and Los Angeles: University of California Press.
Kluckhohn, C.
    1942. 'Myths and Rituals: A General Theory', *The Harvard Theological Review* 35 (1): 45-79.
Kroeber, A. L.
    1925. *Handbook of the Indians of California*, Bureau of American Ethnology, Bulletin 78, Berkeley.
    1948. 'Seven Mohave Myths', *Anthropological Records* 11 (1), Berkeley.
Kunike, H.
    1926. 'Zur Astralmythologie der nordamerikanischen Indianer', *Internationales Archiv fur Ethnographie*, 27: 1-29, 55-78, 107-134.
La Barre, W.
    1970. *The Ghost Dance: Origins of Religion*, Garden City, N. Y.: Doubleday and Co.

Lévi-Strauss, C.
> 1958. 'La geste d'Asdiwal', *L'annuaire* 1958-59, Ecole pratique des hautes etudes, pp. 3-43. Paris.
> 1967. 'The Story of Asdiwal', pp. 1-47 in *The Structural Study of Myth and Totemism*, ed. E. Leach, Tavistock Publications.
> 1969. *Claude Levi-Strauss och strukturalismen*, Stockholm: Cavefors.

Matthews, W.
> 1902. 'The Night Chant', *Memoirs of the American Museum of Natural History*, vol. 6, New York.

Moore, J. H.
> 1974. 'Cheyenne Political History, 1820-1894', *Ethnohistory* 21 (4): 329-359.

Parsons, E. C.
> 1926. 'Tewa Tales', *Memoirs of the American Folklore Society*, vol. 19. Boston.
> 1939. *Pueblo Indian Religion*, 2 vols. Chicago: University of Chicago Press.

Powell, P. J.
> 1969. *Sweet Medicine*, 2 vols. Norman: University of Oklahoma Press.

Radin, P.
> 1923. 'The Winnbago Tribe', *37th Annual Report of the Bureau of American Ethnology*, Washington.
> 1926. 'Literary Aspects of Winnebago Mythology', *Journal of American Folklore* 39: 18-52.
> 1948. 'Winnebago Hero Cycles: A Study in Aboriginal Literature', *Memoirs of the International Journal of American Linguistics*, vol. 1, Bloomington; New York.
> 1956. *The Trickster: A Study in American Indian Mythology*, New York: Philosophical Library.

Reichard, G. A.
> 1947. 'An Analysis of Coeur d'Alene Myths', *Memoirs of the American Folklore Society*, vol. 41, Philadelphia.

Roheim, G.
> 1952. 'Culture Hero and Trickster in North American Mythology', pp. 190-194 in *Indian Tribes of Aboriginal America*, ed. S. Tax, Chicago.

Rooth, A. B.
> 1957. 'The Creation Myths of the North American Indians', *Anthropos* 52: 497-508.

Thompson, S.
> 1919. *European Tales among the North American Indians*, Colorado College Publications, Language Series II, no. 34: 319-471.
> 1953. 'The Star Husband Tale', *Studia Septentrionalia* 4: 93-163.

Waterman, T. T.
> 1914. 'The Explanatory Element in the Folk-Tales of the North-American Indians', *Journal of American Folklore* 27: 1-54.

Wheeler-Voegelin, E. and Moore, R. W.
> 1957. 'The Emergence Myth in Native North America', pp. 66-91 in *Studies in Folklore*, ed. W. Edson Richmond, Bloomington.

Widengren, G.
   1968. 'Mythos und Glaube im Lichte der Religionsphanomenologie',
      Theologische Forschung 45: 129-149, Hamburg.

Respondent: J. W. E. Newbery

In responding to Prof. Hultkrantz, I am conscious of many limitations, since I am neither anthropologist nor sociologist; what I have learned about myth and native world view generally I have learned from the people themselves. And it is out of this that I make my response. I do think it is important, as Dr. Hultkrantz said, to distinguish between myth and legend and tale and I know that that is very often not done. You hear people speaking as if it were all the same kind of oral tradition. I think that Dr. Hultkrantz has led us to understand that myth is distinct from such other phenomenon as legend and tale. One of the things that I was told and has always remained in my mind about myth as told by an Indian Holy Man is that myth is a verbal re-enacting of a creative event, of a creative action, and it is distinct from legend and tale because of that. The myth is, as I say, a verbal way of re-enacting something that happened, of an event in primordial time in the supernatural world performed by those beings of which Dr. Hultkrantz spoke. As the myth is told the event takes place again in that verbal form and that is the reason it is regarded with particular sacredness. There are times in the year when it is not proper to tell the myths and when they *are* told they have to be told with special care because a momentous thing is taking place during the telling. I spoke to an Indian man about the propriety of discussing these things here in this conference at this time of the year and he said it is proper to talk about them but not to relate the myths themselves in such a context and in such a time.

The second thing relates to what Dr. Hultkrantz has said in his paper regarding myths as providing a kind of chart for our understanding of the world and of the ordering of that world. They relate to us what Indian people sometimes say are the "original instructions" that were given to us about the world in which we live and about our lives in that world. They detail the way it was in the beginning—the way it was intended to be. I suppose it isn't simply by chance that at the very heart of Hebrew Torah, for example, is myth. The myths of Genesis are the heart of Hebrew law. They explain what was in the beginning and what is intended to be in human life. So, like other myths, Native American myths offer a prototype of world order. They tell us about a "fall" in creation. They tell us about human suffering and the reasons for it. They tell us about a saving action that has been taken in order to recover man and creation from the fall. And as the myths are related these actions take place again and human life and human society recover and are reinstated and recreated during the telling.

I suppose it is here that myth and ritual are very close together. Myth is the *verbal* reenactment of this recreating event and the ritual is the dramatic expression of it. The original design is restored in the telling of the myth. The disaster of the fall is avoided and the means of salvation are secured. It seemed to me that this phenomon is very important to native people today. I think it's important to other people, for example, Britain in this stage in her history is in a state of anxiety; a nation which was once a great empire, she has had to adjust to being a second rate world power. Isn't it true that in Britain today there is a return to the mythological traditions of the people? Tolkien in his writings, it seems to me, is an indication of an attempt in Britain to go back to roots, to those mythological roots of the nation. I think too, of the writings of Mary Stuart going back to the days of King Arthur or T. H. White's new book that has just been published on "A Once and Future King." There are illustrations of an attempt of a nation to recreate itself, to try to orient itself to this period of difficulty. Or, recall Greece during the days of its change from its archaic to the classical period, when the myths blossomed and became so important in the Delphic oracle, etc. Likewise, it seems to me that in this time of the re-emergence of the native people of this continent from paternalism and disadvantage to self-determination, the myths which carry the people back to their beginnings, which tell them the way things were intended to be, are going to be of immense importance again. I think, for example, of the people of the Nass Valley in British Columbia where the Nishka land claims are being made. There people are trying to establish their aboriginal claim on that beautiful valley. What means are they using to do that? They're going back to the myth which tells how the land was given to them. On one occasion at an interview with an old Holy man in the Nass Valley, he related that myth as evidence. He said if you go up to the top of the mountains there you can see in the rocks the wedges that were driven there by those who anchored their rafts after the great floods began to subside. And from that time the land became ours.

One question that came to my mind as I heard Dr. Hultkrantz's paper concerns the relationship between myth and religion. Although Dr. Hultkrantz said quite properly that myth is a religious concept and its place and its meaning must be sought first of all there, yet I am not quite sure what he means by distinguishing between myth and religion at the conclusion of his paper. His treatment does not seem to one to be consistent at this point and I think further discussions should follow on this.

The Immediacy of Mythological Message: Native American Traditions

by

Joseph Epes Brown

"If we knew and understood fairytales—and by extension the myth—we would not need the scriptures." This insight of profound implication by G. K. Chesterton is indicative of a certain change from previous centuries when myth was synonymous with fable, fiction, poetic invention, an account which was interesting and often amusing, but nevertheless always untrue, a connotation which "myth" still conveys in the popular language of today.

Writing of the Huron in the 17th Century, Pére Raguenau well summarizes the generally accepted and oft repeated opinions of that era:

> "To speak truly, all the nations of those countries have received from their ancestors no knowledge of a God; and, before we set foot here, all that was related about the creation of the world consisted of nothing but myths." (*Relation*, 1647-48)

It is due to a growing number of more enlightened and objective contemporary scholars that we, who generally live outside of oral mythic traditions, have come somewhat closer to an understanding of the realities and truths of mythic statements as understood by those people themselves who still live by their sacred traditions. Such peoples find in their myths, and oral traditions generally, models for human behaviour, statements told and ritually enacted which tell of the origins and ultimate realities of existence, accounts and acts which define the sacred, and make it immediate in all its mysterious modes of operation. It is in the spirit of this new understanding that the great oriental scholar, Ananda Coomaraswamy, has written:

"Myth embodies the nearest approach to absolute truth that can be stated in words." (*Hinduism and Buddhism*, pg. 33, note 21). Or, "...the Myth, the penultimate truth, of which all experience is the temporal reflection. The mythical narative is of timeless and placeless validity, true nowever and everywhere." (ibid, pg 6). Or, "Myth is to history as Universal is to particular."

It is from this perspective that I propose to discuss here selected aspects of the mythologies of Native American peoples which relate to my chosen theme, that is, the immediacy of mythological message. I am also very much aware of other possible orientations and uses of the myth, such as the functionalist and structuralist approaches of the contemporary anthropological sciences, approaches, incidentally, which often tend to be poverty-stricken exercises, but which may hold value where they serve to clarify and elucidate those sacred dimensions of the mythic statement or accompanying ritual act as such are understood and lived by the Native peoples themselves. Those who have read the writings of Mircea Eliade or, above all, who have actively participated in the myths and sacred rites of legitimate Traditions, will understand of what I speak.

There are obviously great diversities in the mythologies held and lived by Native American peoples, as well as in the cosmologies, world views, religious and ritual expressions, all of which have their origin and reinforcement in the myth. Central and all important to this rich diversity, however, is a common perspective which particularly deserves our attention, and which I have purposefully selected as focus for this paper. I am referring to a concept of time manifest in all real myths, and which is continually expressed in those profound ritual enactments of mythic themes and sacred events. We are dealing here with time outside of time, if one may so put it, that is, the sacred time of the *hierophany* of the now. The recitation of a myth defining creation, for example, is not experienced in terms of an event of lineal time past, but rather of a happening of eternal reality, true and real "nowever" and forever, a time which is on the knife edge between the past and the future.

To illustrate this theme of the immediacy of mythological message, as I believe it occurs across the Native Americans' experience, I have selected from an enormous range of possibilities the myths of three groups, distinct linguistically, culturally, and geographically: The Algonquin "Earth-Diver" myth because of its profound expression of a form of theism which is typically and pervasively experienced by many Native American peoples, and which particularly expresses the perspective of an immediacy of experience. Secondly, I have chosen three interrelated selections from translations of Navajo creation myths which express immediacy in other modes, specifically through the perspective of individual identification. I then propose to utilize portions of a northern Washington Kathlamet Chinook text, known as "The Sun's Myth", recorded in 1891 by Franz Boas from Charles Cultee. The immediacy of this message is here expressed in terms of a perennial statement concerning the nature of man's soul, of desire and pride, of punishment and subsequent reconciliation set in the context of the changing events of time. Finally, I wish to stress how the immediacy of the message is conveyed through the use and understanding of language, through the rich and creative variety of means by which myths, and oral traditions generally, are transmitted by the teller.

The "Earth-Diver" myth of the Algonquin peoples of Eastern Woodlands and the Plains are well known in several of their many versions. The creation of land where everywhere there is only water takes place not out of "nothingness", but within the perspective of cyclical process, for land was there before this particular deluge, and thus is now underneath the waters and must be recovered. Further, an Earth-Maker figure, *Manabush* or *Nanabozo*, the "Great Hare" among the central Algonquins, or Old Man (*Napi*) among the western Algonquin, is already there upon these waters. In some versions he is holding the peoples' most sacred pipe, often identified with creation and creative power, as among the Algonquin-speaking Arapaho (Carter 1938). Indeed, all the aquatic birds and animals are there with Earth Maker who instructs them to dive down under the waters to find even a small grain of earth from which new land may be made. Typically, the otter, beaver and mink take turns diving under the waters, each being unsuccessful in the missions. After much suspense in the telling of the account, it is always the fourth being, most often the muskrat[1], who finally surfaces, after four days under water, with a little bit of earth on his paws. Often this earth is placed upon the back of a turtle, as among the southern Ontario Ojibwa, where the turtle itself represents, or is, the earth as well as fertility. Through the agency of breath Earth Maker then fashions and enlarges the earth, establishes its features and contours, until it is again a suitable habitation for all the beings of water and land, and including finally man.

Key themes in this grand account which speak to our thesis of a message of immediacy are the following: First: creation here occurs not once out of nothingness in lineal past, but is an event ever

occurring and recurring in cyclical fashion, just as the observable
cycle of each day or the seasons speak of death and rebirth, or as
with each form of creation, the mystery of this creative cycle of
birth, life, death and life is immediately and continually manifest to
one who is attentive. Secondly, the myth informs us that certain
beings, already created, participate and cooperate with the Creator
Figure in the act of creation. This fact again shifts the orientation
away from creation understood as a single event of time past, to the
reality of those immediately experienced processes of creation ever
happening and observable now throughout all the multiple forms
and forces of creation.

There are those who might insist that such accounts of a creator
cooperating with creation compromise a more ultimate belief in a
supreme Principle transcendent to all creation, or that the account
implies a *deus absconditus* or a *deus otiosus*. Closer examination of
Algonquin beliefs reveal that this is not the case. Among the
Blackfeet, for example, it was "Old Man" (*Napi*) who requested the
animals' cooperation in creating. *Napi*, however, may refer to many
perspectives within creation; he is a trickster and bringer of
important cultural forms, and his is also a name for the Sun
understood in its creative role (Grinnell 1913: 145-155). But this
visible sun, it is believed on a more ultimate level, derives its
creative power from an invisible source transcendent to the realm
of manifestation and is thus an ultimate Principle. This ultimate
principle is referred to by the Algonquin Ojibwa as *Kitchi Manitou*,
usually translated as Great Spirit, as distinct from a *manitou* which
has reference to one of a number of qualitatively differentiated
spirit beings or powers. There is a splendid Winnebago account
which may serve to clarify this question:

A young man blackens his face and fasts in retreat for four days,
for he sought to dream of nothing less than the Earth-Maker. "He
persevered until he had dreamed of everything on the earth or
under the earth, or in the air; he dreamed of the whole world, but
he never saw *Ma-o-na*", the Earth-Maker. Even though the Spirits
told him that he *had* dreamed of *Ma-o-na* because he had dreamed
of all his works, the young man still was not satisfied. Finally the
youth was given to understand the mystery of the fact that *Ma-o-na*
in Himself cannot be seen, and yet at the same time all the visible
and experienced forms and forces of creation that he had dreamed
of are not other than *Ma-o-na*, nor therefore is he other than that.
(Curtis 1907: 262-265).

In what has been stated above it is evident that Native American mythologies express as profound and powerful insights as the Judeo-Christian form of theism which tends to insist on a monotheism understood in a singular sense. Such tendencies, at least at a certain level of understanding, encourage a remoteness from the mysteries of Nature as observable in all her modes of operation. Certainly, students concerned with the problems of environmental abuse and degradation have pointed to the ramifications of this possibility (Nasr: 1968). It is instructive to note, for example, that no less than Arnold Toynbee, the great historian of western religions and civilization, wrote the following in the *New York Times* of September 16, 1973— one of his last writings before his death:

> "For premonotheistic man, nature was not just a treasure-trove of 'natural resources.' Nature was, for him, a goddess, 'Mother Earth,' and the vegetation that sprang from the earth, the animals that roamed, like man himself, over the earth's surface, and the minerals hiding in the earth's bowels all partook of nature's divinity. The whole of his environment was divine . . . . My observation of the living religion of eastern Asia, and my book knowledge of the extinguished Greek and Roman religion, have made me aware of a startling and disturbing truth: that monotheism, as enunciated in the Book of Genesis, has removed the age-old restraint that was once placed on man's greed by his awe. Man's greedy impulse to exploit nature used to be held in check by his pious worship of nature. This primitive inhibition has been removed by the rise and spread of monotheism."

Native American beliefs in what has been called animism, so indirectly applauded by Toynbee, but continually criticized by representatives of the historical monotheistic traditions, need to be understood within the context of larger perspectives. For neither animism, animatism, nor indeed expressions of polytheism, as they appear in Native American traditions, need exclude underlying concepts of monotheism, or beliefs in an ultimate Principle by whatever name this may be called. If animistic beliefs be understood in this manner, that is, as becoming ultimately attached to a unitary Principle, then a way is open for the mysteries of creative process, witnessed through every form and force of nature, to be immediately experienced in the *hierophany* of the Now. This is precisely a perspective which has become lost to the world today, but which needs to be regained as Toynbee, among others, has suggested.

Native American languages are joined to those other sacred
languages of the world in the sense that words are not here
conceived simply as symbols assigned arbitrarily to other units of
meaning, as tends to be the case with our own English language.
Rather, words in themselves are experienced in an immediate
manner as units of power. Thus, to name a being or any element of
creation is actually to make manifest the power of quality, soul or
spirit, of that which is named. It is for this reason that words and
personal sacred names are used carefully in Native languages; one
avoids using one's own or another person's sacred name, and, out
of both respect and awe, especially the name of a deceased person.
It is due to such a concept of language that N. Scott Momaday has
titled his recent autobiography *The Names*, for he tells us here that
". . . a man's life proceeds from his name, in the way that a river
proceeds from its source." (1976: Preface). Thus he goes on to tell
us that his identity is achieved through his name which is that point
in the river of the generations preceding him. It is in similar
manner that the words which comprise language, and which are
the vehicle of the orally transmitted myths, speak with special force
to our theme of immediacy.

It is in this manner that among the Athabaskan Navajo the words
of their chantways have compulsive creative power; to name the
Yei, for example,—which we inadaquately translate as gods—is to
compel those who are named to be actually, immediately, present.
Similarly, with the visual counterpart to the audible, the sacred
beings of the dry paintings are actually present in their
representations. It is thus that sacred curative powers are
transmitted, through word and form, not just to the patient for
whom the rites are performed, but these powers, having been
ritually drawn into a centre, eventually effect all life as they expand
ever outwards as do ripples on the surface of the water when a
pebble is dropped.

Against the background of these comments on the language of
the Navajo, I propose to illustrate the theme of mythological
immediacy through presenting brief excerpts from four separate
Navajo chantway texts involving myths of creation. Although
separate texts have been selected out, it will be noted in their
arrangement that they interrelate to each other in cumulative
manner (Wheelwright 1942).

The first selection is a "sweathouse" song, for among the
Navajo, as well as for other Native American peoples, the
sweatlodge and its rites are associated with creation.

1.

The earth has been laid down, the earth has been laid down
   The earth has been laid down, it has been made.

The earth spirit has been laid down
   It is covered over with the growing things, it has been laid
   down
The earth has been laid down, it has been made.

The sky has been set up, the sky has been set up
   The sky has been set up, it has been made.

The mountains have been laid down, the mountains have been
   laid down
The mountains have been laid down, they have been made.

The mountain spirits have been laid down
   They are covered over with all the animals, they have been
   laid down
The mountains have been laid down, they have been made.

The waters have been laid down, the waters have been laid
   down
The waters have been laid down, they have been made.

The water spirits have been laid down
   They are covered over with water pollen, they have been
   laid down
The waters have been laid down, they have been made.

The clouds have been set up, the clouds have been set up
   The clouds have been set up, the clouds have been made.
   (136-137).

With elements of the earth established with their spirit
counterparts, recounted here with that creative repetitive rhythmic
force that is typical of Navajo chantways, the following selected
second chant now extolls the beauty, harmony, and peace of this
earth referred to in microcosmic anthropomorphic terms:

2.

The Earth is beautiful
   The Earth is beautiful
   The Earth is beautiful.

Below the East, the Earth, its face toward East, the top of its
   head is beautiful

The soles of its feet, they are beautiful
　　Its legs, they are beautiful
　　Its body, it is beautiful
　　Its chest, it is beautiful
　　Its breath, it is beautiful
　　　　Its head-father, it is beautiful
　　The Earth is beautiful. (161)

With an earth of beauty created, and also the directions of space extolled in the remainder of the text which has been omitted, the following third selection now speaks of an ideal interrelationship between man and aspects of this created universe:

3.

The Earth is looking at me; she is looking up at me
　　I am looking down on her
　　I am happy, she is looking at me
　　I am happy, I am looking at her.

The Sun is looking at me; he is looking down at me
　　I am looking up at him
　　I am happy, he is looking at me
　　I am happy, I am looking at him.

The Black Sky is looking at me; he is looking down on me
　　I am looking up at him
　　I am happy, he is looking at me
　　I am happy, I am looking at him.

The moon is looking at me; he is looking down on me
　　I am looking up at him
　　I am happy, he is looking at me
　　I am happy, I am looking at him.

The North is looking at me; he is looking across at me
　　I am looking across at him
　　I am happy, he is looking at me
　　I am happy, I am looking at him. (149)

In the final fourth selection, which now speaks with special and eloquent force to the perspective of immediacy, an identity is established between macrocosm and microcosm, between man and an earth which is of beauty, peace, and harmony, qualities which are expressed in the Navajo word *hozhoni*.

4.

> Hozhoni, hozhoni, hozhoni
> Hozhoni, hozhoni, hozhoni
> The Earth, its life am I, hozhoni, hozhoni
> The Earth, its feet are my feet, hozhoni, hozhoni
> The Earth, its legs are my legs, hozhoni, hozhoni
> The Earth, its body is my body, hozhoni, hozhoni
> The Earth, its thoughts are my thoughts, hozhoni, hozhoni
> The Earth, its speech is my speech, hozhoni, hozhoni
> The Earth, its down-feathers are my down-feathers,
> hozhoni, hozhoni
>
> The sky, its life am I, hozhoni, hozhoni —
>   The mountains, their life am I —
>   Rain-mountain, its life am I —
>   Changing-Woman, her life am I —
>   The Sun, its life am I —
>   Talking God, his life am I —
>   House God, his life am I —
>   White corn, its life am I —
>   Yellow corn, its life am I —
>   The corn beetle, its life am I —
>
> Hozhoni, hozhoni, hozhoni
> Hozhoni, hozhoni, hozhoni. (142)

As a third example of the perspective of immediacy in mythological message, a synopsis will be given of a Kathlamet Chinook text known as The Sun's Myth. In this case the myth speaks of man's perennial pride, desire, and of subsequent punishment and final reconciliation, a theme which certainly speaks to every man of any time.

The Chief of a village determines to take a journey to find the sun.[2] After using up ten pair of moccasins and ten pair of legging made for him by his wife, he finally arrives at the very large house of the sun. Entering, he meets a prepubescent girl, and finds the house filled with painted elkskin blankets, mountain goat blankets, dressed buckskins decorated with dentalia shells, and all the beautiful articles prized by these peoples of the Washington coast itemized in great detail and in repetitive manner. The girl informs the man that these are the things that are being saved for her maturity by her grandmother. Every evening the grandmother returns to the house and hangs up a beautiful object that is shining all over. The Chief finally takes the young girl and is thus offered all the beautiful things hanging in the house. He desires, however, only that one shining object which the grandmother continually refuses to give to him. Finally he becomes homesick and, wishing to depart, insists with increasing persistence and anger on taking the shining object with him. After several refusals and many warnings, finally the grandmother hangs the shining object on him, gives him a stone axe, and tells him to depart. She also says she had tried to love him. As the text of the myth continues:

He went out
　　now he went,
　　　　he went home.
　　　　　　He did not see a land.
　　　　　　　　He arrived near his uncle's town.
Now that which he held shook.
　　now that which he held said:
　　　　"We two shall strike your town.
　　　　We two shall strike your town,"
　　　　　　that which he held said.
His reason became nothing,
　　he did it to his uncle's town.
　　　　he crushed, crushed, crushed it,
　　　　　　he killed all the people.
He recovered:
　　all those houses are crushed,
　　　　his hands are full of blood.
He thought,
　　"O I am a fool!
　　　　See, it is just like that, this thing;
　　　　　　Why was I made to love it?"
　　　　　　He tried in vain to wrench it off,
　　　　　　　　and his flesh would be pulled.
Now again he went,
　　and now he went a little while,
　　　　now again his reason became nothing.
He arrived near another uncle's town.
　　Now again it said,
　　　　"We two shall strike your town,
　　　　We two shall strike your town."
　　　　He tried in vain to still it,
　　　　　　it was never still.
　　　　He tried in vain to throw it away,
　　　　　　always his fingers closed.
Now again his reason became nothing,

now again he did it to his uncle's town,
  he crushed it all.
He recovered:
  his uncle's town (is) nothing;
  all the people have become dead.
Now he cried.
In vain he tried in the fork of a tree,
  there in vain he would try squeezing it off.
    it would not at all come off,
      and his flesh would be pulled.
In vain he would try striking what he held on a stone.
  it would never be crushed.
Again he would go,
  he would arrive near another uncle's town.
    now again that which he held would shake:
      "We two shall strike your town,
      We two shall strike your town,
His reason would become nothing,
  he would do it to his uncle's town,
    crush, crush, crush, crush.
      He would destroy all his uncle's town,
        and he would destroy the people.
He would recover,
  he would cry out,
    he would grieve for his relatives.
He would try in vain diving in water,
  he would try in vain to wrench it off,
    and his flesh would be pulled.
      He would try in vain rolling in a thicket,
        he would always try in vain striking what he held
                    on a stone.

He would give up.
  Now he would cry out.
Again he would go,
  Now again he would arrive at another town,
                an uncle's town.

Now again what he held would shake:
  "We two shall strike your town,
  We two shall strike your town."
His reason would become nothing.

He would do it to the town,
    crush, crush, crush, crush,
      and the people.
He would recover.
  All the people and the town (are) no more.
    His hands and arms (are) only blood.
He would become,
    "Qa! qa! qa! qa!"
    he would cry out.
He would always try in vain striking stones,
  what he held would not be crushed.
    He would always try in vain to throw away what he held,
      always his hands enclosed it.
Again he would go,
  Now next (is) his own town,
    he would be near his own town.
      He would try to stand in vain,
        see, his feet would be pulled.
His reason would become nothing,
    he would do it to his town,
    and he would destroy his relatives.
He would recover.
  His town (is) nothing.
    The ground has become full of corpses.
He would become,
    "Qa! qa! qa! qa!"
    he would cry out.
He would try to bathe in vain,
  he would try in vain to wrench off what he wore,
    and his flesh would be pulled.
Some times he would roll about on stones.
  He would think,
    perhaps it will be broken apart.
He would give up.
  Now again he would cry out,
    and he wept.
He looked back,
  now she was standing there, that old woman.
"You,"
  she told him,

"You.
I try in vain to love you,
  I try in vain to love your relatives.
Why do you weep?
  It is you who choose,
    now you carried that blanket of mine."
Now she took it,
  she took off what he held.
Now she left him,
  she went home.
He stayed there.
  He went a little distance.
    There he built a house, a small house.[3]

The strength of this account of a perennial condition of man's soul is intensified and made all the more immediate for those who told and heard the myth, for it apparently arose out of a culture at a time when the traditional values and cultural forms of these people were being lost and destroyed through contact with an alien European culture of conflicting values. Further, the fact that the Chief of a village should choose to leave family and village, for whatever purpose, is itself a violation of an ancient prohibition. The theme is thus timeless and universal, but is also of special import within a particular historical time and for a specific people.

"He built a house, a small house."

The immediacy of the message of mythological statement has here been illustrated through three examples each of differing perspective: the polysynthetic theological implications of the Algonquin myth, which speaks of a continuum of experience of the sacred through the manifest forms and forces of a creation ever creating; the perspective of personal wholeness, thus holiness through identity with an ideal world of beauty, peace and harmony of the Navajo myth, and finally the powerful Kathlamet Chinook myth, relating to a particular time and cultural condition, but exposing that universal drama of man's soul, of error, punishment-suffering, and final reconciliation. Such treatment of these myths, however, remains incomplete without reference to the fact that an important dimension of our theme of immediacy lies in the very medium through which the message is transmitted. I refer to the force of oral transmission, to what Dennis Tedlock has well termed "verbal art". In clarifying certain contours of this art I draw heavily, in these concluding comments, on two of Tedlock's most seminal articles: "Verbal Art" which appears in Chapter 50, Volume 1 of the *Handbook of North American Indians*, and "Towards a Restoration of the Word in the Modern World" which appeared in the *Journal Alcheringa*, Volume 2, 1976.

In addition to the special nature of the Native Languages themselves, as was indicated in the discussion on Navajo chantways, there should be mentioned first of all that the recounting of the myth is made special, thus immediacy of the message is heightened, through insistence that the telling of the account is serious and potentially dangerous, so that there then must be both appropriate time and place for such telling. Among Native American peopes generally true myths may be told only after dark and normally in the winter season, after the last thunder of summer and before the first thunder of spring. It is at this time that beings of possible dangerous influence are absent, bears, snakes and spiders among some peoples, for example. Indeed, severe punishments may occur if such custom is transgressed. The Kiowa, for example, believe that if anyone tells a story about their Trickster figure during the day, he will then bite their noses off; or, others believe that one may become a hunchback, or perhaps a snake will come and wrap itself around the teller of the story.

Myths often commence with the phrase, "In the long ago . . . ". This "long ago", it should now be clear, does not refer to a historical period of a lineal time past, but usually has reference to a qualitative condition of earlier existence which, through the telling of the myth, may be mysteriously reintegrated and realized in the immediacy of the timeless now. Analagous to such reference to mythic time is the "Once upon a time . . ." of European fairytales which may be translated as "nowever and forever".

A multitude of rhetorical devices are used by the good teller of stories to convey immediacy. He may use the first person, in present rather than past tense, thus telling the account as if he were really present, even actually engaged in dialogue with the figures of the narrative. As a Zuni once told Tedlock, "You're right with that story, like you were in it." Indeed, I still remember vividly those *Iktomi* (Spider) stories old Black Elk liked to tell; you felt that you were right there present with *Iktomi*.

Attention is paid to precise detail, with events in the narrative occurring at specific geographical sites well known in the immediate environment of the listener. Artful utilization of the human voice conveys the sounds of the animals of the narration, and lengthening of vowels in adjectives and verbs convey the sense of duration or distance. Intensity of voice is adjusted to fit the particular action being described, or silence may be used to heighten tension or suspense, or may indicate that the narrator is engaged in personal prayer. Skillful manipulation of language and delivery is utilized to fit the character in question. Rich use of metaphor as well as metonymy—where something is named through a distinctive attribute—serves as a stimulus to the listener's reconstruction of the episode. The beaver, for example, may be referred to, as among the western Shoshone, as "big-tail owner". I have already referred to those rituals relating to drypaintings accompaning Navajo chantways; in addition are those enactments which often accompany the mythic account, or use of a multiplicity of props, hand gestures, mnemonic devices such as the birch bark scrolls of the Ojibwa. Songs may be interjected which are specific to a sacred being of the account, or even a personal sacred song of the narrator may be used. There are a variety of techniques for bringing the audience into the story, and there are careful means for ending the story to insure the constructive and safe return of the listener from mythic time to the present moment through relating and integrating the one into the other. The concluding use of the "that's why" line again contributes to the impact of experiential immediacy. In versions of the Earth-Diver myth, for example—and to return to where we started—Earth-Maker holds muskrat up by his tail in order to take from his webbed feet that soil with which the earth is made, and in so doing stretches out his tail, just as one can see it is today.

The endings of Native American accounts, whether of myths or stories, do have moral force, but this is achieved through use of analogy, or indirectly through the negative activities of coyote or some trickster figure who engages in all those disreputable things that everyone enjoys hearing about, but always knows is improper conduct. In their great wisdom, Native American accounts, whether of myth or just stories, know where to stop. They never, for example, risk alienating their audiences with drawn out moralizing summaries. In that spirit I shall stretch out no further the muskrat's tail, but shall simply end by saying: "It is so . . . ".

Notes

1. A trait of the muskrat, obviously observed by the people, is to build his house in the waters out of mud, dome shaped and circular as is the earth.

2. The solar journey, in other myths, may express the opposite of this present theme, for a hero may travel to find the Sun, or the house of the Sun, which is his solar origin. Cf., for example, *Where the Two Came to Their Father*, Bollingen Series 1, Princeton University Press, 1942

3. I have used the unpublished excellent analysis and arrangement of this myth by Dell Hymes, based on the Franz Boas text.

Bibliography

Carter, John G.
    1938. 'The Northern Arapaho Flat Pipe', *B.A.E., Bulletin* 119.
Curtis, Natalie
    1907. *The Indians' Book*, Harper & Brothers Publishers.
Grinnell, George Bird
    1913. *Blackfeet Indian Stories*, C. Scribner's Sons.
Momaday, N. Scott
    1976. *The Names*, Harper & Row, N. Y.
Nasr, Seyyid Hossein
    1968. *The Encounter of Man and Nature*, George Allen and Unwin, Ltds., London.
Wheelwright, Mary C.
    1942. *Navajo Creation Myth*, Museum of Navajo Ceremonial Art, Santa Fe.

An Approach to Navajo Mythology

by

Karl W. Luckert

Introduction

A discussion of an approach to Navajo mythology can only have
a limited aim. Traditional Navajos know the meaning of their myths
without our help. An incidental benefit of my labours could
perhaps be that some young native Americans, who have stepped
into Anglo-American culture, may find my comments useful for
building their own bridges across what has come to be called the
'culture gap.' In any case, these same young Indians will have to
examine for themselves my suggestions and decide about their
usefulness. The immediate goal of this essay, however, is far more
limited; it is to open a door of understanding for non-Navajos to
the traditional Navajo world.

Most Navajo myths are narrated to explain rituals of healing or
rites which aim at obtaining general blessings. While rituals consist
of "doing," myths are "talk about doing"— and talk about the
ontological or cosmological context which preceded and still
surrounds all human activities. In brief, still today myth and ritual
belong together in most instances in Navajo tradition; they are two
sides of the same coin.

Mythology and the construction of a methodology with which
to approach that mythology are two different things. One learns the
content of a people's mythology by listening, by conversing, and by
reading; methodology, on the other hand, comes as a result of a
student's personal reflection and hindsight. What I am able to say
about an 'approach to Navajo mythology' must therefore be
regarded as my personal reflections on what I presupposed—or
should have presupposed—while researching four projects in the
field.

From phenomenology the historian of religions has accepted the
concept of *Einklammerung* or "bracketing," namely, the suspension
of judgments until the point is reached where the gathered data

add up to a reasonably complete world picture. But as I observe students these days, I find it necessary to expand this suspension of rational judgments to also include the suspension of certain feelings.

This is not to say that we should be insensitive to the feelings of people in another culture. On the contrary! But unchecked emotions never have been a good substitute or basis for actual learning. While in the famous words of Longfellow, "it is the heart, and not the brain, that to the highest does attain," it must also be said that these heights attained by the heart, by themselves, remain quite out of reach of lingual symbolization. Consequently, I will never know, nor be able to express exactly, how a Navajo medicine man "feels;" nor, for that matter, will he know precisely how I feel; nor is all of that very important. No teacher of mine, Anglo or Amerind, has ever made a certain feeling a pre-condition for his willingness to teach me. A sincere love for the subject matter is all that was ever required of me.

When the work of the mind is done—say, for example, after I have rationally grasped the attributes and activities of the Navajo Talking-god—then I do indeed have an idea of how my informant "feels" toward this particular deity. Nevertheless, emotions which I have experienced in the presence of other deities may return to me and influence my response to this Talking-god. This margin of error, of personal supplementation, is unavoidable in any learning process. A Navajo apprentice would face the same difficulty. Moreover, among themselves Navajo medicine men regard ceremonial learning, very soberly, as a business transaction. They, too, communicate primarily in the realm of *logos* or of "rational structure."

Understanding a foreign world comes easier if at the outset the learner perceives some compatible outline or "structure." The issue at hand is not whether or not we want to be structuralists. All acts of rational comprehension, Indian and otherwise, require structure. The question becomes merely *what* auxiliary structure or scaffold should be used in rebuilding the native world-picture from mythic narratives. It is obvious that the scaffold must not obstruct the space in which the reconstruction is to grow. And then, the resulting world-portrait must in the end, when it is narrated back, be recognizable to the original informant; it must look authentic to him, even though he may forever remain unaware of auxiliary concepts or structures.

Moreover, as the size of the scaffold must match the scope of the building project, so our field of vision should match, approximately, that of the native story-teller. For instance, the Navajo narrator of myths is not aware of rules of phonology, morphology, syntax, and semantics—as unaware of them as a non-specialist. Navajo medicine men and visionaries do not go deer-hunting with microscopes. Binoculars may occasionally prove useful during the chase, but the size of the hunting grounds which bare eyes perceive is generally quite adequate. That same scope of vision is also quite adequate for narrating what can be said or known about the lesser and greater realities which surround humankind.

It now seems that the task of understanding and interpreting Navajo myths requires of me no new concepts which are not present when I try to understand, say, the ideological history of Germany. The same structures of space and time suffice. A historian of religions will readily recognize, in the approach which I propose, Joachim Wach's division of *Allgemeine Religionswissenschaft* into the tasks of *Religionsgeschichte* (the study of religious developments, longitudinally, in time) and *Systematische Religionswissenschaft* (the study of religious phenomena, cross-sectionally, in space)—(Wach 1924). The time-space duality, which has proven so useful in understanding culture-portraits given by historians of religions, if applied to the culture-portrait which I obtained first-hand from Navajo narrators, is sufficient to explain the structure of the world in which I met and communicated with my Navajo friends. I need only describe my everyday, simple awareness of space and time.[1]

Proportional Space

If time can be visualized as the current of a stream, it is possible to imagine space as a cross-section of that stream, namely, as a moment of its flow, with me caught in the middle. My space contains all the realities which touch or affect me at any present moment. This means that the stories which I tell about my so-conceived realities constitute my mythology. I know of no other knowledge aside from mythic knowledge, or that which is communicated through story-telling. Mythology is only another word for "ontology" or "theory of being."

In conversing with Navajo traditionalists, I have found that their ontology, like mine, has the same proportional structure. Here among us are our equals to whom we respond with sharing; then, there are so-conceived less-than-human portions of reality to which we respond with scientific analysis, experimentation, and control; and then there are greater-than-human realities to whom we respond with gestures of religious awe and submission.

Among religious experiences and responses, surrender and fear are the most intense; awe ranks next; and fascination blends across the balance point of humanistic trust and familiarity into scientific curiosity and ambitions. At the scientific side of the experiential teeter-totter, fascination becomes curiosity and analysis, then becomes hypothetical re-arrangement, experimentation, and finally control. All the while, I am fully aware of the fact that "religion" and "science" can be distinguished from one another and can be defined in other ways. Many people will maintain that, for them, religion is something else. For me, religious phenomena become understandable when I think of them as responses to greater-than-human configurations of reality—and I use the term "science" to refer to the opposite dimension.

The Flow of Time

Experiences in "pure space," without awareness of the flow of time, remain unintelligible emotions. Awareness of the "longitudinal" flow of time permits the perception of change, and along with an eye on the past, enables us to infer causes; with an eye on the future it enables us to infer purposes. In this manner, all ontological awareness becomes involved in the mental grid along which we visualize the flow of time. All human experiences in space and time, whether they are reflections on ancient events, or whether they are conclusions to recent scientific experiments, must necessarily be communicated in historical narrative. Moreover, historical narratives—scientific reports about minute details, as well as sketches of nearly universal scope—always contain or imply information about mythic beginnings, developments, and hopes for the future.

The Navajo medicine man too reaches for his historical orientation back as far as memory and hearsay together will get him—back perhaps two, three, or four generations. If the man can read, historical documents will help him reach a little further. But from the furthest point in discernible history his narrative leaps to the beginning of all things and he tells the events forward, as time flows. A Navajo hunter may start with describing the condition when men still dwelt together with the gods and with the animals in indistinguishable prehuman flux. A Navajo singer of Blessingway, or of some other later ceremonial, may begin with telling a variant of

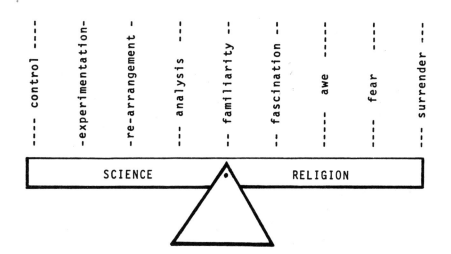

the Pueblo myth of emergence. By contrast I, a child of Western civilization, am accustomed to beginning my mythic narrative either with the Garden of Eden or with the Big Bang, depending on who is listening. Mythic prehistory and the future easily blend into one narrative, because in these stretches of time the counter-thrust of memory, which is so important for understanding history, does not interfere with the natural direction in which time seems to flow.

Only two moments in the flow of time can be pin-pointed—the present, and the beginning of all things. Of these, the present moment is the least stable. It constantly changes and keeps moving forward. Only the point of general origins remains constant in our awareness of time. It is no wonder, therefore, that everywhere in ontology, stories about origins tend to steal the show. But a much deeper cause than the manner in which we visualize "time" underlies this phenomenon. The basic questions of human existence are "what?" and "why?" These cannot be answered without changing them first into the easier historical questions of "how?" and "when?" From the answers, which a multitude of origin myths have given to these historical questions, mankind has managed to squeeze some much-needed postulates regarding the "whats" and the "whys" of existence.

The Continuity of Time and Proportional Space

Originators of Mythic narratives can be classified, cross-sectionally, into three groups. Toward the end of the teeter-totter, on one side, move the mystics; the activities of scientifically-inclined tricksters weigh at the other end. The middle ground is occupied by humanistic and priestly minds, by people who are willing to compromise and who, guided in their relationships to others by the Golden Rule, reach out to embrace as much as possible of the wisdom which lies in either direction. It is such wise men who have taught innumerable generations of Navajo hunters how to be tricksters; these hunters are taught to kill, and at the same time to find salvation from the guilt of killing by surrendering to an exemplary trickster god.

The respective positions of mystics, tricksters, and priests, at different places on the scale, produce for each of these personality types a different life perspective. Each person travels, so to speak, on one or more "tracks," longitudinally, with the flow of time—seldom on all of our nine tracks at once. The teeter-totters of societies or individuals gain and lose their balance continually, depending on where at a given moment human occupants rest

the beginning   the present

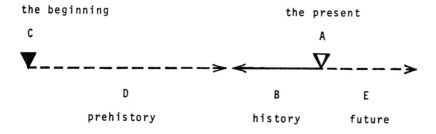

C   A

D   B   E

prehistory   history   future

their weights. If, for the sake of a simplified diagram, we choose to stablilize this teeter-totter, and if we plow its nine-point scale along the dimension of time with nine shares, a somewhat useful graph results.

Plotting a Myth in Time and Proportional Space

The scaffold is ready; now let us reconstruct the edifice—a dynamic picture of the early Navajo hunters' world. To facilitate this discussion I will be using coordinates which are designated by upper and lower case letters. Let me emphasize that these letter symbols designate coordinates; they are not formulas to which the Navajo hunters' world can be reduced. Consequently, their sole purpose is to help situate the listener, temporally and spatially, in the world of the narrator at approximately the place from which the statements flow. In other words, the myth itself is what is important; our graph is auxiliary. We are challenged to appreciate, with increased awareness, how the narrator tries to balance his personal teeter-totter and at the same time also the teeter-totter of his culture.

The myth which I am going to plot on our graph narrates "the release of the game animals." At one time this myth explained for the archaic hunter the origin of human hunting, hunting rules, and the justification for having to kill animal kinfolk. (Luckert 1975). I will be plotting several paragraphs of the narrative in detail, statement by statement. Then, after this method has been sufficiently demonstrated, I will summarize the remainder of the myth. To begin, it may be interesting to note how in the first two paragraphs of the narrative the familiar landscape, lying there before us at the present moment, becomes a sort of permanent bridge to understand the beginnings. The eventual killing of game animals, an "i" response, is carefully being prepared for by weighing down the teeter-totter religiously at "a." Every "i" is atoned for, is justified, or balanced with an "a."

Ae   — There is a place called Graystreak Mountain.
Ca-d   — It was the time when the gods or Holy-people were alive. There were no Navajos yet. Human beings had not been created yet.
Aa-d   — Graystreak Mountain is the place where the gods live;
Ae   — it looks as though a gray streak of sand extends up the side of this mountain. But the name of the mountain is not derived from its colour. It was not named that way because it is gray; rather, it was named after the colour of game animals, such as deer.

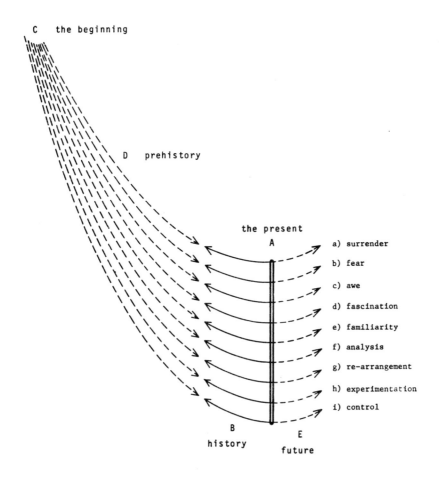

C   the beginning

D   prehistory

the present
A

a) surrender

b) fear

c) awe

d) fascination

e) familiarity

f) analysis

g) re-arrangement

h) experimentation

i) control

B

history

E

future

Ae	— Nearby is a house—now a low hill—
Ca-d	— which was the sweat lodge of the gods. This is where they lived (the prehuman divine hunters, such as Wolf and Mountain-lion);
Ce	— and they would build a fire to make the rocks very hot for the sweat bath.
Dd	— When everybody was about ready to go into the lodge, they kept noticing a black person that would come. After everybody had gone inside, the black person would come in.
De	— He came in once. He came in twice.
Df	— And the third time the people started asking: "Who is he?" "Where is he from?" "What is he?"
Dg-h	— The fourth time they set a trap for him.
Dc-h	— The trap was set so that gods would find out from where and who he was. Two divine persons, Red-tailed Hawk and Robin, were stationed outside the sweat lodge to watch for the black person.
Ce	— For this occasion, inside, the gods began singing this song by Talk-god:

The last sentence of the preceding paragraph is an introduction to the song which follows; it refers to the song's origin and identifies Talking-god as its author. The hunter, as he chants this song, identifies himself with its divine author—a mystic union which takes him back to the beginning. The coordinate "C" is therefore implied with every statement of the song.

CAe	— I am standing nearby. . . .
CAa-e	— I am the Talking-god,
CAe	— I am standing nearby. . . . I am standing atop of Black Mountain, I am standing nearby. . . .
CAa-f	— A son of Male Wind stands nearby. . . .
CAe-i	— I have a black bow in my hand as I am standing nearby. . . . I have a feathered arrow in my land as I am standing nearby. . . .
CAe	— A male wind with a sensitive ear, I am standing nearby. . . . With my feet ready to go anywhere, I am standing nearby. . . .

I am a son of Light Feather,
CAe   — I am standing nearby. . . .
CAi   — I am standing nearby, na-ya-yeh!

    With a measure of reflection the choice of coordinates for most lines of this song will become apparent. However, the choice of "i" for the last line requires an explanation: All the hunting songs by this informant end with "yeh!" When a deer is shot and falls, the sound is "yeh!" Understood in the context of the entire song and myth, this means that the human hunter *did* and at the same time *did not* kill the deer that fell. It was the Talking-god who did it. Now that I have demostrated how each statement can be plotted approximately on the grid, I shall summarize the remainder of the myth.

Ce   — The next song, one by Black-god,
CDg-i   — was chanted to lure its divine author himself toward the sweat lodge.
De   — He arrived in the form of a common crow.
Ai   — Nowadays human hunters use this song to get deer to come close.

De   — Before entering the sweat lodge the Black-god took off his clothes.
De-f   — While he was inside, some children discovered deer meat in his pockets; the god who had been hiding the game animals was found out.
De-i   — Four songs and four days of sweating later the prehuman hunters had found the home of Black-god, inside Yale Point. It turned out that this was the hiding place for the animals.

    The number "four" in the Southwest refers to the four cardinal points and generally means "completeness." In this instance it implies an ambition for complete control on the part of the would-be hunters—therefore the coordinate "i" is assigned. Two paragraphs later, we shall see how "four" divine deer, standing up against a hunter, become for him an "a" of submission—submission to their divine laws.

Dg-h   — One of these prehuman hunters disguised himself as a puppy. His friends left him behind at a campsite near the Black-god's home.
De   — The Crow family came and adopted the puppy as their pet.
Di   — In due time the disguised trickster released all the game animals.

Ci — Hunting as a way of life was so made possible.

Cd-f — But this was also the event by which the game animals became sensitive to odours and to sounds—all the things which make hunting difficult.

Ae — In a ravine near Graystreak Mountain and the Sweat Lodge hill, right here,

Dg-h — the trickster who formerly had been a puppy waited in ambush.

Di — When the first buck arrived the hunter had his arrow on the bow, ready to shoot.

Dc — But at that very moment the deer transformed himself into a mountain mahogany bush.

Dc-c — A mature man stood up from the bush and revealed to this first hunter the rules of hunting.

Da-b — The deer-man's laws were repeated by a doe, a two-pointer, and a fawn. All together four deer spoke.

CAb-i — These hunting laws were revealed for the benefit of human hunters who were to appear later, to establish a correct way of life for hunters.

De — Then the divine Deer-people travelled far and wide throughout Navajoland,

Ce — and they named many geographical sites.

Da — In the end the deer returned into the very mountain from which they had escaped. As formerly they had escaped from their keeper, the Black-god, so they had now escaped the hunters.

CAd-f — New deer come from there every year. Some deer, however, still originate from mountain mahogany bushes.

DAe-f — When the deer and the pursuing hunters had returned to the Black-god's house, they observed inside that mountain sheep were grazing in the south. In the west they found maize, squash, and other food plants.

DEb — In the north stood the Fawn as bringer of snow and as wielder of punishments for all careless hunters who would come along in the future.

Ce — A song and a prayer were made then,

Ea-i — which could be sung and prayed at a time when its use should become necessary to remove the consequences of these punishments.

In Conclusion

I should perhaps explain how the Time-Space structure of this hunter myth is related to the Time-Space structure of my own world.

Claus Chee Sonny, our primary informant, understood the present (A), and he anticipated the future (E) almost completely the way I do. As his opening words during our first recording session reveal:

Ae   — All right, my children (Navajo interpreter and author), that is the way it goes—asking questions about the old ancient stories. That is what you have asked about. I like that, and I am happy.

Be   — I have hoped that somebody would ask me these very questions.

Ae   — Nobody asks me these questions anymore, and I am getting very old.

Ef   — And if I would die, not telling these stories, then nobody would know them. Then there would be nothing, no stories, no songs, no life.

AEe   — Now this is a new beginning for people who are going to school, for young people from all over the world.

Eg   — My children will want to know these stories and will live by these stories. And I thank you for it.

His understanding of the immediate past (B) spans essentially the same stretch of time during which the Navajo tribe has moved into the light of our written history—about three generations:

Be   — I learned the Deer Huntingway from my father, the Very Tall One. He learned it from his father, the Stick-dice Player—my grandfather. My grandfather learned it from Mister Rope.

Immediately after this reminiscence in the realm of history (B), he leaps all the way to the beginning (C) of his hunting ceremonial:

Ce   — The first people who taught the Deer Huntingway were the gods.

Some of the conclusions which I have been able to reach by comparing this myth with existing written sources were, of course, out of Claus Chee Sonny's reach. For instance, it is not difficult for me to see that the literary ages of some elements in this myth belong to relatively recent times. Since it seems that the Navajos had not come to Graystreak Mountain and had not seen Yale Point before A.D. 1750, the geography of the myth can be no older than that. The reference to maize at the end of the narrative can be no older than the 16th Century, because the earliest known Navajo settlements in Gobernador Canyon were built during that century. (When we played our tape to another medicine man, he praised the original narrator for "updating" the Deer Huntingway). The basic theme of hiding the game animals and their release, however, appears to have belonged to Apachean mythology before their arrival in the Southwest.

Claus Chee Sonny's theory of origins (C) and his prehistorical follow-up narratives (D) differ obviously from mine—not irreconcilably, however. Personally, I ascribe small-animal hunting to our prosimian-like ancestors of over 70 million years ago. Intentional hunting, with manufactured tools, was pursued by australopithecines perhaps as early as 3 million years ago. In contrast to me, Claus Chee Sonny gets along without this far-flung chronology altogether. I am convinced that this priestly thinker was intelligent enough to do chronology as well as I can. But he has chosen instead to focus on the ontological dilemma with which the act of hunting burdens us at present—whenever it might have begun: hunting one's animal kinfolk is a practice that must have started before humankind existed, with the gods. Only so can our guilt of killing them be shed. Whether it was my australopithecus with his stick or stone chopper, or whether it was Claus Chee Sonny's trickster-hero who aimed his bow and arrow, the relational crisis between the self-conscious hunter and his animal victim was the same. Hauntingly this crisis leaks from the innocent eyes of every animal which the reflective hunter is about to kill. Innocent blood stains the hunter's conscience, burdens him with guilt, it demands justification and some sort of reconciliation.

If I reflect carefully on my own manner of thinking, I must confess that by explaining the origin of hunting chronologically, I have but scattered my very deficient awareness of "C" over my stretch of "D." My realm "D" is only slightly better furnished than Claus Chee Sonny's, because it contains a sprinkling of archaeological data from my realm of "B." Suddenly it begins to dawn on me, that I have not even touched the real "origin" of hunting after which Claus Chee Sonny and all his teachers have groped. The real question for a hunter who turns philosopher is: "Why and how did our ancestors develop a craving for animal flesh?" or "Why are some creatures anatomically equipped to capture and to eat the flesh of other creatures?"

Evasively and from a distance I may insist that Nature or God has willed it so. The real hunter must stalk real animals through the woods, must face them at close range as their killer—and must watch them die. A rational being, he, like the rest of us, is doomed to reflect on what he does. What can it possibly mean to him when academicians—such as I—who buy their meats cellophane-wrapped in supermarkets, wonder about the beginning of hunting somewhere in history? His life is involved in real, not imaginary, proportional space: Here, but for the exemplary presence of some hunter gods—such as Wolf and Mountain-lion—a deer could be an untouchable ("taboo") greater-than-human personage. The alternatives for the traditional hunter are not many. He can stop hunting and starve with an easy conscience; or, he can respond to such natural hunters as Wolf, Mountain-lion, or the Talking-god as his arche-typal tutelaries—eat, and still be forgiven.

Notes

1. Ten months after presenting this paper—as the collection approaches publication in the form of a book—an important point of information can be added. The conceptualization of space and time, which according to this essay Navajo elders and Westerners have in common, has now been documented also for Hopi tradition. My colleague, Ekkehart Malotki, a linguist with seven years of experience in Hopi, informs me that the Hopi language does have an even better device than English—a suffix—for referring to future time. Had the influential Benjamin Lee Whorf discovered English before he philosophized about Hopi, we all could have come out, by his method, as having a less defined sense of history than the Hopis. It turns out that linguistics is not always the infallible bedrock for religious studies which it is frequently made out to be. Whorf's theory and its descendants in many current textbooks remind us still too much of Levy-Bruhl's "primitive mentality" from which he had the wisdom to back away later in life. Thus, for trying to understand people of different traditions, it is still better to begin with assuming a common ground of logical structure, rather than by committing oneself to a search for differences.

Bibliography

Luckert, K.
   1975. *The Navajo Hunter Traditions*, University of Arizona Press, Tuscon.
Wach, J.
   1924. *Religionswissenschaft*, Leipzig.

Respondent: Sam Gill

I find it notable that this is a conference of many tongues. Last night we were addressed in English, in French, and in Cree. This morning we have heard the language of Cree prayer and witnessed their language of ritual. Besides these we have heard another language, a subset of English peculiar to academicians. Professor Luckert has offered to us his view of certain aspects of this language in the hope of extending our understanding of native American mythology. It seems to me that the existence of a number of languages is precisely the issue we face in this conference. We are really here to learn something about one another, yet we do not all speak the same language. So we're concerned that we are not being understood adequately or correctly.

Professor Luckert and I have known each other for quite some time and in a way it's unfair that I should have to respond to his paper. We have found that we approach the same subject in different, perhaps complementary, ways. We have argued this out privately and will continue to do so. I would prefer then to make but a few general remarks which are stimulated in a way by his paper. Professor Luckert, in his approach to the understanding of native American mythology, begins, I think, with a kind of presupposition that is not unusual in academic studies, but is one that I personally have not found to be acceptable. He feels, if I understand him correctly, that his view of time and space is adequate as a basis for understanding native American concepts of time and space. I find quite convincing the kind of evidence that Joseph Brown has given us this morning about the immediacy of the notion of time in the context of mythology and I have been frequently struck by the way in which many native American languages reflect categories of time and space quite differently from my own. I am told that in Lakota and other Sioux dialects, as well as in some California languages, distinctions between time and space are not made in the same way as is common in Western languages. When and where are not distinguished from one another. In Hopi language time is not accounted for through the use of tense as we ordinarily think of it, while in Navajo language the system of tenses is very elaborate and much more precise than in English. So simply on the basis of evidence in but a few native American languages I have found it necessary to expect quite different views of reality, of the nature of time and space, in the study of native American mythology and ritual. That is a question that we may wish to discuss at some length. It seems to me that the major issue is how we can be sure that we understand the messages of mythology as they are intended to be received, not as they are filtered through our own world views.

Ritual Section

Ritual in Native North American Religions

by

Åke Hultkrantz

It has often been said that the North American Indians "dance out" their religions. Their religious convictions are expressed through the medium of dances, songs, repetitive movements. Lowie pointed at the central place of what he called "ceremonialism" in Amerindian culture (Lowie 1915: 229 ff.). Perhaps we should remember that at the time he wrote his article on the subject the ritualism of more complex societies on the Plains, in the Southwest, and on the North Pacific Coast had just been investigated. The cultures of technologically more "simple" tribes were as yet less well known (particularly in the Great Basin and western Canada (interior) and Alaska). These cultures have later proved to lack the intricate ceremonialism of the more complex societies. Nevertheless, the recent westward expansion of Plains Indian cultural traits gradually changed the picture in the Great Basin, and the attraction of Northwest Coast cultural features has, to some extent, had a similar effect among Athapascan Indians of the Mackenzie (cf. Gunther 1950 and Swanton 1904).

Ritual is thus a prominent part of North American aboriginal religion, and to behaviourists (like most American anthropologists) it is the foremost religious document of a primal people. This is not the place to challenge this view, although I do not share it: personal confessions, beliefs and legends are in my eyes important records of what people really hold. A ritual is a system of fixed behaviour, and it sometimes tends to move away from the belief system that once motivated it. We know this to be the case in stratified societies where the official cult may have very little relation to the living beliefs. We also know that members of tribal societies act ritually in a certain way because this was the way their forefathers did it. In North America many strange ritual actions cannot be explained symbolically by the Indians, because they had simply been taught in dreams by their guardian spirits (or the guardian spirit of the first owner of the ritual) to enact the ritual in just that manner. The ritual has always an ulterior background in religious experiences and religious beliefs, something that is rather easily observed in Indian North America.

At the same time ritual forms follow a well-established pattern and, as socio-cultural phenomena, they take part of the same dynamics as other institutional forms of society. This is why they have become favourite objects of social-anthropological studies: kinship systems, political systems and other structural forms of society are reflected in and models for a ritual organization, ritual expressions and ritual values. Of late, however, anthropologists interested in cognition and symbolism have approached the ritual in a new spirit. I think particularly of such scholars as Victor W. Turner, Mary Douglas and Melford Spiro. Their analyses come close to what could be wished for by scholars of religion, with the additional caveat that the "symbolism" may have been more easily revealed had more references to religious problems been evident(cf. for instance, Turner 1967 and 1969).

In contrast to anthropologists, students of comparative religion have for a long time been absorbed by the problems of interrelationships between myth and ritual. If only they had taken seriously native North American materials, their onesided interpretation of one with the other would never have occurred. Regrettably, students of religion have been interested in native American religions only marginally. There is now a more positive trend in this respect. Perhaps this will lead up to a more modulated opinion on rituals.

In this short lecture I shall try to see the North American Indian rituals from the point of view of religion, that is, as an expression of religious beliefs. In that connection a succinct survey of prominent types of ritual in North America will be supplied. The theme I have chosen is of course enormous in scope, and only some very general observations can be presented. To a large extent they also hold, I presume, for rituals in other parts of the world.

Types of Ritual

Ritual is, then, a fixed, usually solemn behaviour that is repeated in certain situations. Anthropologists like to call the latter "crisis situations", but there is not always any crisis involved. It would be better to speak of "sacred situations", in Durkheim's spirit. Although not all rituals occur in a religious setting (e.g. receptions to secular order societies in Europe or American Indian rites of greeting), most rituals in tribal cultures are symbolic expressions of religious thought, feeling and will. They usually correspond to human needs and desires, and they are instrumental in carrying them out. There is no reason why we should discuss here the problem then arising as to what extent a ritual is either religious or magical. This is a major problem in itself. I shall avoid it in this presentation.

There are rituals that consist in prayers, harangues and songs, as for instance, many of those found among the Navajo. However, the characteristic thing about most North American Indian rituals is that action reinforces the word, thereby giving more palpability to religion. The word is a poor symbol of all the individual thinks and feels when confronted with the supernatural. By dancing it out he is relieved of the tension caused by verbal deficiency. At the same time, the action is palpable and concrete with the number of participants enhancing this feeling of reality and realization. The ritual may have its origin in a visionary dream, in a dictate by a culture hero or a mythic event in cosmogonic time, or it may stem from a neighboring tribe to serve as an institution that makes "good medicine". The important thing is that ritual, if truly integrated in a living culture, does not exist as an independent phenomenon. It is always a vehicle of religious aims which alone can legitimize its occurrence.

Rituals may be systematized according to various scales (see e.g. Wach 1947: 55 ff.). Here are some examples.

(1) Quantitative scale: observance—rite—ceremony. The observance is the smallest unit. It is an observance, for instance, to avoid visiting a tabooed place, like the spouting geysers of the Yellowstone Park (Hultkrantz 1954). A ritual is a simple ritual, or a part of a complex ceremony. For instance, the actual sandpainting is part of the lengthy Navajo ceremony of two to nine nights (see e.g. Matthews 1897: 43 ff.).

(2) Sociological scale: there is a difference between a personal, private ritual and collective, institutional ritual. In complex societies the latter may be divided into folk, official, and secret ritual. A clan ritual may belong to either of these three categories.

(3) Psychological scale: attitudes of veneration contrast with attitudes of self-assertion. To many this is the difference between religion and magic. It would, in this connection, be more advantageous to emphasize the line between rituals that are the gift of gods and rituals that are acquired through training. To the former belong most cultic acts that seek divine or spiritual help; to the latter rituals of shamanism.

(4) Temporal scale: rites of transition, calendar rites, crisis rites. This is Honko's classification, presented at the methodological

congress for the study of religion in 1973, and it comes close to
Spiro's classification from 1970 (Honko 1975, Spiro 1970: 206 f.). The
rites of transition are van Gennep's well-known *rites de passage*,
with their three phases (van Gennep 1909). Calendar rites are, I
think, primarily typical of agricultural societies. In North America
the Iroquois and Pueblo calendars regulate the rhythm and the rites
of the vegetational year (Fenton 1936, Hale 1883, Parsons 1922 and
1933, Fay 1950). On the other hand, there is archaeological evidence
that hunting societies might have observed solstices and the exact
yearly cycle, probably for ritual purposes (Kehoe and Kehoe 1977).
The appearance of salmon on the Northwest Coast and in the
Plateau rivers and the growth of luscious grass on the Plains were in
a way calendrical marks for festive religious occasions among the
hunters and gatherers living there. Crisis rites, finally, are arranged
when an unforeseen crisis jeoardizes the welfare of the individual
or the people.

There is no doubt that this scheme is of great value to our
interpretation of rituals. It is certainly the best one among those
here proposed. At the same time it tends to disregard certain
categories of ritual action, such as ancestor rites. These may belong
to all three types of ritual, but are at home in none of them.

(5) Structural scale: ritual drama—ritual address—ritual
meditation. The ritual drama has two different faces. Firstly, it may
be an imitation of the cosmological primeval events, with the
partakers impersonating (with or without masks) the mythic beings.
The Pueblo Machina dances are a good example (Anderson 1955).
Ritual myths usually serve as texts for such dramas. Secondly, the
ritual may be an actual ride into the unseen world, performed by
the shaman, and watched by a number of observers. This is a real,
in some details, unforseen drama; the imitation is limited to the
shaman's symbolic references to the course of events during the
act. The ritual address takes the form of a prayer, an offering, or
other divine service. It presupposes a direct mutual interaction
between the god and his devotees. Ritual meditation is
characteristic of the vision quest, for instance. It may be defined as
wordless prayer within a ritual frame.

The ritual drama and ritual address have a vague likeness to
Spiro's commemorative and expressive rites, but there is certainly
no exact affinity. Apotropaeic or preventive rites may be subsumed
under all the three categories here suggested. For instance, the
Navajo have detailed apotropaeic rituals which may be termed

ritual drama (cf. Haile 1938). (They also convey a positive identification with the universe, and are thus only indirectly apotropaeic.)

We could also classify rites according to their contents, but such classifications will remain unsystematic if they are not correlated with a typology of the kind presented above.

One term has been avoided here quite consciously: cult. There is an unfortunate habit among American anthropologists to use the words cult and cultic as equivalents for religion and religious. It seems that Kroeber was the first to introduce this linguistic designation when, in his Handbook on Californian Indians, he discussed the "Kuksu cult" (Kroeber 1925: 364 ff.). Later new religious movements, such as the Peyote religion, have been acclaimed as cults. Even archaeological complexes have been designated as cult: we could mention the so-called Southern Cult in the Southeast, presumably the predecessor of the harvest feast, the *busk* ritual, among the Creek and their neighbours (cf. Howard 1968). A cult is indeed not a religion but a ritual of supplication directed to a divinity. We should therefore be cautious in our use of the term. Many rituals are cults, but not all.

The Belief System of the Sun Dance

If a ritual expresses religious beliefs it cannot be reduced to a collection of ritual traits. Certainly, there is, as Jensen has pointed out, a development between spontaneous rites and an intricate pattern of traditional rites handed down through the generations (Jensen 1963). The latter may have little in common with the beliefs that once energized it.

Still, the rites give a general response to the particular beliefs held, and a ritual has a motivation that keeps it going.

This was overlooked when at the beginning of this century Clark Wissler organized the field collection of Sun Dance rituals for the publication department of the American Museum of Natural History in New York. Scholars like Goddard, Lowie, Spier and Wissler himself assembled all information they could among the different Plains tribes (see the papers in the museum's anthropological series, vol. XVI). Spier made a meticulous distributional study of the traits and trait complexes (Spier 1921). However, the import communicated by the ritual was lost behind all the details. Writes Fred Eggan many decades later,

> despite all the studies of the Sun Dance we still do not have an
> adequate account giving us the meaning and significance of the
> rituals for the participants and for the tribe. One such account would
> enable us to revalue the whole literature of the Sun Dance
> (Eggan 1954: 757; cf. also Hultkrantz 1976: 90).

This was written in 1954. Since that date some more congenial
works on the Sun Dance have appeared like Peter Powell's study of
the Cheyenne ceremonial and Joseph Jorgensen's of the
Shoshoni-Ute rituals (Powell 1969, Jorgensen 1972). Still, the Sun
Dance is mostly seen as a ritual with a compound of aims, like
fulfilling a vow, healing the sick, gaining a particular favour, making
good war or hunting medicine, and so on. In other words, the fixed
point is the ritual, whereas the motivations differ. I think that the
basis of this attitude is, beside the general behaviouristic approach,
the ahistorical, "flat" perspective that domineered when Wissler
and his colleagues were writing about the Dance (Hultkrantz 1967a:
102). The fact is that archaeology, documentary research and
comparative investigations —in short, "ethnohistory" — could lend
us support for deeper penetrations into the historical past. In this
way the original ideological complex of the Sun Dance could be
revealed.

Thus, there are indications that the Sun Dance ritual is an
instance of the North American Indian new year rituals, best known
from Northwest California as world renewal ceremonies and the
Lenape or Delaware Indians as the Big House Ritual (Kroeber and
Gifford 1949, Speck 1931). Additionally, the Plains ritual has its close
counterpart in the new year festival of the Siberian Tungus. This
festival was a celebration of the renewal of nature, but it also
included, like the Sun Dance, the initiation of new shamans. The
central ritual attribute was the offerings pole, decorated with skins
of sacrificed animals, and with two coloured pieces of cloth at the
top. This pole, symbolizing the world-tree, resembles the center
post of the Sun Dance lodge (Anisimov 1963: 92, 93, 116). There
must be some connection here between the Plains and the Tungus
ceremonies, perhaps even a common heritage.

These comparisons, if accepted, suggest that the new year, or
new creation, is the central feature of the Plains ceremony. Of
course, if we consider the motivations given by the different
sun-dancing tribes they are most diverse. However, through his
distributional tabulations Spier suggested that the Cheyenne and
Arapaho were the originators of the Dance. Precisely among these

two tribes the Sun Dance is a ceremony of new creation, the lodge is the world, and its center post the world-tree, the communications channel between man and the powers above (see Hultkrantz 1973: 8 f.). This central idea practically explains the whole Sun Dance ritual in all its variations. With the dissemination of the Dance to tribes with other cultural traditions a variety of other motives came to the fore. Among the Dakota, for instance, the Sun Dance has turned into a shamanic ritual, an initiation ceremony for young candidates of the shamanic profession and for other visionaries, while the self-torture so conspicuous in the Dakota and Blackfoot Dance seems to have been in harmony with their military ethos.

This kind of analysis, focussing on the ideological premisses of the rituals, opens up these rituals to us and makes them meaningful. So many American Indian rituals are just a jumble of ritual elements and ritual movements to the spectators (and the scientific observers among them). It is time for us to try to discover their real import, their message.

Survey of Major North American Indian Rituals

It is now time to present a short descriptive survey of some historical ritual forms in Indian North America. What follows is thus no classification, but an enumeration and characterization of rituals that have played a major role in North America. It is a representative selection, for the rituals among the North American aborigines have been legion. Those mentioned here are all traditional rituals, that is, they have not as such been influenced by white American culture.

(1) New year rituals. These may also be called thanksgiving rituals. They reiterate the cosmic creation, and are thus dramatic performances of the mythic events at the beginning of times. The lodge or house where they are held is a replica of the universe, and the length of the celebration corresponds to the progress of the cosmic creation. Thus, the Sun Dance is a creation drama during four successive days, and the Lenape Big House ceremony lasts twelve days. In this case also another interpretation is current: "The belief that each day's performance lifts the worship a stage higher in the series of twelve successive sky levels until on the final day it reaches the Great Spirit himself" (Speck 1931: 61). The Hupa Indians and Karok Indians of northern California have a sweat house as their cosmic building, and its construction symbolizes the creation of the world (Kroeber and Gifford 1949).

(2) Hunting rites. The northern Californian new year ritual is combined with the custom of honouring the first salmon that has been caught in the season. This ritual exists independently among many tribes on the North Pacific Coast and the Plateau (Gunther 1928). Veneration of the killed game, called animal ceremonialism, is known all over North America (see e.g. Paulson 1959, Heizer and Hewes 1940). Best known of the hunting rituals is the historically connected bear ceremonialism in northern North America (Hallowell 1926). Rituals promoting the growth and access of animals have been rather general and occur even in agricultural regions like the Pueblo area (Underhill 1948).

(3) Fertility rites. These belong to the agrarian cultures in the Southwest, some Plains tribes and Eastern woodlands populations from the Iroquois to the Creek. The rituals are determined by a calendar, resulting in a cycle of ceremonies. The Zuni, for instance, have dances in the summer to please the rain gods, while the winter dances are held by societies specialized in promoting fecundity and in curing diseases (Bunzel 1932). Also the Iroquois year was divided into a series of rituals, the most important of them being the Midwinter ritual which, like the Creek harvest festival, was associated with a rite of new fire — the token that it may derive from a new year ritual (Speck 1949).

(4) Moiety rituals. The idea that there is a dual cosmos, divided between the powers above and the powers beneath, or two sacred world halves, has generated the moiety systems. The moieties of the tribes perform rituals for collective aims in such a reciprocal way that the cosmic unity is secured. Moiety rituals occur in the Southwest, Southeast and on the Prairies (see, for instance, Fletcher and La Flesche 1911).

(5) Initiation rituals. There are tribal initiations, as in California, initiations into clans, as among the Prairie Tribes, and into secret societies, as among the Kwakiutl and Ojibway. The Apache of the Southwest arrange great puberty rituals for girls that refer to the creation. We even find adoptions of foreign groups into a relationship of friendship through rituals, called the *hako* among the Pawnee, *hunka* among the Sioux. This ritual includes the famous calumet dance, once distributed from the Plains to the Iroquois area (Fenton 1953). Finally we have the initiations into sacred professions, for instance, shamanhood.

(6) Bundle rituals. Rituals around sacred bundles are common in the Plains-Prairie area. They may involve the whole tribe, as the ritual of the sacred arrows of the Cheyenne (Powell 1969), or segments of the tribe, as the opening rituals of most inherited

family bundles and the rituals that have been formed in clubs joined by visionaries who have procured visions and bundles from the same spirits (e.g. Ewers 1955).

(7) Shamanic rituals. These may be roughly divided into vision rituals, associated with the quest for guardian spirits, which are common in North America outside the Pueblo area and concern most men (Benedict 1923), and the divination and healing rituals which are performed by the recipients of specific powers, the medicine-men and shamans. The most widely-known divination ritual is the Shaking Tent ceremony, in its Sioux form called *yuwipi* (Hultkrantz 1967b). The healing rituals vary from ecstatic pantomimes of the shaman's soul-flight to the nine-night curing ceremonies of the Navajo. (The idea of a ceremony of nine nights has been taken over from the Pueblo Indians.)

(8) Death rites. These include mourning rites (blackening of face, mutilations, various taboos) and burial rituals. So-called secondary burials (in which the bones were cleaned from flesh and deposited in a new grave) at one time occurred in the east, for instance, among the Huron. Proper ancestor rites are lacking in North America, unless the Pueblo *kachina* rituals should be named thus: the *kachina* are supernatural beings recruited, at leastly partly, among the dead.

The North American Indian ceremonials are often preceded by ritual cleaning, either through induced vomiting (the Southeast), or through sweat baths (for instance, on the Plains). Ceremonies are usually ended by general feasting.

All these rituals have one thing in common: they serve religious ends.

Ritual Persistence and Ritual Change

Finally, some words should be said about the dynamics of rituals from the point of view of religion. It was said before that although rituals are provoked by religious experiences they tend to become self-operative, cultural mechanisms. Disregarding influences from outside there are two possibilities for their development: either they remain integrated with the goals and values of the society, or they show the inclination of becoming rigid systems indifferent to, indeed, conflicting with tribal ideology. For instance, among the Wind River Shoshoni there are some doubts whether the old vision quest should be upheld when "spontaneous" visions may be acquired through the Sun Dance (Hultkrantz 1969: 30). The rule is however that a ritual endures as long as it is serving the prevalent religious ideology.

Since Robertson-Smith's days it has been taken for granted in some circles that of the three genres of religions materials, myths, rituals and beliefs, only the first two resist the change of times, whereas beliefs are too vague and too brittle to remain for a longer time. This view, still held by many scholars, is actually without foundation. The state of affairs is more complicated.

While beliefs may concern peripheral things such as divers "superstitions", they often mediate value judgments and basic convictions at the very core of religion (cf. Hultkrantz 1968). It is therefore exceedingly difficult to measure their rate of change. Probably most beliefs partake in the fate of the rituals: at least among the Eastern Shoshoni they have changed with the cultural premises (Hultkrantz 1962: 551 f.) In contradistinction to rituals however they seem to linger on for some time.

Myths may give the impression of being less tenacious, in particular in preliterate societies such as found in North America. Indeed, migratory myths may have only a weak hold if they do not refer to fundamental issues. However, in comparison with rituals, myths seem more permanent. Or, as Kluckhohn put it, "taking a very broad view of the matter, it does seem that behavioral patterns more frequently alter first" (Kluckhohn 1942: 53). There are reasons to suppose that a mythology that is not built around central cultural values, and thus is less submitted to change, is more conservative than other parts of religion (Hultkrantz 1962: 552).

Rituals, on the other hand, change with their cultural premises. When the eastern Plains Indian technology, value pattern and ceremonial complex was imprinted upon Shoshoni culture their old thanksgiving ritual, in a round dance, was supplanted by the Sun Dance (Hultkrantz Ms). On the other hand, the Navajo did not accept the Ghost Dance because their old value pattern with its outstanding fear of the dead had remained intact (Hill 1944). Hence, ritual change is another indication of the links that exist between ritual and basic religious tenets.

Bibliography

Anderson, F. G.
1955. 'The Pueblo Kachina Cult: A Historical Reconstruction', *Southwestern Journal of Anthropology* 11 (4): 404-419.

Anisimov, A. F.
1963. 'The Shaman's Tent of the Evenks and the Origin of the Shamanistic Rite', pp. 84-123 in *Studies in Siberian Shamanism*, ed. H. N. Michael Toronto: Arctic Institute of North America.

Benedict, R. F.
1923. 'The concept of the Guardian Spirit in North America', *Memoirs of the American Anthropological Association*, no. 29.

Bunzel, R. L.
1932. 'Introduction to Zuni Ceremonialism', *47th Annual Report of the Bureau of American Ethnology*, pp. 467-544, Washington.

Eggan, F.
1954. 'Social Anthropology and the Method of Controlled Comparison', *American Anthropologist* 56 (5): 743-763.

Ewers, J. C.
1955. 'The Bear Cult among the Assiniboin and Their Neighbors of the Northern Plains', *Southwestern Journal of Anthropology* 11 (1): 1-12.

Fay, G. E.
1950. 'A Calendar of Indian Ceremonies', *El Palacio* 57: 166-172.

Fenton, W. N.
1936. 'An Outline of Seneca Ceremonies at Coldspring Longhouse', *Yale University Publications in Anthropology*, no. 9, New Haven.
1953. 'The Iroquois Eagle Dance: An Offshoot of the Calumet Dance', *Bureau of American Ethnology, Bulletin* 156. Washington.

Fletcher, A. C. and La Flesche, F.
1911. 'The Omaha Tribe', *27th Annual Report of the Bureau of American Ethnology*, Washington.

van Gennep, A.
1909. *Les rites de passage*, Paris.

Gunther, E.
1928. 'A Further Analysis of the First Salmon Ceremony', *University of Washington Publications in Anthropology* 2 (5): 129-173. Seattle.
1950. 'The Westward Movement of Some Plains Traits', *American Anthropologist* 52 (2): 174-180.

Haile, B.
1938. 'Navajo Chantways and Ceremonials', *American Anthropologist* 40 (4): 639-652.

Hale, H.
1883. *The Iroquois Book of Rites*, Philadelphia.

Hallowell, A. I.
1926. 'Bear Ceremonialism in the Northern Hemisphere', *American Anthropologist* 28 (1): 1-175.

Heizer, R. F. and Hewes, G. W.
1940. 'Animal Ceremonialism in Central California in the Light of Archaeology', *American Anthropologist* 42 (4): 587-603.

Hill, W. W.
    1944. 'The Nahavo Indians and the Ghost Dance of 1890', *American Anthropologist* 46 (4): 523-527.

Honko, L.
    1975. 'Zur Klassifikation der Riten', *Temenos* 11: 61-77.

Howard, J. H.
    1968. 'The Southeastern Ceremonial Complex and Its Interpretation', *Memoirs of the Missouri Archaeological Society*, no. 6. Columbia, Missouri.

Hultkrantz, A.
    1954. 'The Indians and the Wonders of Yellowstone', *Ethnos* 19: 34-68.
    1962. *Religion und Mythologie der Prarie-Schoschonen'*, *Proceedings of the 34th International Congress of Americanists*, pp. 546-554, Wien.
    1967 a. 'Historical Approaches in American Ethnology', *Ethnologia Europaea* 1 (2): 96-116, Paris.
    1967 b. 'Spirit Lodge, A North American Shamanistic Seance', pp. 32-68 in *Studies in Shamanism*, ed. C.-M. Edsman, Scripta Instituti Donneriani Aboensis, vol. 1.
    1968. 'Miscellaneous Beliefs', *Temenos* 3: 67-82.
    1969. 'Pagan and Christian Elements in the Religious Syncretism among the Shoshoni Indians of Wyoming', pp. 15-40 in *Syncretism*, ed. S.S. Hartman. Scripta Instituti Donneriani Aboensis, vol. 3.
    1973. 'Prairie and Plains Indians', *Iconography of Religions* 10 (3), Leiden.
    1976. 'The Contribution of the Study of North American Indian Religions to the History of Religions', pp. 86-106 in *Seeing with a Native Eye*, ed. W. H. Capps, New York: Harper and Row.
    Ms 'Mythology and Religious Concepts [of the Great Basin Indians]'. To be published in the *Handbook of North American Indians*, vol. 10, Smithsonian Institution.

Jensen, A. E.
    1963. *Myth and Cult among Primitive Peoples*, Chicago and London: University of Chicago Press.

Jorgensen, J. G.
    1972. *The Sun Dance Religion*, Chicago and London: University of Chicago Press.

Kehoe, Th. and Kehoe, A.
    1977. 'Stones, Solstices and Sun Dance Structures', *Plains Anthropologist* 22 (76): 85-95.

Kluckhohn, C.
    1942. 'Myths and Rituals: A General Theory', *The Harvard Theological Review* 35 (1): 45-79.

Kroeber, A. L.
    1925. 'Handbook of the Indians of California', *Bureau of American Ethnology, Bulletin* 78. Washington.

Kroeber, A. L. and Gifford, E. W.
    1949. 'World Renewal', *Anthropological Records* 13. Berkeley.

Lowie, R. H.
   1915. 'Ceremonialism in North America', pp. 229-258 in F. Boas et al.,
      Anthropology in North America, New York: G. E. Stechert & Co.
Matthews, W.
   1897. 'Navajo Legends', *Memoirs of the American Folklore Society*, no. 5. Boston.
Paulson I.
   1959. 'Zur Aufbewahrung der Tierknochen im nordlichen Nordamerika',
      *Amerikanistische Miszellen, Mitteilungen aus dem Museum fur
      Volkerkunde in Hamburg* 25: 182-188. Hamburg.
Parsons, E. C.
   1922. 'Winter and Summer Dances Series in Zuni', *University of California
      Publications in American Archaeology and Ethnology*, vol. 17: 171-216.
      Berkeley.
   1933. 'Hopi and Zuni Ceremonialism', *Memoirs of the American Folklore
      Society*, no. 39. Boston.
Powell, P.J.
   1969. *Sweet Medicine: The Continuing Role of the Sacred Arrows, the Sun
      Dance, and the Sacred Buffalo Hat in Northern Cheyenne History*, 2 vols.
      Norman: University of Oklahoma Press.
Speck, F. G.
   1931. 'A Study of the Delaware Indian Big House Ceremony', *Publications of the
      Pennsylvania Historical Commission*, vol 2. Harrisburg.
   1949. *Midwinter Rites of the Cayuga Long House*, Philadelphia: University of
      Pennsylvania Press.
Spier, L.
   1921. 'The Sun Dance of the Plains Indians: Its Development and Diffusion',
      Anthropological Papers of the American Museum of Natural History, vol.
      16 (7): 451-527. New York.
Spiro, M. E.
   1970. *Buddhism and Society: A Great Tradition and Its Burmese Vicissitudes*,
      New York.
Swanton, J. R.
   1904. 'The Development of the Clan System and of Secret Societies among the
      Northwestern Indians', *American Anthropologist* 6 (4): 477-485.
Turner, V. W.
   1967. *The Forest Of Symbols: Aspects of Ndembu Ritual*, Ithaca, New York.
   1969. *The Ritual Process: Structure and Anti-Structure*, London.
Underhill, R. M.
   1948. 'Ceremonial Patterns in the Greater Southwest', *Monographs of the
      American Ethnological Society*, no. 13. New York.
Wach, J.
   1947. *Sociology of Religion*, London: Kegan Paul.

Respondent: Joseph E. Brown

Professor Waugh has put me in a most embarrassing situation here. As a student at the University of Stockholm of Professor Hultkrantz, I do not feel in a position to do anything but simply applaud his elegant statement. I spent a good deal of last night reading it. Let me simply applaud then first his reservations on those earlier students of native American life and religion, such as Wissler, Leslie Spier, who, incidentally, was also a former professor of mine, and others because it seems to me very clear that there is enormous poverty in the material types of classifications that they endeavour to achieve in distributional studies (e.g. Spier). I think also it helpful to *scholars* in this area to have both Prof. Hultkrantz's schema for systemization and his categorization of historical ritual form.

Concerning the Sun Dance there is one emphasis I would like to suggest here, and that is certainly the assertion that the renewal of world and life—re-creation—is essential. I would also like to emphasize , in the same context, that one should not forget this renewal also applies to man. That is to say, the man who undertakes the Sun Dance also goes through the process of interior regeneration, rebirth, renewal, and this is quite evident. I would also like to stress that the categories which Prof. Hultkrantz has suggested here are useful categories for scholars, but I wish that there were time to come up with categories that were meaningful to the native American people themselves. It seems to me that this is very important. I am not saying that the academic type of categories are redundant or useless but I do feel that it is most important to understand this kind of material as the people themselves do and I therefore look forward very much to a discussion of this during the afternoon sessions.

Finally, I have a minor request for clarification. It has to do with the suggestion that there could be or is considered to be a primacy of belief over ritual. As Prof. Hultkrantz puts it, the action supplants the word. I would rather use the term *supports*. It seems to me that the word supports the ritual act. The rite should not be separated off (as the term "supplants" suggests) from the supporting word that comes in the form of chant or song. This is a theme I like to return to again and again and it can be expressed as the importance in native traditions of the *word*, whether this be expressed in verbal prayer or chant or song. The key dimension here, as many native people have explained to me, is the fact that the word proceeds ultimately from the realm of the heart, from the lands which produce the breath. The breath then proceeds to bear the word. As we are all aware, the breath is ultimately sacred in native traditions. Hence there is a special quality to the word which is very difficult for those of us to understand who do not participate in these kinds of sacred languages. So I see their relationship more in terms of mutual support and I would hesitate to establish a kind of priority of one over the other.

Prof. Hultkrantz

You have noted that I stressed the primacy of action over word and that isn't true when it comes to North American Indians—the word supports the ritual act. Yes indeed. I have written action supplants the word and that is perhaps giving the wrong idea. Actually what I had in mind is this—there is a mystery here that is something very difficult for us to fathom. When you experience it words are not enough to describe what you see. And it is this fragility of the word, this fragility of our way of expressing our religious experiences that can be handled through ritual action. That was the thought behind it. But I understand it can give the wrong impression so I think I should change it in my manuscript so no misinterpretation will occur. All the other issues you mention are correct and I accept that. (Change has been made in paper—Ed. note).

Whirling Logs and Coloured Sands

by

Sam D. Gill

For some time I have been intrigued by Navajo sandpaintings, which is to non-Navajos the most visible and broadly known aspect of Navajo ceremonialism. It is a bit curious that sandpaintings should be so commonly known since in Navajo religious traditions they are not glued down and saved, but are destroyed during the ritual. To record or photograph a sandpainting is not often recommended or allowed and the designs have been retained in the minds of Navajo singers who chose to acquire that sacred knowledge and not as patterns to be copied from books. Still, hundreds have been recorded and published. Recently Navajo artisans have begun to recognize the monetary value in making permanent sandpainting-like pictures which are sold as authentic Indian art in department stores everywhere.

When I look at the many picture books of sandpainting, I am impressed with their beauty, and I find it difficult to understand the Navajo aesthetic which can tolerate their destruction only moments after they are completed. And in the context of publications containing dozens of them the details fade and I see only a parade of blurry mandalas. I have read explanation of the rituals of sandpainting which tell of a magical osmosis effecting an exchange of the good in the sandpainting for the evil in the person sitting upon it, but I remain puzzled about the role of the many complex patterns, and how the person sitting on the sand perceives this osmosis effect. I also wonder if this explanation, based on a dichotomy of good and evil, accurately reflects Navajo religious thought.

It seems to me that an appreciation of the life and meaning of Navajo sandpainting for non-Navajos must begin with an extended view of a single sandpainting seen in its ritual, mythological, and cultural contexts. This is, after all, how traditional Navajos experience sandpaintings. Navajos do not decorate their hogans with sandpaintings nor do they publish picture books. The Navajo experience associated with a sandpainting is one of intense personal involvement and quite specific personal need. It requires the investment of considerable time and wealth. Perhaps it is ironic that we should be perplexed at the short life of these paintings.

What I propose to do in this paper is to focus on a single sandpainting done in an actual performance of a Navajo ceremonial. I would like to view the sandpainting from several angles by considering the process of its construction, the rite performed upon it, elements in the greater ceremonial context, and the associated mythology. I want to attempt to move closer to the perspective of the Navajo and to illustrate aspects of Navajo religious thought, yet due to my own background and the analytical style of academics, I will obviously be using a very different approach and language than would the Navajo.

The sandpainting which I have chosen for consideration is the whirling logs sandpainting done during the Nightway ceremonial. The choice is fortuitous, but only partially so. While I have access to an extensive collection of photographs taken of this sandpainting by David Perio in 1963, I feel that it is one of the most broadly known among Navajo people. It has been commonly depicted in Navajo tapestries, and in paintings by Navajos.[1] The American Museum of Natural History has a display depicting a Navajo sandpainter completing the Whirling Logs painting (cf. Underhill 1956: 80). The Nightway ceremonial is commonly performed during the winter months and undoubtedly the whirling logs painting is frequently a part of it. The sandpainting has been published by both Matthews and Stevenson (1902: Plate VI; 1891: Plate CXXI).

The sandpainting process has been frequently decribed, and needs only to reviewed here (Newcomb and Richard 1937; Reichard 1939; Kluckhohn and Wyman 1940). The center of the ceremonial hogan is cleared and the fire is moved to the side. A layer of clean sand is spread upon the floor and smoothed out with weaving battens. The sandpainters make a guide for long straight lines by stretching a string over the area and snapping it to make an indentation in the sand base. The sandpainting is constructed from the center outward under the direction of the hataaxi, or singer, who does not usually participate in the sandpainting. The black cross which represents the whirling logs is constructed first upon the center which may be formed by burying a shallow bowl of water so that the surface is even with that of the painting.[2] The center represents the lake upon which the logs float. The logs are outlined in red and white. The crushed coloured materials used in making the sandpainting are held in bark containers.

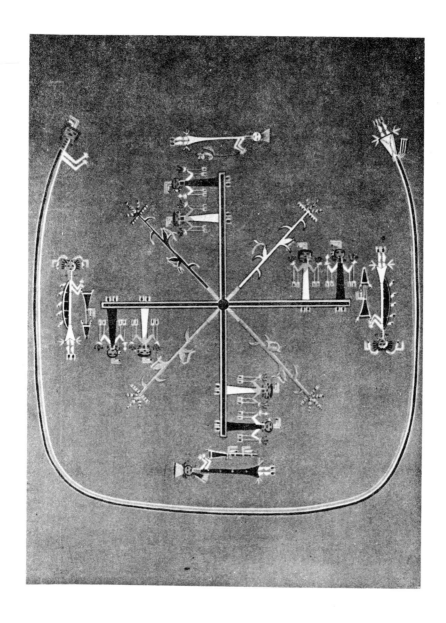

As the last arm of the cross is being completed, the roots of the corn plants which lay in each of the four quadrants are drawn with their beginning in the central representation of the lake. Navajos have said that this is so because the corn needs water in order to live. The corn plants constructed in each quadrant are of the four colours—white, yellow, blue, and black. Each is outlined in a contrasting color. Two ears of corn are shown on each stalk.

On each of the four arms of the whirling logs sit two *yé'ii* or masked holy people. The outer figures are male and wear helmet-like masks with two eagle plumes and a tuft of owl feathers. They carry gourd rattles and spruce branches. The inner figures are female carrying spruce branches in both hands.

When the inner portion of the sandpainting is complete, *yé'ii* figures are drawn adjacent to the ends of each of the arms of the cross. To the west is *hashch'é ooghwaan*, or Calling God, who is dressed in black and wears a blue mask ornamented with eagle and owl feathers. He carries in his hands a black wand decorated with representations of feathers of turkeys and eagles. The skins of blue birds are depicted as being attached to the wand. The figure on the east side is *hasch'é ti'i* or Talking God. He is dressed in white and wears a white mask decorated with eagle feathers tipped with breath feathers and a tuft of yellow owl feathers, with a fox skin under the left ear. He carries a gray squirrel skin pouch on a string. His eye and mouth markings are distinctive, but the sandpainting representation does not include the corn symbol on the face as does the mask.

The *yé'ii* to the north and south are *ghwą́ą'ask'idii* or Humpbacks. They wear blue masks with a zigzag line of white lightning around them and red feathers representing sunbeams radiating out from the masks. The masks are topped with blue horns which identify them with mountain sheep. The hump on the back is a representation of a sack laden with goods. These *yé'ii* carry black staffs. The anthropomorphic rainbow guardian figure circumscribes the painting on all sides but the east. Plumed wands, which represent holy people, are erected around the periphery of the sandpainting.

In the hands of the rainbow guardian are placed cups of herbal infusion which will be used in the sandpainting rite. A cedar twig is laid upon the shell cup with which to administer the medicine. This completes the construction of the sandpainting (Matthews 121-123).

The Nightway ceremonial during which this sandpainting is made is performed according to a Holyway-type ritual process. This indicates that it is performed for a person suffering a predicament whose cause is attributed to one of the *diyin dine'é* or holy people of the Navajo. The ritual process is bent upon reestablishment of proper relationships between the one over whom the ceremonial is being sung, that is, the one-sung-over, and certain of the holy people. The expected results of these renewed relationships are that the malevolence will be withdrawn and the person may then be rightly remade or recreated. The sandpainting rites take place on the fifth through the eighth days of a nine-night ceremonial. It should be noted that Nightway is one of the ceremonials in which the holy people make appearance by means of masked impersonators.

When the rites on the sandpainting are about to begin, the one-sung-over enters the ceremonial hogan and the singer begins the whirling logs songs. The one-sung-over, carrying a basket of corn meal, stands to the east of the painting and sprinkles corn meal upon it. This gesture of blessing is repeated on the south, west and north. Then meal is scattered all around the periphery. While the one-sung-over prepares to enter the sandpainting, a *yé'ii* enters the hogan whooping, and proceeds to sprinkle the picture with the herb medicine using the cedar twig. The application of medicine is done systematically and carefully. The one-sung-over enters the sandpainting and sits down. The *yé'ii* approaches her with the shell cup of medicine from which she drinks. Some of the medicine is put on the hands of the *yé'ii* and with this moisture he picks up sands from the feet, legs, body, and head of each of the figures in the sandpainting including the cornstalks and applies them to the corresponding body parts of the one-sung-over. After each application, the *yé'ii* lifts his hands toward the smoke hole. When the application is completed the *yé'ii* yells twice into each ear of the one-sung-over and leaves the ceremonial hogan. The one-sung-over then leaves the sandpainting. The plumed wands are removed and what remains of the picture is carefully erased by the singer using a feathered wand. The sandpainting materials are blanketed out of the hogan to be correctly disposed of. The Whirling Logs songs are sung until the *yé'ii* departs.

The mythology is too extensive and complex to recount in detail. The principal myth is about four brothers and a brother-in-law who go on a hunting expedition. The next to the youngest brother is the protagonist and is unique because he is a visionary. His name, *Bitaháatini*, means "his imagination" or "his visions." The myth opens with a conflict between the visionary and

his brothers because they do not believe the authenticity of the
vision experiences and refuse to listen to *Bitahátini*. The two eldest
brothers and a brother-in-law leave for a hunting trip and the
visionary decides to follow them the next day. While camping by
himself he overhears a conversation between two groups of crows
in human-like forms. He learns that his brothers have killed a crow,
a magpie and twelve deer. Since the crow and magpie are the
owners of the deer, the crow people decree that the brothers will
get no more game. Proceeding the next day the visionary catches
up with his brothers and tells them what he has heard. Only the
brother-in-law listens to him. The elder brothers continue to hunt
for several days, but the visionary's prophecy proves correct; they
get no more game. On the way home mountain sheep are spotted
and the visionary is sent to kill them. As he attempts to do so, he
finds that he is unable to release his arrows and he shakes violently.
He makes several attempts until finally, the sheep reveal to him that
they are really holy people. They are Fringe Mouths in disguise, and
they give him the guise of a mountain sheep and take him into a
canyon. The place to which he is taken is no ordinary canyon and
here the Fringe Mouths enact the archetypal performance of
Nightway and teach *Bitahátini* its songs, prayers, and procedures. In
an attempt to help recover their lost brother, the elder brothers
have left offerings of jewels and pollens in baskets at the cliff edge.
These are used in the ceremonial performance.

   During the performance, the visionary is captured by *hasch'é
ayói*, or Superior God, and taken to his home in the sky. Talking
God is dispatched on a journey to recover the visionary. The
ceremonial continues.

   Finally, after testing the visionary's powers and his knowledge of
Nightway songs and prayers, the holy people allow him to return to
his home in order to teach what he has learned to the youngest of
the four brothers. After the younger brother becomes proficient in
the ceremonial performances, *Bitahátini* disappears and it is
believed that he has gone to live in the home of the holy people.[8]

   Washington Matthews, who studied the Nightway ceremonial
for twenty years during the late nineteenth century, recorded a
sequel to this story which he entitled "The Whirling Logs." In many
ways it is a more complex and fascinating story than the other. The
protagonist, once again, is *Bitahátini*, the visionary. Having seen the
picture of the whirling logs when he learned the Nightway, he is
driven upon a quest for this place of the whirling logs. The visionary
prepares a hollow cottonwood log for travel down the San Juan

River in search of this place of the whirling logs. Upon launching his vessel, it immediately sinks and *Bitahátini* fears that he will lose his life. When they find that he is gone, his family seeks the help of holy people in finding him.

Upon rescuing him from the bottom of the river, the holy people ask what he was attemping to do. He reveals his desires to visit the place of the whirling logs and to learn of the mysteries there. His persistence overcomes the reluctance of the holy people to assist him. They prepare a hollow log with crystal windows and launch him down the river. Several holy people accompany his journey to keep him floating in mid-stream and to assist him past obstacles. After a journey of many incidents, the log enters a lake and upon circling it four times, lands on the south shore. The visionary is allowed to leave the log and enter the house of the Fringe Mouths of the Water where he learns from them their sandpainting. He reenters the log and it carries him around the lake four times again to land on the north shore where another sandpainting is revealed to him. Back in the log, he is carried out of the lake and along a stream leading to the whirling lake. Landing on the south shore, *Bitahátini* finally sees the whirling logs upon the lake. The story says, "He beheld the cross of sticks circling on the lake. It did not move on its own center, but turned around the center of the water. The log which lay from east to west was at the bottom; that which lay from north to south was on top. On each of the logs, four holy ones were seated—two at each end. . . . Many stalks of corn were fixed to the log." (Matthews 183-184) As he watches, the log cross on the west shore and the holy people who were transported by it enter a house. The visionary proceeds along the shore toward the west and he too enters the house. The holy ones are prepared for him and already have placed the picture of the whirling logs upon the floor. They reveal to him the rites of the painting.

The visionary is then given a ride around the lake on the cross of logs with the holy people.

Taking his leave the visionary starts back to the south shore where he had left his log vehicle, but on the way he discovers an area which would make a good farm. His pet turkey whom he had left behind appears there and produces seeds of four colours of corn and many other plants from various parts of its body. The turkey protects and comforts *Bitahátini*. The seeds are planted and they grow to maturity in four days. Holy people appear to help with the harvest and to instruct the visionary on how to harvest, cook , and eat the foods he has grown. They build him a house and perform a harvest ceremony.

Left alone, the visionary soon becomes lonely, yet he is reluctant to leave his stores of food behind in order to return home. Again the holy people assist him by spreading clouds upon the ground and wrapping his foods in them. This makes several small bundles which he can easily carry home. His journey is made upon a rainbow and he is escorted by Talking God, Calling God, and Water Sprinkler.

Upon his return he teaches his younger brother the mysteries of the whirling logs so that his knowledge of Nightway will be complete and he divides the vegetables and grains among his relatives for use as seeds. The story explains that before this heroic venture the Navajo people had no corn or pumpkins (see Matthew 171-197).

Beginning now with some comments upon these myths, I would like to work my way back to the sandpainting rite, including a discussion of the sandpainting, in an effort to relate more closely the significance this sandpainting rite has for Navajos. An outstanding feature at the surface of these stories which accounts for the tension and drama in them is the existence of two kinds of worlds very different from each other. In the Nightway myth there is the world of the hunters and the game animals and there is the world of the holy people and the owners of the game. In the whirling logs myth there is the world of the visionary's home and family, and there is the mysterious world of the holy people and the whirling lake. From the very beginning of both stories it is clear that the drama is focused upon the visionary because he has some knowledge of both worlds, while other Navajos apparently have little or no knowledge beyond their mundane world. As they unfold, the stories follow similar patterns. The visionary is in the world of ordinary reality and then travels to the other world where he acquires knowledge. In the end he returns to relate this knowledge to those left behind. It seems that the holy people are free to visit the world of ordinary reality, but it is unusual and difficult for an earth surface person to visit the homes and world of the holy people. During the arduous journeys the visionary enters dangerous territories, he undergoes difficult tests, he suffers imbalance and fear. Yet, as a result of his journey he gains knowledge, courage, and balance. Through him knowledge of the other world comes to the Navajo people. This knowledge often reveals facts basic to the subsistence of the Navajo people. It shows that the elements of sustenance—game, corn, and other foods—are ultimately owned by or dependent upon the world of the holy people. The journey of the herioc visionary provides a means by which the double view of reality which is held at the myth's beginning is integrated and unified.

It is notable that the holy people keep the pictures which are the models for sandpainting on *naskhá*, a cloth or spread, sometimes specified as a cloud. During the archetypal performance, these cloths are spread upon the floor for use and later folded up. In revealing the pictures to *Bitahátini* the holy people explain, "We will not give you this picture; men are not as good as we; they might quarrel over the picture and tear it, and that would bring misfortune; the black cloud would not come again, the rain would fall, the corn would not grow; but you may paint it on the ground with colors of the earth." (Matthews 165) In another place the visionary is told, "Truly they [Navajo people] cannot draw a picture on a cloud as we do; but they may imitate it, as best they can, on sand." (Ibid 182-183). Here too the existence of two kinds of worlds, and of two kinds of peoples is emphasized.

This double-imagery is interwoven dramatically throughout the sandpainting ritual. The hogan in which the sandpainting is constructed is blessed at the outset of the ceremonial and set apart from the world outside of it. The ceremonial hogan is identified with the hogan in which the world was created and consequently with the very structure of the universe. The sandpainting, done within this sacred enclosure and in the context of many other ritual acts, provides an identification with the events in the primal era when the heroic visionary lived. It replicates the picture revealed to him in the canyon where he learned Nightway and in the house of the holy people on the shore of the whirling lake. It also represents the whirling logs which he observed on the lake and upon which he rode with the holy people. The very shape and design of the sandpainting echoes the shape of the hogan and the quarternary structure of the universe. The plumed wands erected around it intensify the sacrality of this space.

The design of the sandpainting incorporates a complex dual imagery. On each arm of the log cross sits a male and a female *yé'ii*. By the very nature of the cross, the quaternary division of the world along the cardinal directions, east and west, north and south, is given representation. The paired Humpback *yé'ii* are set across from one another as are Talking God and Calling God. The Navajo colours—white, blue, yellow and black—are set across from their complements in the corn stalks. Contrasting colours are used as outline.

In design, the sandpainting is similar to the log cross inscribed within the circle which has often been noted as an important symbol in native American cultures. Discussing this symbol Joseph Epes Brown shows that it reveals the nature of the native American concept of man and his relationship to the universe, a relationship which he says is characterized by a reverence for life (1964: 14-16; also Ridington and Ridington 1970).

An interesting variation in the Navajo form of this symbolic design is the openness of the inscribing circles. The rainbow guardian and the arch of plumed wands never completely enclose the sandpainting. It is through this opening that the one for whom the ceremonial is performed enters and through which the yé'ii enter and leave. This is essential to the purpose of Navajo sandpainting rites and to the very meaning of the Navajo word for sandpainting, iikhááh which means "they enter and leave." This entryway, sometimes flanked by sandpainted guardian figures, is aligned with the entryway of the ceremonial hogan which faces east. This suggests that the Navajo recognize an essential communication and interdependence between the sacred world of the ceremonial hogan and the ordinary world outside. This is precisely what the myths have shown in a different way.

Stylistically, something may be said about the way in which the double-imagery is presented. In the myth the log cross is contained within the sacred lake while in the sandpainted representation it projects out of the lake reaching into the enclosed sphere. This seems to expand the significance of the log cross to more global dimensions and to suggest that it is not limited to the sphere of the lake. Still the major holy people stand beyond it and control its movement with the staffs they hold. The corn plants which appear in the four quadrants are rooted in the lake from which they gain their sustenance, but they project into the areas of each quadrant thus also forming a cross joined at the center in the lake. The details of the myth correspond closely with the structure of the sandpainting. The revelation of the whirling logs painting and the origin of agriculture are represented in the picture, one by the cross of logs, the other by the cross of corn. In the myth, the log cross on the lake was described as having stalks of corn affixed to it which suggests an interrelationship between the whirling logs and the origin of agriculture. This interrelationship is maintained in the sandpainting, for both crosses are based or rooted in the lake in the center.

The sandpainting is, at one level, a reminder of the events of the story of a heroic adventurer who obtained knowledge of the Nightway ceremonial, who experienced the mysteries of the whirling logs, and who introduced agriculture to the Navajos. At another level, the sandpainting is a geometric projection of the essential pattern of order in the world.

The tension of the double-imagery gains further complexity in the rite which takes place on the sandpainting. The earth surface person walks upon the painting and sits amidst the holy people. This entry to the sandpainting reenacts the visionary's journey in that it brings the two worlds together. A yé'ii enters the hogan and walks on the sandpainting to administer the rite. The masked appearance is another instance of the coincidence or integration of the two worlds. The yé'ii offers to the one-sung-over the medicines that have been fed and applied to each of the holy people in the surrounding picture. Then with the aid of the moisture of the medicine on the hands of the yé'ii, the one-sung-over is ritually identified with each one of the holy people by being pressed at the sacred spots on his body with sands from the corresponding parts of all of the holy people who surround him. This act of identification is clearly described in a common prayer which goes:

> His feet have become my feet, thereby I shall go through life.
> His legs have become my legs, thereby I shall go through life.
> His body has become my body, thereby I shall go through life.
> His mind has become my mind, thereby I shall go through life.
> His voice has become my voice, thereby I shall go through life.

In this way he is identified with the very forces of the universe. He has become one with gods.

It is too little to say that for the person involved this identification with the gods must be a very significant event. His position on the logs identifies him with the hero as he was escorted on the mystical ride around the lake. He too can experience this mystery. While it may well be beyond all description, his experience surely must be related to his position in the center of the sandpainting and, therefore, symbolically at the center of the world. The visual perspective of one sitting in the center of a sandpainting is unique. From this position, only portions of the sandpainting may be seen at any one time and these only from the center outward, and perhaps upward. I would think that this visual perspective introduces a depth and movement to the picture that cannot be enjoyed from any other place. Consequently, this translates into a heightened experience of truly being at the center. And by being at the center of the sandpainting, this map of cosmic dimensions, the person who perceives its cosmic design becomes the integrative element within it. In the person on the sandpainting the double-imagery meets and its tension is resolved. To sit upon the sandpainting and to be identified with its many elements is to experience the point common to all of them and therefore to see the unity and wholeness of the universe. The sandpainting event accomplishes a re-creation of the person and the universe. The world which may have seemed at odds with itself, experienced in the person as physical or mental suffering, is unified and reintegrated in the sandpainting rite where it is acknowledged that the whole drama of the universe is repeated in the human being.

In the complex representation through the double-imagery in the sandpainting and the ritual acts, the person who is the subject in the ritual may achieve a unity transcending this duality, an integration of the many to the one. This opens to the person an experience of reality which permits him to grasp the spiritual powers which are present in it and one with it.

In the sandpainting rite, the person comes to experience the truth in the myth which is that there are not two worlds, but one world composed of parts which are complexly interrelated and interdependent. Order and disorder (*hózhó* and *hóchó* in Navajo) are interdependent as are health and sickness, life and death, spiritual and material.

Once this truth is experienced the sandpainting can no longer serve as a map. The one-sung-over has found his way from within the sandpainting and by becoming a part of it it has disappeared by becoming a part of him. With the experience of the unity of the world, the sandpainting, as a depiction of the order of the world, cannot exist. So the destruction of the sandpainting during its use corresponds with the dissolution of the double-imagery it presents. When the one-sung-over arises and leaves the sandpainting his experience of unity is confirmed in a way by the destroyed sandpainting. The many colours have dissolved into one as the sands and the one-sung-over return to the world.

Notes

1. I have seen paintings of this sandpainting by Harrison Begay at the Museum of Northern Arizona and by Tony Begay at the Navajo Tribal Museum.

2. There are also occasions when a bowl of water is set upon the centre of the completed sandpainting.

Bibliography

Brown, Joseph Epes
    1964. 'The Spiritual Legacy of the American Indian', *Pendle Hill Pamphlet* #135, Lebanon, Pennsylvania.
Kluckhohn, Clyde and Wyman, Leland C.
    1940. 'An Introduction to Navajo Chant Practice', *American Anthropology Association, Memoirs*, no. 53, Menasha, Wisconsin.
Matthews, Washington
    1902. 'The Night Chant, A Navajo Ceremony', *American Museum of Natural History, Memoirs*, vol. 6, New York.
Newcomb, Franc J.
    1937. *Sand Paintings of the Navajo Shooting Chant*, J. J. Augustin, New York.
Reichard, Gladys
    1937. *Sand Paintings of the Navajo Shooting Chant*, J. J. Augustin, New York.
    1939. *Navajo Medicine Man: Sandpaintings and Legends of Miguelito*, J. J. Augustin, New York.
Ridington, Robin and Ridington, Tonia
    1970. 'The Inner Eye of Shamanism and Totemism', *History of Religions* 10.
Stevenson, James
    1891. 'Ceremonial of Hasjelti Dailjis and Mythical Sand Painting of the Navajo Indians', *Bureau of American Ethnology*, 8th Annual Report, Washington, D. C.
Underhill, Ruth
    1956. *The Navajos*, University of Oklahoma Press, Norman.

Respondent: Karl Luckert

My response will be brief. I will attempt to explain to this audience, Indian and non-Indian, the situation in which Dr. Gill and I find ourselves. We have not come to Edmonton to show off to the Indian peoples of Canada the length of Navajo ceremonials. We only thought you might want to know something about them. We were invited to come to the University of Alberta to perform something like an academic ritual. The ritual is called Improvement Through Lecture Criticism. One person explains his thinking and another person criticizes him. The purpose of this ritual is to improve and to sharpen our thoughts so that we could be better teachers in the future. We know very well that we are doing all of this before the eyes of the Great Spirit. He surely knows all the myths and rituals of all the peoples on this earth. Moreover, I am convinced that this Spirit knows also more than anyone here about academic mythologies, and surely has chuckled about many foolish things which we said during this symposium. Sam Gill and I came to Edmonton prepared to finish our rituals, to criticize one another. But yesterday while I was reading my paper something happened to Dr. Gill. The Great Spirit God spoke to him and told him that he should not finish the most intimate portion of our ritual, that he should wait till we are back in Arizona and there finish improving me with his criticisms. Likewise, the Great Spirit spoke to me this morning, not to finish this academic ritual with Dr. Gill because many in the audience would not understand and appreciate what we are doing. We will finish also this ritual back in Arizona. Instead, I wish to offer you our greetings and our peace. We thank you for having invited us to share with you some of the ways of the Navajo people. The sacred tobacco smoke which rolled into the air this morning, which all of us in this room have breathed, the sanctified air which we inhaled and which gave us life, it has made us friends, not to be able to forget one another anymore forever.

The Universe At Prayer

by

J. W. E. Newbery

The sacred pipe is, I suppose, the best known symbol and the ceremony of the pipe the most wide-spread sacrament of the American Indian people. Much has been written about it and much scholarly work done to which I cannot add. I come simply as a witness and a worshipper who hopes to share the spirit of this ceremony. It is important I believe for this Native ceremony, and others, to be understood as true religious expression. Perhaps there is a place for a non-Native person to say why.

My intention then is to report the experience of prayer with the pipe in which I have been a participant. The right to say these things is greater for some of you than it is for me. That I recognize. But again I propose to say only what I, as in some ways an outsider, have seen and to some extent understood.

1. Differing from the set times as in some other religions, it is always some *need* that brings people together for the ceremony of the Sacred Pipe. It may be the need to give thanks for a successful journey or venture, for a recovery from illness or the like. It may be the need for help: rain, relief from suffering, prospering in a venture and so on. Or it may be the wish to honour someone alive or dead, to strengthen ties with the spirit world, to fulfill a pledge. The pipe is sought as the means by which these needs will be satisfied. It is the medium of prayer given especially to the Indian people. It is a "pontifex" as Schuon says, a contact point between the spirit world and this. It is the agent of renewal as, stuff of the earth itself, it becomes an altar on which the sacred plant is offered and through which its fumes are drawn into the suppliant's body and puffed out on his own breath as evidence of his inner desire and bearing it up to the spirit of power.

Anyone may take the initiative to call for a pipe ceremony. He or she will approach the pipe carrier or holy man with tobacco and a request for prayer. The request cannot be refused nor can those who are invited decline except for the soundest reasons. The call of the pipe is compelling. It is the call of the spirit and men must obey.

When the time has been arranged the invitation goes out to those who may share the concern.

2. *The Gathering.*

The place for the ceremony may be a tipi, an open space, a tent, the room of a house. The time of the gathering is given in the invitation but the time of beginning is the "proper" time: the time when all are ready,—the preparations, the people, the spiritual atmosphere. No clock or bell dictates the time to begin.

Some non-Native students had been invited to a recent ceremony. One was a young woman who had left her household and her children in the keeping of her husband. She arrived promptly at the time given. As the time passed she grew restless. At last she asked the officiant, "when are we going to begin?" "In awhile" he replied quietly. And witnessing this little interchange one had a sense of fitness in what was going on. It seemed reasonable to the questioner that when the indicated hour had arrived the ceremony should begin. But evidently more was involved in such a decision than the clock. The readiness of the gathering had to be sensed. And this included the unseen as well as the seen participants. It would be improper and ineffective to begin until it was felt that all was ready.

The gathering as it assembled had seated themselves in a circle on the ground or floor; a circle oriented to the East. The "Eastern" door-way is marked by placing an eagle feather there.

The circle form is, of course, basic. It is the natural form, the perfect form, the therapeutic form, the sacred form. "Everything" said Black Elk, "tries to be round". Thus the circle is the form for prayer because into it all things are readily drawn and into it all things are renewed in their relationship to one another. Oriented to the East all movement in the circle follows the sun, East to South to West to North, that is to say "Clockwise". The offering of the purifying sweet grass, the passing of the pipe, and bowl of water at the close, in fact any action in the circle proceeds in this way, harmonious, as is thought, with universal motion.

There are ceremonials and times when a counter-clockwise direction is followed. But this is the negative part, the complementary action, in life's duality. It is the *unwinding*, as it were, of the cycle in order to begin again with new power.

3. *The Preparation.*

As the time proper for beginning approaches, the officiant prepares the "Altar" for the ceremony. A skin or blanket is spread at the western doorway of the circle. The fire has already been burning at the centre of the circle where it symbolizes those powers of the Spirit to attract and to repel, which, in perfect balance, create the sacred hoop. The officiant kneels at the blanket facing the fire and beyond it the Eastern doorway. He takes the materials for the ceremony from their coverings and arranges them before him.

It should be indicated that these materials may in some respects differ from place to place and from one officiant to another. So also the ceremony may be quite simple or more complex, lasting for hours according to the occasion or the person in charge. I am describing a usual ceremony as I have seen it with Ojibwa and Cree people in Northern Ontario.

At this time of preparation participants often remove their shoes and don mocassins. Sometimes also they remove such other articles of western culture as are thought to be foreign to the spirit of the gathering: watches, pens, and jewellery. Sometimes they are invited to lay upon the blanket close to objects there, such sacred articles as they carry in order that there they may be renewed in their power.

Upon the blanket the eagle feather fans are placed on one hand and on the other of the officiant. The fans are used by the celebrant and his assistant to quicken the fire and to disperse the smoke of the sweet grass as it is offered to the worshippers for purification. The eagle feathers used for whatever purpose in the ceremony, carry something of life and prestigious powers of the great bird from which they came: the spirit, the vision, the protection, the solar qualities of the eagle. They are at the Eastern doorway through which the eagle flies every morning at dawn to look for the rising smoke and listen for the sacred songs of prayer. They are also present to fan the offering fire and disperse the purifying smoke of sweet grass.

An eagle-bone whistle is laid on the blanket in front of the officiant and a rattle made from bone or shell to one side of him.

Just beyond the edge of the blanket are placed the four folds of cloth in the colours red, black, yellow and white. They represent the 4 races of the earth and they offer the prospect of their representatives gathering into the sacred hoop to make it complete. The Ojibwas prophecy of the seven fires gives emphasis to the presence of this symbol in the praying community. That ancient prophecy tells of the coming to this "Island" of a white-skinned

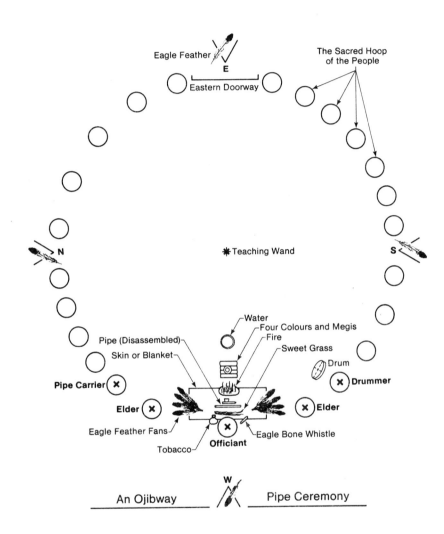

Eagle Feather

E

The Sacred Hoop of the People

Eastern Doorway

N

✳ Teaching Wand

S

Water
Four Colours and Megis
Fire

Pipe (Disassembled)

Sweet Grass

Skin or Blanket

Drum

Pipe Carrier ✗

✗ **Drummer**

Elder ✗

✗ **Elder**

Eagle Feather Fans

✗

Eagle Bone Whistle

Tobacco

Officiant

W

An Ojibway   Pipe Ceremony

race from across the sea, of their depredations here and the sorrows they would bring to the original dwellers in the land. The seventh fire, or stage, in the original people's pilgrimage comes with the time of opportunity for reconciliation, the time when the white is given the chance to change their possessive ways and listen to the Native wisdom they have scorned. If they can do so the seventh fire will lead to the eighth, a time of peace and well-being for all. If not the sorrows that that race has visited on others will befall themselves. These folds of coloured cloth, like the coloured cloths tied to the Sundance pole witness to a vision of peace and unity among humans that is prevalent in Native religious expression in most of its forms.

On top of the four folds of cloth is placed the megis shell. This shell is one of the stirring symbols in the ceremony. It is the focus of Ojibwa history and hope. It connects the prehistoric past with the people and times that are coming toward us now. The traditional historic home of the Ojibwa is the area around Red Lake, North West of Lake Superior. There the people are found who carry the *Megis*. It is a sea shell. The sacred scrolls of the Midewiwin tell of this shell arising out of the great eastern sea to lead the people. Through five long periods of their history it led them westward. In each of these stages its leadership was nearly lost. The people fell away and became disobedient. But revival was given. The shell led on into a new stage and to a new stopping place. The Red lake region was the last area where the people under pressures from the fur trade from the East and obstructed by the Sioux in the West, dispersed southward into Michigan, Wisconsin, Minnesota, and when the pressures from the East subsided some of them were able to filter back eastward. But the Midewiwin again almost disappeared. Masters of the Society, like James Redsky, surrendered to the forces of acculturation. The Scrolls were lost. Redsky's were sold. But there lingered here and there the sense that a new revival and a returning migration Eastward would come when the sacred shell would be carried back to its origins. We see the shell in the pipe ceremonies along the shores of Georgian Bay. It has been carried from there as far East as Montreal. The return journey is a fact. The day of revival has come. There is the shell on the 4 folds of coloured cloth witnessing movingly to the completing of this great cycle which will revive the ancient power of the people and unite all the people of this island and of the world.

Beyond the cloths and the shell is placed a bowl with water, the selected symbol of mother earth for it is the blood that flows in her veins and gives life to her children. To this symbol we will refer later. A pouch of sacred tobacco, wild tobacco grown and prepared for the purpose of worship, is laid on the blanket. Finally, the separated pipe is taken from its wrappings by the officiant and placed immediately in front of him. Flanking the officiant may be elders, men or women who by age and wisdom are recognized as such. It may be that one of them has brought his own pipe which later he will invite the company to share with him in prayer for some special concern. Beside the elder on the one side may be a drummer and assistant to the officiant who will administer to the worshippers the rite of sweet grass purification and accompany the leader's prayer with the drums or rattle. Beyond the elder on the other side may sit the person who is carrier of the pipe if that differs from the officiant himself or one of the elders. The main pipe in a community may have come there by special means and some one may have been indicated as its carrier—the one who takes care of it. Such a person thus sits close to it at the ceremony.

The pipe is now purified, in sweet grass smoke, assembled and charged with sacred tobacco. The stem of the pipe and its bowl are carefully passed through the smoke especially their junction points since this is the point where the bowl-altar in which the sacrifice of prayer is offered up and the worshipper with the stem in his mouth, come together.

The officiant now takes from his pouch a pinch of the sacred tobacco. He passes it through the sweet grass smoke and offers it to the East and then places it in the pipe pressing it down with a thin fragment of bone. Another pinch is taken, purified and offered to the South and placed in the pipe. Likewise to the West and North. Then a pinch is lifted up and offered to the powers above and deposited. Then one is touched to the earth and finally one to the officiant's breast area.

These seven gestures in charging the pipe recognize the three, the four, the six, the seven "grandfathers" or power places of the Universe which are soon to be involved in the *prayers*. They are the *four* directions, the four winds, seasons, classes of life both human and other than human into which life in this world is divided, the *six* directions of space: the four of the horizontal plane plus heaven and earth of the vertical. The *three* worlds (the heavens, the 4 directions, the horizontal plane as it were), and the *seven*,—that is the six plus the point where they all *intersect*. This is the here and now,—the worshipper's own heart.

When the pipe has been thus charged, it is again passed through the cleansing smoke from each of the four directions and laid upon the blanket.

The attendant now takes up the smoking braid of sweet grass and proceeding sun-wise (from left to right) offers it one by one to the circle of worshippers, fanning the smoke toward each with the eagle feathers. Meanwhile, the officiant may speak about the importance of the purifying act.

It is understood that women at the end of their menstrual cycle do not sit in the circle nor do those who have been drinking alcohol or who have otherwise contaminated themselves. The sweet grass cleansing has about it a sense of lurking evil forces which may have worked their contamination and from which the smoke delivers. But today the stress is laid upon cleansing from negative and harmful thoughts and selfish desires, before the unseen guests are called and gather in the circle. The worshippers gather up the wafted smoke and "wash" themselves with it, hands, head and heart.

4. *The Teaching.*

In the attitude of expectancy that has been created and before the great gathering for prayer begins, the officiant may take some time for teaching. Perhaps he will use the teaching wand (see diagram) as his lesson and will speak of the universe of the seven powers soon to gather and focus here in common prayer for the concerns that have brought the group together. From the four corners of the world the great powers will be called. They represent the forces that are active in the great winds and the four seasons. In their quartering they represent the four classes of creatures that live on the earth and in those classes every living thing. They represent also the four character-divisions of the human species and the four stages of human life. They represent the four colours also. Thus when they come into the sacred circle they bring all these with them to pray with us.

From the heaven also the great forces of Sun and Moon, the Thunder Beings and their storms, the Spirit World where the departed live, all these will be invoked, the masculine power of the sun, the feminine power of the moon, the cleansing power of the flashing lightning and the crashing thunder. And from the earth her providential powers to feed and nourish life.

These too will come and meet and focus, as in the teaching wand, in this moment of prayer, in this here and now, around the needs of this group of worshippers. To say it again, upon this point

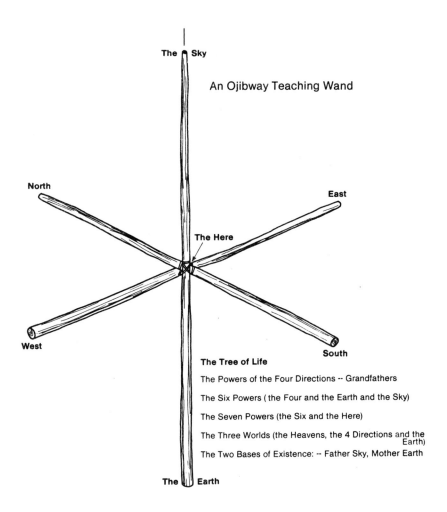

The Sky

An Ojibway Teaching Wand

North

East

The Here

West

South

The Tree of Life

The Powers of the Four Directions -- Grandfathers

The Six Powers (the Four and the Earth and the Sky)

The Seven Powers (the Six and the Here)

The Three Worlds (the Heavens, the 4 Directions and the Earth)

The Two Bases of Existence: -- Father Sky, Mother Earth

The Earth

of the manifested, this past and present with its heritage of good and bad, will come to focus the unmanifested, the intention of providence, the pity of the Creator, the destiny hidden in the six powers.

This great community for prayer may also be movingly taught by the device of the Medicine Wheel (see diagram). Here again, the Universe is portrayed as a sacred hoop quartered and divided into its varieties yet complete and unified as a circle. Its centre is the drum speaking with the thunderous voice of the sky, throbbing with the heart beat of the earth. All will be called, all will come. In their coming we will be united again in the whole of which we are each one a fragment. All you engage with us in prayers of gratitude and in petition for our needs and in intercession for one another. One has in such teaching the strongest kind of expectation, confidence, hope and comfort.

5. *Invocation*.

And now the invocation begins. The piercing eagle-bone whistle alerts the heavens and the earth and all that is in them. The *great gathering* has begun. The officiant sings the invocation beginning with a song to the spirit power of the East.

The invoking of the six great powers, the six grandfathers, is done in songs because it is a sacred thing, and a very solemn act.

I am not permitted to write down these songs in Ojibwa, nor to utter the names of the grandfathers in that language outside the act of prayer. I therefore give only an approximation of what the songs contain. One part of them, a Mide song, I have been asked not to speak of at all.

The songs are remarkable, not only for the way they gather together into the act of prayer all the creatures and powers of the universe, but also in the way they compass the whole life and history of the Universe. For they reach as you will see into the original creative acts, they join hands with the myths, they re-enact and renew the process of creation. All this is brought into the sacred hoop of prayer.

In these ways, you will see, the songs have kinship with the restraints of Hebrew worship and with the recital nature of the Hebrew scriptures, particularly the great psalms which celebrate creation and the mighty acts of Jahweh. "What you did in the past, do now again for us here!"

Kneeling, bowed, to the beat of the rattle in the hands of his assistant the holy man calls, in his songs, the spirits of the sky, and

The Medicine Wheel
"All My Relations"

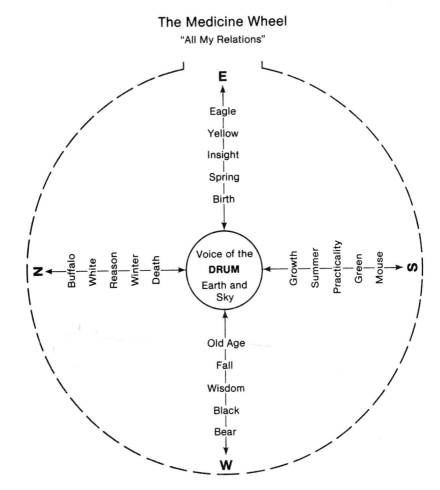

the earth, the spirits of the four directions, East, South, West and North, to come with all their powers, to join with us in the sacred circle, to share this concern of ours and grant to us the things we need.

Hear, Father Sky, Grandfather, home of our brother the Sun and our sister the Moon and all the Wheeling Stars, home of the clouds and the strong thunder begins, of the rain and snow and cleansing winds, Grandfather, Great Spirit of the Sky

Have pity, Grandfather
Grandfather, have pity
Come and give to your children what we need.

Hear, Mother Earth, Grandmother, dressed in the green of trees and grasses, decked with the beautiful flowers, through whose veins the waters run and from whose bounty food is given to all, gathering in your arms all creatures large and small,

Have pity Grandmother
Grandmother have pity
Come and give to your children what we need.

Hear, Spirit of the East, Great Spirit, source of light, place of the sun's rising, from whom the solar eagle flies through the crack of dawn calling to prayer for a new beginning and blue day, great spirit come as in the beginning, at the dawning of the world you came, bringing light and illumination, insight, vision and hope. Come with all the creatures of your direction, with all that gives light to men.

Have pity, Grandfather
Grandfather, have pity
Come and give to your children what we need.

Hear, Spirit of the South, beautiful one, Great Spirit of new life and growth from whose keeping the birds return as they came in the beginning to scatter the seeds of all the plants, spirit of warmth and pleasantness and providence, renew your creative act.

Have pity Grandfather
Grandfather, have pity
Come and give your children what we need.

Hear, Spirit of the West, Great Spirit of the sun's decline and setting, spirit of wisdom and old age, spirit of the people's past, and the knowledge they have gained, traditions, and ceremonies, doorway to the departing.

Have pity Grandfather
Grandfather, have pity,
Come and give your children what we need

Hear, Spirit of the North, the place of flint, Great Spirit of the strong winds and the cold, spirit of testing and ordeal, spirit of discipline and cleansing, spirit of healing and strength, come as in the beginning to contest with your brother and bring balance and harmony to the world.

Have pity, Grandfather
Grandfather, have pity
Come and give your children what we need.
Mercy, Mercy, Mercy, Mercy

One has the feeling now that, as in the Sundance Ceremony, the sacred hoop has been restored, and now there can be a new beginning. The moment for prayer has come.

6. *The Pipe Prayer.*

The people are invited to put into words the concerns that they have brought to the gathering. The voicing of these concerns moves from the officiants' left sunwise about the circle. Each one speaks, in Ojibwa or in English, or other language, even if the utterance is only a murmured "Meegwetch". Little children are encouraged to respond also. No one should remain outside this hoop of confession. As the testimony moves around the circle the strong sense of community grows. The joys and sorrows of each one are shared as they choose to express them. One speaks of the burden of alcoholism, another of failure as husband, wife or parent, a boy gives thanks for his dad. The sick and afflicted are mentioned. There are tears and rejoicing. The special announced concerns of the gathering are also remembered.

When the cycle is complete the officiant takes up the sacred pipe and the high moment of the prayer has come when all that has gone on before is focussed in the tobacco sacrifice and made actual in the ascending smoke. The worshipper puts the proffered pipe to his own lips, draws the smoke of the sacrifice into his own body and sends it out upon his own breath. He thus identifies himself, *his own life* with his brothers and sisters and with the great universe of creatures and powers here gathered and linked together. The experience is one of deep renewal and often of overwhelming power.

The pipe is ignited by a coal from the fire or by the burning sweet grass and, carried by the attendant, is passed from mouth to mouth. After the pipe has been offered to and smoked by each supplicant, it is rotated or circled through all the directions thus to offer it also to all the powers, all the creatures and all the times. And the supplicant says "All my relations" to acknowledge that in his proffered prayer everything in the universe is joined. The worshipper identifies himself again with the great company of the sacred hoop, those seen around him and the unseen of whom he has become conscious in the ceremony, the seven Grandfathers and all their hosts all united in the sense of the one Great Spirit, one *whole* in which he is a member.

When the pipe has completed its cycle the attendant takes up rattle or drum and to their rapid beat the officiant prays for all here gathered. The prayer is often repetitive in its phrases, highly ecstatic and deeply moving in its power. Often a strong sense of spirit presence is felt, visions are seen, messages are given as the worshippers are lifted to new heights of consciousness. When the prayer is ended the officiant sometimes will invite the people to share with the others any visions or message that have come to them in the ceremony. One hears at these times of the sense that has come of the eerie presence of the spirit worshippers, of lights that have been seen, of the touch of an unseen hand, of the presence of loved ones, of words of forgiveness and reunion with estranged family and friends. It is a time of great seriousness and eagerness and deep confidence as this sort of sharing goes on. One feels the bonds of fellowship tighten and a great love develop as hearts are opened in this way.

7. *The Conclusion*

When the prayer is ended the officiant invites an elder or some other participant to give thanks for the water and the food if that has been provided. In this prayer the strong sense of Native people of their close connection with the earth is usually heard. The water and food are passed around the circle and all share until they are consumed. There is talking, laughing and release from the tension of the ceremony in this act. Those who have brought tobacco may come now and make their own offering in the fire, or cigarettes may be passed around for such an offering. Then the officiant separates the pipe and the ceremony is complete.

Summary

In the Sioux myth of the gift of the sacred pipe the beautiful Wakan woman, the white buffalo women who brought the pipe to the people, concluded her instruction with these words: "when you pray with this pipe you pray for and with everything". Then she touched the foot of the pipe to a round stone which lay on the ground and said, "with this pipe you will be bound to all your relatives".

This I confess *is* the experience of the pipe ceremony. One has the strong and inspiring sense that gathering into the sacred hoop are all the powers, all the creatures of the universe. All are there to witness your concern and to pray with you. It is the sacred hoop indeed that is created and in the hoop health and happiness are given to each worshipper and to the whole community of creatures human and other-than-human.

In writing this witness I have had in mind also the following:

Alexander, Hartley Burr, *The World's Rim*
Brown, Joseph Epes, *The Sacred Pipe*
Schuon, Frithjof, *Light From the Ancient Worlds*, and
Schuon's introduction to the French version of Brown's *Sacred Pipe*
Storm, Hyemeyohsts, *Seven Arrows*

Respondent: Cal Dupree

I have been asked to make my response short, so what I could do is say thank you for having me sit up here with you while you were making your presentations. But being a warrior, a Lakota, a Sioux, born and raised in South Dakota I have to respond, not to Professor Newbery's presentation, but to Professor Newbery and to all of you. Instead of reading a response on and on for a whole hour (which you all could read if you had copies) I can only say that I think we have forgotten how to respond spiritually to each other. I am not an Ojibwa so I cannot respond directly to the paper. I'm a Lakota. I can only respond favourably to my friend, Professor Newbery, even though I have never met him, never was introduced to him, and have never even seen him before, but I know that the Great Spirit has told me that all two-leggeds are my brothers, that all four-leggeds are my brothers, that all the winged and the finned creatures are my brothers, that all of nature, the rivers, the mountains, are all my brothers. I have to treat them all as my friends. The only way that I could respond to the Pipe Ceremony of the Ojibwas is through my own experiences with the Pipe Ceremony of the Lakota. I've had several of them. I carry my pipe with me. I even have it with me today. Those of you who would like to share it with me sometime today can join me and we'll go out and sit around out here on the campus and have a real spiritual ceremony. I want to thank you very much for listening to me, even though you didn't have me on the program, and even though I was asked to make my response short. I would like to invite you to share with me the Native People's version of "short". I would like to share with you some slides of a Lakota Sun Dance. The Sun

Dance that I went through for five years to complete my
commitment for all of you. I danced for five years for each and
every one of you, to bring us together to rebuild this hoop, the
sacred hoop of life of which we all are a part. I hope that you will
come and share this experience with me.

The Pigeons, a Society of the Blackfoot Indians

by

John C. Hellson

Like most Plains tribes, the Blackfoot possessed an age-graded system of religious and military societies. Among the three divisions of the Blackfoot Confederacy, we are aware of the existence of at least 15 societies, although some were confined to one division only, with occasional members coming from the other two. These societies were ranked in age seniority; the youngest participants entered at the bottom of a series of societies and progressed by ritual transfer up through each one over a period of about four years per society. In later years, the age-graded system collapsed and it was common to find elderly persons in societies once reserved for the young—and viceversa. Traditionally, Blackfoot societies were active all year round, but recently, with the passing of camp life, they have become inactive most of the time, appearing in their traditional roles only at the annual Sun Dance. The Pigeon society (also known as the Doves or "Kakoiks", probably the more proper form) is the subject of this paper. Although the Pigeon society was considered by Wissler (1913:375) and others to be the most recently formed age-graded society, and therefore the lowest in the series, it was in fact flourishing by the mid-nineteenth century. Examples of truly recent societies are the Crow Has Waters society and the Kaispa society (Ibid: 436).

The earliest mention of the Pigeon society in anthropological literature comes from Curtis (1907: 19) where he states that "The society of the Doves was first formed among the Piegan in 1855 or 1856 in imitation of a similar organization then existing among the Blackfeet and Bloods." Then Wissler, through his field worker Duvall (who advised Wissler in a letter dated May 2, 1911), states that Bearskin, a South Piegan, was a member of the Pigeons about 1853 (op.cit.: 375). McClintock (1970: 449) simply says that "The society originated in recent years among the South Piegans." These are the only dates we have in establishing the historical origin of the Pigeons; further difficulties arise in determining the pattern of origin of the Pigeon society. First, one of Duvall's informants—Bear Skin, a South Piegan, claimed that the society originated among the Blood and that he and a few others were the originators of the society for his people (see letter above). In other words, it was a Blood who had the dream (the usual motivation for creating a society) while Bear Skin and his friend actually organized it about 1853. This contradicts McClintock's observation that the Pigeon society was first dreamt in recent years by a South Piegan named Change Camp (Ibid: 449). Curtis claims through his informants Tearing Lodge and Painted Wing, however, that the society originated among the Piegan in 1855-1856 in imitation of a similar organization then existing among the Bloods. Maximillian, writing about 1833, made no mention of the Pigeon society—but that is not evidence that the society did not exist, because it is possible he did not list all of the societies existing at that time. The best information, gathered by the author in recent field work, supports the historical origin of the Pigeons among the South Piegans. One informant (Spopee) stated that a South Piegan brought the Pigeon society to the Bloods, and that it came from the east.

Pattern of Development

Fieldwork in 1956, following Wissler (1908: 105), showed that the simplest organized aspect of the society was said to have originated among the South Piegan in this manner:

> Once, a man spent a night on the top of a hill. The pigeons spoke to him and gave him a dance. When he returned to camp he organized the dance; the dancers were called Red Pigeons.

The first stage, among the South Piegon, formed the basis of the society to which were added other segments of membership by other South Piegan members so that, even early in its career, the society was structured by a complex of origin myths attributed to the visitations of several supernatural animal beings. Thus, to the original myth, were added the officers of the society, themselves the result of separate origin myths. Sources suggested that South Piegan originators added the distinctions of Yellow and Bear Pigeons, the office of the Coyote owner, Rattle owner, and the Smear Staff to the basic structure. Blade Roast is credited by my informants with introducing the Smear Staff, which is linked to the Bears; Wolf Trail brought the Coyote and Rattle positions; Turtle[2] contributed the Bear belts. Saiyii, a South Piegan, introduced the Yellow Pigeons. At first they had only one office, but Saiyii later added others.

What is most interesting about the origin of the Pigeon society is that it did not follow the prescribed pattern of development expected of an institutional, authentic society (in the Indian sense) such as the Front Tails, Bulls, or Kit Foxes, which are attributed directly to supernatural forces. Instead, the subsequent organizations of the Pigeons was secondary, not immediately based on the founding dream. It was considered manmade and therefore more closely related to military and secular institutions. For this reason, the Pigeons did not use a sweat lodge for purification purposes. In spite of this, as we shall see, the Pigeons were considered to be a very powerful society that could easily instill a great deal of fear in anyone not connected with it.

There were six membership positions in the Pigeon society. In order of rank, they were:

Officers:	1) Coyote owner
	2) Rattle owner
	3) Yellow Pigeons (four members)
	4) Smear Staff owner
	5) Bear Pigeons (four members)
Ordinary members:	6) Red Pigeons (indefinite number)
Associated members (non-ranked):	
	Old Men Comrades (two persons)
	Women Comrades (two persons)

The usual age for joining the society was in the late teens (17 and 19) and membership was held for about 4 to 5 years. Until recently, members (not associates) were painted all over their bodies (including the soles of the feet), with the exception of the Coyote owner, Rattle owner, and Smear Staff owner. Pigeons were painted by others at the transfer ceremony, after which they were allowed to paint themselves.[3]

Bundles were associated with the various society positions. In addition to their intra-society significance, Pigeon bundles were known to be used for non-Pigeon activities; for example, an informant described to me how a Bear Pigeon bundle belonging to Willy Scraping White was used in curing the sick.

Coyote and Rattle Bundles

The Coyote and Rattle bundles belonged to the two leaders of the Society and were used together.[4] Wissler (1913: 376) says that the Coyote owner was the assistant leader, but Duvall's informant (*Ibid*) states that the Rattle owner was the assistant. My informants agree that the Coyote owner was the leader and the Rattle owner was second in command; however, the two officers always performed their duties together and the two bundles were kept in the same parfleche. This may account for the ambiguity of status. As well, each had a like-painted assistant.

The Coyote bundle consisted of a complete skin of a coyote with seven eagle tail feathers attached to it as well as a wad of human hair. The human hair represented enemies killed in the battle. The nose of the coyote skin was painted vermillion and the forehead was painted with a red ochre known as Seventh Paint. A small segment of the power root (*Angelica dawsonii*) was attached near the head.

The power root was an important element in the Pigeon society, as in other Blackfoot societies. The root was tied to a headpiece; it was removed and used during most Pigeon activities—in fact, without chewing the power root, a society member would not dance or perform any of the society functions. There was also a small headpiece made from the underwing coverlet feather of an eagle, painted red, with a piece of power root attached. Wissler (Ibid: 371) mentions that the Coyote owner wears an eagle-feather headpiece. However, none of my informants agreed with this.

It is noteworthy that Pigeon customs, positions, and para-phernalia were created by a process in which individuals simply extended their own power, thereby expanding and enhancing the charismatic aspect of the society. Informants claim that when the Bloods acquired the society, they used a round drum instead of the traditional hides, to show off. Among the Plains tribes and in the Blackfoot confederacy, a society could be spread among the various divisions by buying society bundles from a tribe and building matching ones. The origin of the powers of each individual is not known.

The items were kept in a cylindrical, fringed, painted parfleche (Figure 1). The facial and body painting worn by the owner of the Coyote is illustrated in Figure 2. He wore no clothes, and the wrists and the ankles were encircled with red paint above the joints applied one finger in width. The skin was painted white, except for the nose, which was red, and the Rattle owner was painted in the same manner. This painting took place during the transfer. The new Coyote owner would remove all of his clothes, and be painted white to symbolize the body of the coyote after it had been skinned. At other times, only the nose, face, and backs of the hands were painted. In later years this tradition of full painting at transfers was discontinued; only the face, nose and backs of hands were painted. When painting the nose of the coyote skin, the owner would pay an older warrior (who had killed), to count four coups before the painting could commence. The red paint on the nose of the coyote skin and the owner symbolized blood on the coyote's nose after feeding from a kill. This connection with food could have the community significance since the coyote bundle could also be used to acquire food for the camp. If the owner sang the songs for his bundle, food would be found shortly.

The Rattle facial painting was the same as the Coyote owner, and the rattle and headpiece were stored in the Coyote's bundle parfleche. The Rattle bundle consisted of a single small buffalo hide rattle and a plume headpiece similar to the Coyote bundle.[5]

Yellow Pigeon Bundle

The Yellow Pigeon bundles, of which there were four, all exactly the same, consisted of a short bow and four arrows (Figure 3) made of silverberry wood (*Eleagnus commutatta*) known as "excrement wood", painted yellow. Two arrows were blunt-ended and two had projectile points. The bow-string, the most important item in the bundle, was made of braided sinew and ochred yellow. There was a plumed headpiece painted yellow similar to that of the Coyote and Rattle owners. All were kept in a cylindrical, fringed, painted parfleche.

The facial and body painting worn by an owner of a Yellow Pigeon bundle is illustrated in Figure 4. Wissler (19: 373) mentions that Yellow Pigeons might have their paint scratched and that they wore eagle tail feathers. My informants disagreed; the eagle plumes were used and the paint was not scratched.

Bear Pigeon Bundle

The Bear Pigeon bundles, again four in number and all the same, consisted of a wide girdle made of semi-tanned bear skin (an uncomfortable garment) to which were attached a number of red-ochred eagle coverlet plumes (Figure 5). Each bundle included a pair of bear skin arm bands with a number of bear claws attached (Figure 6) and a pair of bear skin leg bands (Figure 7). In addition there was a pair of fringed bearskin moccasins that were ochred red (Figure 8). The bundle contained a small plumed bow with four arrows, two pointed, two blunt, again of silverberry wood. The bow-string of braided sinew was ochred red with "real" paint. The usual plumed and painted headpiece with the attached power root was included also. These items were kept in a cylindrical fringed and red-painted parfleche.

Traditionally, bison robes were used by the Bear Pigeons; in later years domestic cow and horse robes were used. The robes were painted red on both sides although Bear Pigeons were allowed to wear any colour robe except white. They were also worn with the fur out. The robes were given in the transfer ceremony. In the tipi a tanned black skin is placed in front of each of the four Bears, between the altar and the bed. The Bears use backrests. The bows and arrows are placed on the skin.

The Bears were the strong men of the society, and exhibited aggressive behavior at society functions, yet, as part of their performance, children would throw manure at them. When mistreated by the Bears, a person was not allowed to show anger. Red Pigeons were shot with blunt arrows for offences such as dancing too slowly; the Coyote owner was not subject to attack by the Bears. These arrows would bruise, but would not pierce the skin. The facial and body painting for an owner of a Bear Pigeon bundle is illustrated in Figure 9.

Smear Staff Bundle

The Smear Staff bundle was a pole of three to four feet in length, cut from alder wood, and coated with human excrement. The staff was stuck into the ground in front of the owner when he was inside the tipi and it was remade every summer. During the society's performance, the Smear Staff owner would dress himself in tattered clothing using tipi pins as buttons. The clothes did not form a part of the bundle and were left in the bush as a sacrifice after the society's Sun Dance performances were over. The facial painting is illustrated in Figure 10.

The Smear Staff owner was given the power to humiliate, by smearing recipients of Pigeon disfavor with human excrement. His duties were to watch the Red Pigeons (who were lowest in status and frequently smeared) and also to smear anyone who prevented society members from stealing food. On certain occasions, the Smear Staff owner would spoil food by smearing; the circumstances surrounding this act are not clear. The position of the owner was officially anonymous. Disguised in old clothes later to be discarded, his head covered, the smearer would hide his identity during performances. He acts as the society orderly, bringing firewood and preparing incense. Young boys were threatened that they could be caught by the smearer and daubed.

The symbolism of the Smear Staff relates to the coyote. When a coyote howls at a kill, birds join in the feast and excrete when full.

This bird excrement is symbolized on the Smear Staff. In later years, after missionary contact, grease was used; the people complained that this would spoil their clothing, and thorns were substituted. In the old days, the Smear Staff owner had a facial painting of a Medicine Pipe owner, in black paint. Like the Coyote owner and the Rattle owner, the Smear Staff owner had an assistant.

Red Pigeon Bundles

The Red Pigeon bundles, of which there could be any number, were exactly the same as those for the Yellow Pigeons, except that they were ochred red instead of yellow. An unfavoured son would possess a Red Pigeon bundle as they were cheap to purchase; in earlier times one round of ammunition or a mink pelt was paid for a Red Pigeon bundle.

Red Pigeons were the slaves to the other members. They were not allowed to cover themselves with their blankets at night (or anytime); if they did, they would be shot with blunt arrows by the Bears. The Coyote would order them to undress down to their breech cloths at night. The facial and body painting of a Red Pigeon bundle owner is illustrated in Figure 11. The two women members had bundles identical to the Red Pigeon bundles. The facial and body paintings were also the same.

Old Men Comrades

Sometimes a retiring society member would volunteer or be asked to remain as an associate of the incoming society members. These men would maintain their association for many years. The main duty of the Old Men Comrades was to teach new members the society dances and rules. There were no bundles or facial paintings associated with the Old Men Comrades, although these persons were sometimes former members who did not relinquish bundles at transfers.

The Pigeon society was functioning at a time when it was still the practice for the entire society membership, which included all Pigeons in one tribe (such as the Bloods), to relinquish their rights in favor of a new group, usually drawn from the population of young men. It was possible, however, for a member to renew his membership in the society and to retain his bundle throughout his life—as in the case of the Old Men Comrades. Such lifetime memberships were rare, and considered irregular.

Dancing Associations

Sometimes younger men of the same age were already loosely organized in a dancing association, a grouping that operated like a social club and was distinguished from a full-fledged society by its lack of regalia and ceremonies. Sponsoring dances and other social events for the public, these dancing associations maintained a friendly rivalry and sense of competition among themselves. The extent of paraphernalia for members was perhaps shirts of the same colour, or specified breech cloths, belts, or other symbols. For example, the Eagle Parted Hairs association had a stuffed eagle as a symbol to display at functions. Each association had a song. The songs, symbols, and simple paraphernalia were not transferable. These were the property of the individual member; when members of a dancing association moved into a society, the dancing association was disbanded and the name never used again. Members of a dancing association could make a vow together to take the society as a group. For example, in 1924, among the Blood, there was a dancing association in the south end of the reserve known as the "Grey Horse Owners ('Akaisikimioutasi')." They had the Pigeon society transferred to them at the Sun Dance that year. At that time, the current members of the society were formerly the Eagle-Parted-Hairs association drawn from the north end of the Blood Reserve.

The Transfer of the society

If a young man wished to join the Pigeon society, he had to undergo a series of ritual procedures that would result in the recognition of his authority and power to act within whatever office he chose. This series of rites was collectively called a "transfer," and the novice would receive ownership of certain society regalia from an acting member soon to retire. First, a prospective member would make a vow to join the society, although often a father would force his favourite son to join the society, believing that it would bring good luck to the family, since the child would be considered a sacrifice. He might make this vow, along with his age mates, in the fall of the year, plans being made to join the society during the winter and spring of the next year. During this time he would receive advice from one of the four Old Men Comrades as to which bundle he should take.

The comrades would investigate the habits of each existing society member and assign novices according to their findings. A person with a light complexion would usually take the Yellow

Pigeon bundle, those with darker complexions would choose the Red Pigeons or Bear Pigeons. A tall, slim man was usually given the Coyote bundle and a short, not so attractive person was usually given the Smear Staff.

In the summer, when the Sun Dance was held, the society transfers would take place. The novices would gather in a tipi, taking up a position that correspond to the bundle each hoped to take. The Pigeon society itself would pitch a tipi inside the circle of lodges, near the centre. In a short while, the leader of the novices would assemble his friends and they would all march toward the Pigeon tipi, led by the Four Old Comrades, singing a song known as the "worried" song, in apprehension that the bundles wanted might not be given to them. They would be joined by the novices, each carrying his own smoking pipe and a number of short painted sticks, known as "horse" sticks. These represented the number and colour of horses that each would pay to the owner of a particular bundle for the privilege of joining the society. Payments for bundles would be in the form of horses, blankets, pelts, ammunition—almost anything. In the case of the Smear Staff, the payment would be old clothing. When they reached the society tipi, the Old Men Comrades would count four coups—not important coups, usually small thefts—and the prospective officers of the society would enter the Pigeon tipi. Novices of lesser rank would remain outside. Inside the tipi, each novice would offer his smoking pipe to the owner of the bundle he had vowed to take, saying "This is your smoke." If the pipe was received, the horse sticks were offered and the novice would indicate what colour the horses were.

The first member of the Pigeon society to be offered the pipe would be the owner of the Coyote. Because the Coyote and Rattle were formally part of the same bundle, the Coyote and the Rattle were given in the same parfleche to the new Coyote owner. Next, the new Rattle owner paid the old Rattle owner, and the Coyote owner gave the Rattle to its new owner, who used it in ensuing ceremonies. After the Coyote and Rattle were used, they were always returned to their joint parfleche. These were the most important positions and always went together.

Any retiring society member who accepted a novice's pipe, would, before smoking, approach one of the Old Men Comrades, who would then pray with the pipe. After the Comrades prayed, the society member would make the receiving sign by passing both hands over the outline of the Comrade's upper body, finishing by drawing the arms to the chest. Then the novice would take the pipe back and return to his sitting place. After all the pipes had been smoked and the bowls emptied, the novices would leave the Pigeon tipi, returning to their own tipi and dismantling it. Then they erected their tipi directly beside the society's tipi. The covers of the two tipis were joined, forming one large lodge in which the complete transfer of the society would take place. Society offices would be transferred in this lodge; transfers for Red Pigeons would take place in other tipis. All goods for payment (or symbols of exchange) would accompany the recipients to the transfer ceremonies, which would require four days and nights for completion. According to my informants, payments for bundles inflated over time.

As soon as the two tipis were joined, each novice would return to his relatives' camp, gather the materials with which he was to pay for the transfer, and return to the double lodge singing a song of rejoicing. Then each would enter and sit beside the owner of the bundle that he was to take, wearing only a breech cloth, robe, and moccasins. When each novice was seated beside a Pigeon member inside the double tipi, the transfer ceremony was ready to begin.

Transfer ceremony

Positions of members in the Pigeon society tipi are diagrammed in Figure 12, which is drawn from informants' descriptions. There were variations of this arrangement, but most informants agreed that the drawing is a good generalization. As shown the doorway faced east. The four Bear Pigeons would sit near it, reclining on backrests. Nearby, the Smear Staff owner—who acted as orderly during the transfer—would set the Smear Staff (covered, to contain the odour). The Coyote owner, Rattle owner, Yellow Pigeons and Bear Pigeons would each have an incense altar. Red Pigeons lined the tipi wall opposite the doorway; there were places for Woman Comrades, wives, and Old Men Comrades (who acted as drummers). This arrangement was complicated somewhat by the presence of bundle recipients and ceremonialists; the arrangement was varied to accommodate different numbers of Pigeons.

In front of each Pigeon member there was a forked stick that had been forced into the ground fork up; the respective bundles hung from these sticks. Also, each Pigeon member would have a ceremonialist sitting beside him. To initiate the ceremony, incense made from willow galls was burned. A Pigeon member would exclaim that his bundle could be removed from the forked stick only after receipt of the promised payment, which he would itemize. The recipient would pay, retrieve the bundle, and place it in front of him on the ground. In the case of the bow-and-arrow bundles, the former owner could make a new set for the recipient or transfer the old set. There was a ritual for releasing the feathers on the arrows, which were tied down; any feathers were used. After this, each ceremonialist would remove the power root from the headpiece, place it in his mouth (without chewing it) while preparing the paint for the facial painting. As he rubbed the paint in his palms, he would spit on the paint in order to strengthen it with the attributes of the power root, and count a minor coup. Then he would apply the paint to each novice's face and body according to the dictates of the bundle. In the cases of the Red Pigeon, Yellow Pigeon, and Bear Pigeons the paint was applied to the entire body, including the feet. With the Bears, a novice's hair was cut in a very rough manner to a length of about two inches across the top of the head. Then it was ochred and greased to make it stand up straight. Before cutting, the former bundle owner would ask the novice how he wanted his hair cut. If he replied "just a little", the owner would cut off a lot, and vice versa.

Each novice then exchanged three items with the Pigeon member: he would give his shirt, leggings, belt, moccasins and breech cloth to the member, who would reciprocate using his own clothing. Then everyone would rise and dance four times to the society's dancing song. The four Old Men Comrades would drum and sing this song, which marked the end of the transfer.

Stealing society tipis

The former members of the society would dismantle the double lodge and disperse, while the new members would sit in a circle nearby in the positions they would hold in a new society tipi. They would discuss which tipi in the camp they would steal as their new lodge. After they had decided which one to choose, they would approach the tipi, led by the Yellow Pigeons, followed by the Bears, Smear Staff owner, Coyote owner, Rattle owner, and the Red Pigeons; the four Old Men Comrades accompanied them last. They would all stand in front of the tipi and the four Old Men Comrades would sing a war song (which was repeated four times, alternately) with counts of coup for tipis stolen or items stolen from inside tipis. The words to this song are "How am I going to die?" The four Yellow Pigeons would divide and walk around opposite sides of the tipi. The rest of the society would follow suit until the lodge was completely circled. Then they would all shout and the Red Pigeons would dismantle the tipi, taking everything—including furnishings. The owner of the lodge had no choice in this matter; should he object he could be shot by the Bear Pigeons' blunt arrows. The society now had a new tipi in which to hold their meetings.

Stealing Women Comrades

When the new tipi was erected, toward the centre of the camp circle, the society would have a meeting to decide who among all the unmarried women of the camp would be suitable as the two Women Comrades. Pretty young women were usually chosen, based on diligence and status. Once each woman was sighted, the society would stalk her, as though she were a buffalo, and when she was captured the society would make a victory call. Sometimes the woman would object and scream, but to no avail: if anyone tried to interfere they would be shot by the blunt arrows of the Bear Pigeons. If she ran away and hid in a tipi, one of the Old Men Comrades would have to count a special coup involving the capture of something or someone from inside a tipi. Then the Bear Pigeons could go in and take her. Usually a woman's parents would welcome her membership in the society since it enhanced her status, but if they objected, they would have to pay to have the girl released and the society would look for another.

George First Rider has given me an account of stealing a woman for the Pigeon society:

> I saw it happen once. Four of us went into the tipi to get the woman we wanted; the girl was George Davis's wife. I told Black Plume to grab her. The girl was crying and kicking. Joe Bull Shields paid a horse and money to get her back, then we had to look for another girl.

New clothing for the women—moccasins, belts and blankets—was supplied by the society. The Bear Pigeons would steal this clothing from anyone in the camp and always sought attractive material because the society wanted to show their women off. Again, any objections were met with the threat of being shot by one of the Bears' blunt arrows. Women members were allowed to keep the clothing stolen for them. They were required to participate in society performances throughout the Sun Dance (four days). On the first day, they were painted red, on the second, yellow, on the third day, red, and on the last day, yellow. They were not painted on the wrists, as were other Pigeons. The duties of the Women Comrades were to clean the society's tipi, to help feed them, and to assist the drummers in singing. They repaired broken paraphernalia. At night, when the society was singing and dancing inside the tipi, they were allowed to dance with the other members.

Pigeon society performances

During Pigeon performances, members were expected to remain awake all night, sleeping only at intervals during the day. This went on for four days and nights, during which the society gave two daytime performances. At night, when members would get drowsy, their leader would encourage the groups to get up and dance; they would sing most of the night. The songs were called "stick tapping songs": each member would tap his bow with an arrow in time to his song. The Red Pigeons were not allowed to cover themselves with blankets at night and if they did so, they were shot by the Bears. Late at night, the women would be accompanied to their tipis by the Bears, who would defeat any attempt by young men to accost them. The Bears would also get the women in the morning.

If any member of the society were to leave during the night, the Bears would also get him. If he refused to return, he was shot with blunt arrows. Also, if any member left the camp the society would take his wife into their tipi and hold her until he returned.

Pigeon informant George First Rider explains:

> Amrose Shouting returned to his wife. Next morning, Nick Striped Wolf, Bob Black Plume, and I searched for him. We searched all (the next) night but we could not find him. Nick Striped Wolf took Shouting's wife prisoner until he returned.

Just before sunrise, the Pigeons would assemble outside their tipi in readiness for their performance. They would maintain the same positions that they held inside and would assemble regardless of the weather. The people of the camp would gather and sit in a large circle to watch them dance (Figure 13). The dance would last between an hour and an hour and a half; it was performed the same way on all occasions. The Old Men Comrades acted as drummers and would start the songs. Traditionally they kept rhythm by beating sticks upon a single rectangular rawhide that lay upon the ground; later, the round drum was introduced and its use spread to all the societies. Before each song, the drummers would make four passes with the drumsticks and strike once, upon which all in unison would give the call of the Pigeons, which was repeated four times. First, they would sing the three "forward" songs, which were really the same song repeated three times. The owner of the Coyote bundle, the owner of the Rattle, and the four Yellow Pigeons would stand facing away from the center of the circle; the others would face in. Only the four Bear Pigeons would perform during these songs, mimicking the actions of a bear. The children of the camp would taunt them and throw pieces of manure at them; The Bears would cover themselves with their blankets, rear up on their knees, and imitate the actions of a bear being aroused and getting ready to attack. The fourth song was the "forward" song repeated the fourth time. This was the signal for the Bears to stand up.

The Red Pigeons would then dance westward, followed by the Bears (who would seem to be herding them in that direction). The Bears would split into two pairs; between them the Smear Staff owner would follow. As the dance continued, these two pairs would make their way around the cluster of Red Pigeons. Their bows would be nocked with blunt arrows aimed in all directions. Later, these arrows were shot into the ground. Figure 14 shows the latter part of these performances. If anyone should slow in dancing, the Smear Staff owner would smear him with human excrement, which was always freshly applied to the staff. In later years, axle grease or cactus was used.

The owners of the Coyote and the Rattle, as well as the Yellow Pigeons, would dance where they stood, watching the group moving westward and the Rattle owner shaking his rattle while he danced. When the Yellow Pigeons suddenly turned about, that was the signal for the Bear Pigeons to move completely around the Red Pigeons, heading them off and driving them back in an easterly direction. The Coyote owner and Rattle owner would turn with the Yellow Pigeons. The Yellow Pigeons always took the initiative in turning and did so at their own discretion, sometimes allowing the cluster of Red Pigeons to dance for a half-mile. This to and fro pattern was repeated four times, to the accompaniment of songs from the Old Men Comrades. The dance step was a hopping gait, the progress being quite slow, but sudden and sporadic. If anyone should fall while dancing, he could not rise until an Old Man Comrade counted coup over him and burned sweetgrass. Such a person would be assisted up by the Smear Staff owner. The Blackfoot feared that misfortune would befall them if coups were not counted to raise a fallen dancer. At the end of each Pigeon song all members would make the sound of a Pigeon cooing. It is said that this sound could be heard at a great distance.

Historical account of performance

The Pigeon Society performed as a group only at the Sun Dance (Okan) festival. At other times, various members would invoke society privilege to acquire possessions or food by ritual stealing. An interesting account of a Pigeon Society performance was given by Calvin McQuesten who attended a Blood Sun Dance in 1907. The last recorded Pigeon Society transfer and performance was in 1924. He took the only known historical photographs of this performance in existence (Figure 15 and 16); as one of the photos attests, he did so at great peril. His written account is quoted below:

One of the most picturesque of them is probably the Pigeon dance.

The dress of the Pigeons is charmingly simple, and would make a Parisian belle in evening dress feel like a colourless prude. It consists simply of a breech cloth and moccasins, with a single feather stuck in the flowing hair, and a full coat of paint covering the body from head to foot. The colour worn by the officers is a brilliant yellow, while that of the rank and file is brick red. The dance, in order to be properly performed, appeared to occupy the time of the devotees for the greater part of the day and night.

The Pigeons begin to assemble in their lodge early in the forenoon. Each one as he arrived proceeded to disrobe and adorn himself, mixing the dry paint in a cup or saucer and applying it with his fingers. Evidently several coats were required to produce the required tint, and it was two or three o'clock in the afternoon before the plumage of all was finally preened to their satisfaction. About this time it was discovered that there was not a sufficient number present, and deputations were dispatched to bring in recalcitrant members, who from laziness or other cause had failed to appear. If verbal inducements proved insufficient, a convenient blanket was brought into use to convey the dissenting gentleman to the post of duty.

When the number was finally completed, and all were duly arrayed, the lithe-limbed dancers gathered their blankets about them, and made a tour of the camp in a body, soliciting contributions of fuel and eatables for the all-night seance. It was about six o'clock in the evening before a sufficiency of supplies was secured, and the Pigeons at last seated themselves in the open space in the centre of the camp, while the tom-tom beaters struck up their monotonous music.

Suddenly, throwing off their blankets, the dancers leaped to their feet as one man, the red fellows standing in one long line, with their backs to the setting sun, while two or three canary-hued half-faced them at either end. For a minute all tripped it where they stood, with a sort of "balance all" movement. Then in a flash the red line faced about, and with their bows extended, and arrows strung, and their black hair flowing about their necks and faces, they seemed almost to fly with winged feet toward the setting sun. At about thirty yards they stopped and turned, and in a moment were once more beside the yellow fellows, keeping in time to the tom-toms. In another minute all were seated on the ground, with their blankets about them, and the first number on the programme was over.

While they rested, three other naked braves performed a bear dance. Squatted on the ground, but with bodies erect, the trio paused for a moment, each with both hands to his ears as if to listen. Then with a quick movement they drew up their blankets over back and head and threw themselves prostrate on their faces, while all the small boys around them pelted them with chunks of mud. For a moment the pelting ceased, and once more the Bears raised their heads to listen, only to throw themselves down again, with blankets drawn over to protect them from the shower of missiles. This was repeated some half a dozen times.

After the final dance the Bear Pigeons would disperse to gather wood from other tipis, for use in their own fire, and relatives of the members would serve lunch to the society. Later, if a Red, Yellow, or Bear Pigeon felt that his bow was not good enough, he would leave it as a sacrifice at the centre pole of the Sun Dance lodge; he would get an Old Man Comrade to make another. The bow string was saved and placed back in the bundle by an Old Man Comrade, who would pray continuously.

Special duties at the Sun Dance

One of the duties of the Pigeons was to build the Hundred-willow sweat lodge for the Holy Woman, sponsor of the Sun Dance. They carried the parfleche of buffalo tongues and helped in their distribution on behalf of the sponsor. Acting as orderlies they would gather firewood and food. Two members were chosen for this role, and received identifying crow-feather headpieces. When the Sun Dance lodge was erected they were expected to enter it and perform the "Dugout Dance," a war dance, assisted by members of the All Brave Dog society. During this they would form on opposite sides of the Sun Dance lodge and dance towards and back from each other, shooting arrows at the top of the centre pole as they danced back. The leaders, the Coyote owner and the Rattle owner, would dance in the doorway of this lodge, and the four Old Men Comrades would count coup for the society. After the dance the leaders would lead the members out of the lodge in single file. Another performance was a mock battle in the Sun Dance lodge, between the Pigeons and the Flies Society. Pigeon society members also acted as orderlies for the Cutting of the Hide ceremony, and the tying of the rafters on the Sun Dance Lodge.

Another duty of the Pigeons was to police the Sun Dance camp at night. Young boys caught disturbing people would be taken prisoner by the society and kept until their parents paid for their release. Other policing duties included the punishment of thieves or adulterers. The guilty person was caught, tied to a travois, and the Smear Staff owner would paint his or her face with human excrement from his staff in the design of a Medicine Pipe owner. An eagle-bone whistle would be tied around his neck to keep it in his mouth.

Ritual privileges

The Pigeon Society enjoyed the right to steal anything for their own use from within the camp. As mentioned earlier, they would steal their society's tipi and furnishings, wood for their fire; and clothing for their women members. During the Sun Dance the Pigeons would steal a society tipi for the four-day period, then abandon it (and its furnishings) for the owner to claim when the Sun Dance was over. Further, they would steal food for their membership. The Yellows, the Bears, and the Smear Staff owner did the actual stealing, the Bears threatening to shoot anyone with their blunt arrows or steal on orders from the Yellow Pigeons. The Smear Staff could also smear with feces anyone who objected. They could steal from anyone, regardless of status: Medicine Pipe owners, Beaver men, or even members of the dreaded Horn society were victims. The Bears always took the material by grasping it in a bear-like manner. When the Bears had stolen food, the owner of the Coyote bundle would imitate the call of a coyote, inviting the other Pigeons to come and feast.

The following is an account of the Pigeon Society stealing at the 1924 Sun Dance, recorded by Bob Black Plume, Bear Pigeon from a personal communication.

> On one occasion our elders told us to go and steal food from the Horn Society; our elders were Little Weasel Calf, Bear Fore Arm (Tom Morning Owl), Red Boy (Billy Heavy Runner) and White Calf (Charlie Good Rider). They kept encouraging us to go to the Horns, but we were afraid, the Horns are holy, a non-member cannot go up to them when they are performing, if he does misfortune will befall

him. At last we walked up to them at their tipi in the centre; they were unloading their food from the wagons. The Yellows took the load and we, the Bears, walked behind with the Smearer. When we got nearer to the food we told the Yellows to grab some meat which they did and we walked away. We had our bows loaded to shoot anyone who tried to stop us.

Sometimes the stealing occurred outside of the Sun Dance. In the days when the Bloods received government beef rations, the Pigeon society was known to have performed outside of the abattoir and each person that came out of the building with his rations was forced to give a piece of meat to the Bears. They also took items that were on display at the canteen.

Another ritual privilege included the shooting of dogs at the Sun Dance. After the dances, the Bear Pigeons would roam through the camp shooting and killing dogs that were either not a recognized breed or that were not marked by their owners. In the dog days, they would even kill a dog pulling a travois. Dogs with grey mouths, shaggy coats, or bobbed tails were spared: these dogs resembled bears; the colour made no difference. If a dog owner wished to protect his animal he would take it to the Bear Pigeons and pay a member to paint the face of the dog with "real paint," a reddish ochre. A plume headpiece would be attached as further identification. If a dog approached Pigeons while they were stealing food, it would be shot—unless it was marked (or of a privileged breed), in which case it would be fed. If a dog should escape, wounded, and run into a tipi, an Old Man Comrade would be required to come and count war coups or stealing coups before the dog could be removed and killed.

The Pigeon Society at war

The Pigeon Society, like many other societies, would often become involved in warfare with other tribes. The society might take the Coyote bundle with them to war; the members of the party would pray all night and hold the coyote skin over a smudge of sweetgrass. Each member holding it, they would pray for a safe return home and victory. The Coyote would also lead them to many horses to steal.

An account of the Pigeon Society at war is well-known among the Blackfoot, but is unpublished. It is given by George First Rider and Dave Melting Tallow:

Blade Roast, one of the originators of the Society and his members, the ones that he taught, went on the warpath. They fought with the Crees; a good battle raged between the parties. Suddenly, the Yellow Pigeons left the rest of the group and charged the enemy. As the shooting got hot, the Yellow Pigeons dodged into a hollow between them and the Cree. The Yellow Pigeons started singing to their own members. Both parties stopped shooting and listened. The Yellow Pigeons gave an invitation call to smoke: "Pure tobacco smokers you are invited. Come and attend." They were inviting anyone who was courageous enough to go where they were sitting. This was an effective tactic, and disconcerted the Cree.

Blade Roast, the leader, who was not with the main party, went around the back of his members singing his war song. He walked to the end, and around in front of the Cree. He walked back and forth in the line of fire; as the rifles started cracking, it seemed to everyone that Blade Roast would be shot down. Yet, he ran past the hollow where Yellow Pigeons were lying low, and this put the enemy on the run.

He killed some of the enemy and ran back. Both parties had regrouped and were shooting; as he got to the Yellow Pigeons and lay down beside them, a smoke was seen. The Yellow Pigeons had started to smoke, after which they sang a Pigeon song. This act of nonchalance threw fear into the Crees. As the pipe burned out, the Yellow Pigeons stopped singing and prepared to disperse. Blade Roast, however, ran the opposite way and again panicked the enemy. But the Yellow Pigeons fled back to their own line. So did Blade Roast.

The next time Blade Roast charged, he got a horse from a Cree who had jumped off his horse and was leading it away on foot. When Blade Roast caught him, the Cree dropped the rein and fled; Blade Roast grabbed the rein and jumped on. This was the last straw for the Cree, who did not return to fight. The Pigeons went home victorious, and the people sang the victory song.

Notes

1. In reference to Wissler's contention that societies were ranked and assumed seniority by historical origin, the author feels that it is an oversimplification to say that newly formed societies were automatically placed at the bottom of the series. While it is true that the Pigeon Society was relatively new, and its membership was young, the society's importance in comparison with others was no less in degree.

2. Turtle was a South Piegan who received power from the coyote in a dream. In his vision, the coyote being appeared and gave him its song "Dead animals smoke up." This song is used in the coyote bundle of the Pigeon Society but his extension of the coyote powers come from this source.

3. Clark Wissler, (1913: 371-376), gives a similar organization but includes two Bear Shirt Owners, four Single Men Comrades (not Old Man Comrades), only one woman member, and four drummers. There is no evidence, either through informants or ethnographic collections, to support the existence of two Bear Shirts. Wissler (19: 371) gives a description of Bear Pigeon paraphernalia. His description, however, does not tally with the information I obtained. This may have been a result of inaccuracies on Duvall's part resulting from mistranslation, or misunderstanding on his informant's part. Duvall was Wissler's main source of information in all his Blackfoot work, and Duvall stated in his field notes that the information he was getting from his informant, Red Plume, on the Pigeon society was mixed with data from at least two other societies. He was not sure which was which.

    Also there seems to be some confusion in Wissler's work concerning the rank of Single Men Comrades. These people were never considered full members of the society because they only possessed the right to participate in the society's ceremonies when an actual member was absent. They obtained this privilege by participating in the transfer of membership with their associated member, during which they would receive the paint, authorizing them to handle the ceremonial regalia. There could be any number of Single Men Comrades and they were common in any society. The four drummers mentioned by Wissler are actually the four Old Men Comrades, one of whose duties was to drum for the society. These men were usually former members of the society, who knew the songs and dances. Wissler, Curtis and McLintock all note one woman member, but our information from reputable informants shows two.

4. Wissler (1913) notes that the Coyote, whom he called the assistant leader, carries a bow and arrow and rattle. Then he gives the leadership to the owner of the Rattle. It appears that he has confused these two offices, which is understandable, because they are always associated. The leader is actually the Coyote owner, who never owns the Rattle for the assistant leader is the Rattle owner.

5. There is no identified Pigeon society Rattle bundle in any collection in the world.

Bibliography

Curtis
  1911-1928. *The North American Indians*, Norwood.
Duvall, D.
  7 unpublished field notes on file at the Glenbow Alberta Institute, Calgary, Alberta, Canada.
Goldfrank, E. and Hanks
  1945. 'Changing Configurations in the Social Organization of a Blackfoot Tribe during the Reserve Period', *Monographs of the American Ethnological Society*, #8, University of Washington Press.
McClintock, W.
  1910. *The Old North Trail*, University of Nebraska Press, Lincoln, Nebraska.
McQuesten, C.
  1912. 'The Sun Dance of the Blackfoot', *Rod & Gun in Canada*.
Wissler, C.
  1913. 'Societies and Dancing Associations of the Blackfoot', *Anthropological Papers of the American Museum of Natural History*.
Wissler, C. and Duvall
  1908. 'Mythology of the Blackfoot Indians', *Anthropological Papers of the American Museum of Natural History*.

Appendix: Membership in the Pigeon Society

These lists have been compiled from informants' notes, and are incomplete. As well, names were changed two or three times during a man's life. Goldfrank and Hanks (1945, p. 40) said that in 1939, of a sampling of 305 adult males—practically the entire adult population of the Blood Reserve in that year—205 had been members of the Pigeon society at some time. If a man was known by another name, that name is given in parentheses. The office of each man in the society is given in italics. Where known, approximate age in 1976 is given as well, or age at death and approximate date if deceased.

Members of the Pigeon Society in 1924

These members were drawn from the Grey Horse Owners' dancing association. They later became members of the Horn society, but did not relinquish their membership in the Pigeon society.

George First Rider (First Rode) *Yellow Pigeon*, 75*
Paul Melting Tallow (Long Time Crow) *Yellow Pigeon*
Dick Wells *Yellow Pigeon, d. 1974, at 60*
Bob Black Plume (Skunk) *Bear Pigeon, d. 1976, at 81*
Nick Striped Wolf (Bear Coming Over The Hill) *Bear Pigeon, d. 1972, at 62*
Emil Good Rider *Bear Pigeon, d. 1975, at 60*
Black Pink Tail Feather *Bear Pigeon*
Dan Chief (Burnt End, Star) *Coyote Owner*, 77*
Jim White Man (Wouldn't Listen) (Owns Holy White Horse) *Rattle owner*
Sam Hairy Bull (Obstinate) *Smear Staff owner*, 75*
Little Weasel Calf *Old Man Comrade*
Tom Morning Owl (Bear Fore Arm) *Old Man Comrade, Drummer*, 79*
Billy Heavy Runner (Red Boy) *Old Man Comrade*, 56*
Charlie Good Rider (Fore Arm White Calf) *Old Man Comrade, Drummer*
Willie Eagle Plume (Glove Man) *d. 1976, at 70*

---

* informant

Ben Brewer (Wailing in the Woods)
Cougar Cub
Could Not Be Shaken By The Wind *Red Pigeon*
Cat Man *Red Pigeon*
White Man *Red Pigeon*
Jim Many Feathers *Red Pigeon*
Albert Wells *Red Pigeon, d. 1974, at 70**
Earth Owl
Grey Horse Rider
Ambrose Shouting in the Middle (Bob Tail) 68*
Moogyoii
Joe Shouting in the Middle
Does He Have a Fine Horse
Joe Young Pine (Slanted Horn Bull) 75*
Crow Spreading His Wings Standing (Many Swans)
Wolverine Cub
Dave Big Water
Jim Belly Fat
Gets His Gun
Cougar Cub *Bear Pigeon*
Bear Coming Over the Hill *Bear Pigeon*
Jim Low Horn *Old Man Comrade, Drummer*
Among Them Steals *Women Comrade*
Red Buffalo Stone *Women Comrade*

Members of the Pigeon Society drawn from the Eagle Parted Hairs dancing association

These members transferred to the Grey Horse owners in 1924.
Mike Yellow Bull *Bear Pigeon, d. 1976, at 80**
Chris Bull Shields *Yellow Pigeon, d. 1976, at 81**. *Transferred to George First Rider*
No Runner *Bear Pigeon, 85**
Chased Back
Shot On Both Sides
Calf Robe
Scabby Robe
Steve Oka (Tall Eagle) Originator of Eagle Parted Hairs association 90*
Emil Wings *d. 1973, at 87**

―――――――――

* informant

Dog Child
Wolf Child *80**
Estogumi
Mike Eagle Speaker *Coyote Bundle owner* Transferred to Dan Chief
Moon

Members of the Pigeon Society draw from the Hard Rider Kaispa dancing association

These members transferred to the Eagle Parted Hairs dancing association (date unknown).

Joe Gambler (Only Full Stomach Rider) *Bear Pigeon, d. 1970, at 85**
A Lot With Ride Bear Pigeon
Yellow Boy *Bear Pigeon*
Blacklooking *Bear Pigeon*
Two Chief *Yellow Pigeon*
Eagle Shoe *Red Pigeon*
Calf Chief *Red Pigeon*
Small Boy *Red Pigeon*
Clear Bad Weather *Red Pigeon*
Good Bachelor *Red Pigeon*
Hide Tanner *Red Pigeon*
Dim Light *Coyote owner*
Off Ground Sleep *Rattle Owner*
First To Crash *Smear Staff owner*
Bull Head *Drummer*
Big Throat *Drummer*
Old Man Bathe *Old Man Comrade*
All Over Kindly Woman *Old Man Comrade*
Five Beaver *Old Man Comrade*
Heavy Head *Old Man Comrade*
Willie Scraping White *Bear Pigeon*

Members among the South Piegan

These Pigeon society members belonged at an unknown date. The list is summarized from work published by Curtis, Maximillian, and Wissler.

Bear Skin
Ghost Boy
Blade Roast

---

* informant

Bear Hump
Sayii (Owns Little Sorrel Horse)
Tearing Lodge
Painted Wing
Scalp Roller
Little Leaf
Bear Heard
Turtle (Fish)
Black Scar Face
Bear Shirt
Bear Head *Rattle owner*
Big Brave *Yellow Pigeon and Coyote owner*

---

* informant

Figure 1: Coyote bundle. Coyote skin above, parfleche below. Photo
courtesy of the Provincial Museum and Archives of Alberta.

SEVENTH PAINT
(red ochre)

MOCHSISAAN PAINT
(vermillion)

Figure 2: Facial painting of the Coyote owner and Rattle owner.

Figure 3: Bow and two arrows of a Pigeon Society member (Yellow Pigeon).
Photo courtesy Provincial Museum and Archives of Alberta.

YELLOW

MOCHSISAAN PAINT
(vermillion)

Figure 4: Facial painting of a Yellow Pigeon.

Figure 5: Bearskin belt of a Bear Pigeon. Photo
        courtesy Provincial Museum and Archives
        of Alberta.

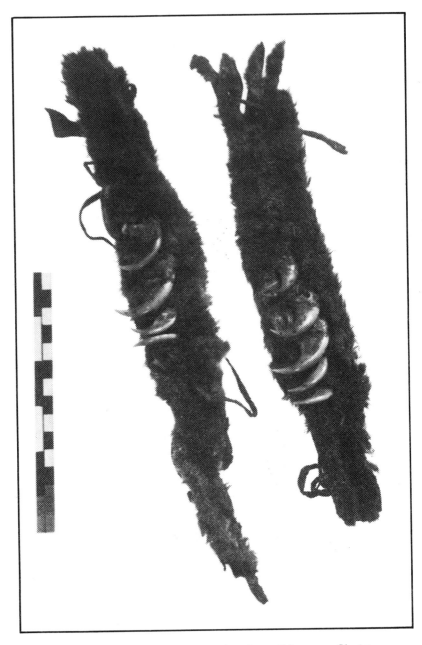

Figure 6: Bear skin arm bands of a Bear Pigeon. Photo
courtesy Provincial Museum and Archives of Alberta.

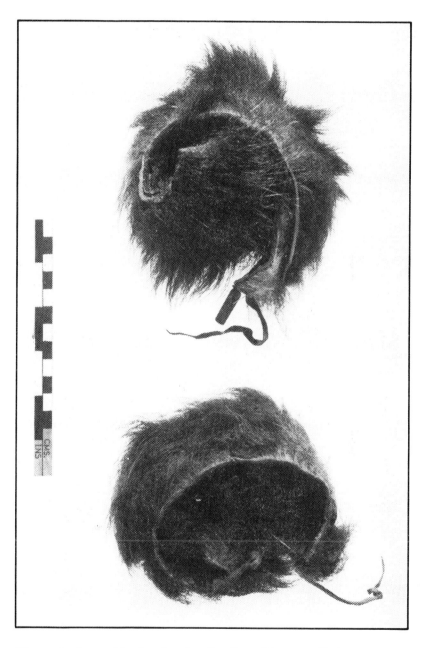

Figure 7: Bear skin leg bands of a Bear Pigeon. Photo courtesy
Provincial Museum and Archives of Alberta.

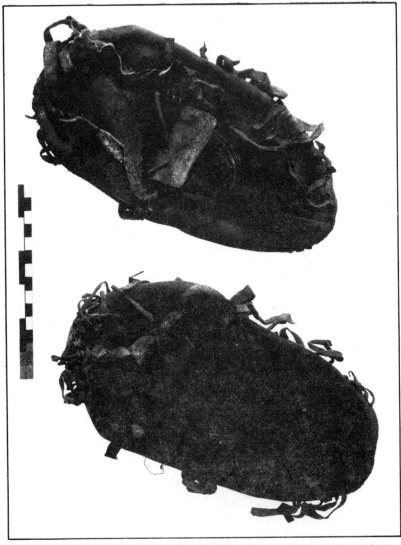

Figure 8: Fringed bear skin moccasins of a Bear Pigeon. Photo courtesy of the Provincial Museum and Archives of Alberta.

REAL PAINT
(red)

BLACK

Figure 9: Facial painting of a Bear Pigeon.

SEVENTH PAINT
(red ochre)

BLACK

Figure 10: Facial painting of a Smear Staff owner.

REAL PAINT
(red)

Figure 11: Facial painting of a Red Pigeon. Women Comrades were painted
in the same manner.

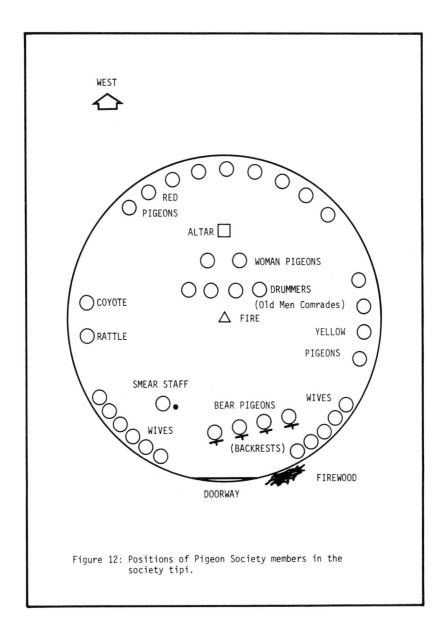

Figure 12: Positions of Pigeon Society members in the
           society tipi.

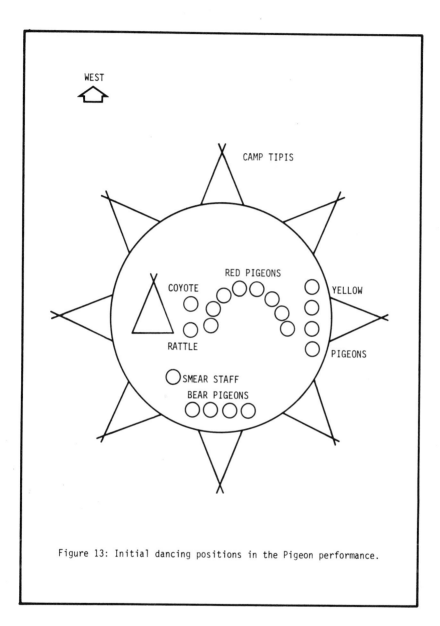

Figure 13: Initial dancing positions in the Pigeon performance.

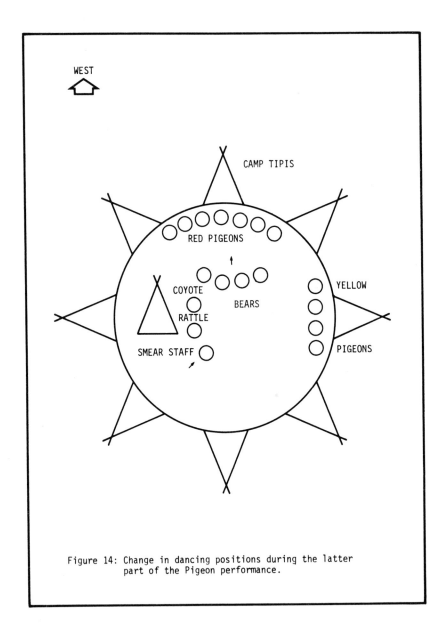

Figure 14: Change in dancing positions during the latter part of the Pigeon performance.

Figure 15: Pigeon Society performing at a Blood Sun Dance in 1907. Photo by Calvin McQuesten.

Figure 16: Pigeon Society member approaching photographer Calvin McQuesten during a Pigeon Society performance, 1907 Blood Sun Dance.

Epilogue

K. Dad Prithipaul

I still remember the persuasive eloquence with which Chief Dan
George reproached the majority of the people of this country for
the great misfortune which has befallen his people. "How dearly
you have made us pay for what you have given us. We have paid
dearly, very dearly. And we continue to pay. We have paid with our
lands, with our traditions, with our culture, with our religion. I
consent to be deprived of all that my forbears have bequeathed to
me. But what I cannot consent to is that you deprive me of my
manhood and my humanity". These words were uttered with great
pride, with a virile authority, but pregnant with a certain gandhian
kindliness, to the crowd of students and teachers who filled the
theatre of the University. They listened to him, in silence,
fascinated, bewildered by the words of the wise Elder who recalled
to them the sad fate meted out to his folk by those who upheld,
perhaps too strongly, perhaps for too long, an ethics of
utilitarianism.

During the centuries following the discovery made by
Christopher Columbus, each time the West has encountered a
civilization different from its own, it has been to weaken it, or to
impoverish it, or to reduce it materially. Since the Renaissance the
West has forgotten how to learn from others. And these violent
encounters have been as many opportunities lost in the course of
the history of mankind. Today no one can pretend that we do not
need one another. It becomes increasingly difficult to believe that a
people, or a culture, can persist in a historical continuity, within a
closed space, without the desire to understand the consecrated
wisdom of the neighbour, without the sentiment of an intellectual
privation which would be eliminated by the serious, rational and
sincere study of his traditions, his metaphysical aspirations, his art.

For too long the West has scoffed at what it did not understand,
or what it did not try to understand. At the same time, one must
not overlook the specialists who have given attention to
inter-cultural problems. But it is nonetheless true that while we
have created new myths (for instance, those of the cinema, of
politics, of international economy) we have not allowed the
legends, the traditions of the pre-Columbian Americans to
integrate themselves within our social life.

The disarray which seems to invade all the sectors of higher studies, and this in a period of the development of high technology, seems to indicate that concerned intellectuals must, before it is too late, strive to bring about a greater understanding of all that is good in the cultures of the other peoples and to ask them to teach us what we have failed to learn. This requires the use of a new rationality which would stretch beyond the academic framework which has, for generations, been dominated by the subjective-objective dichotomy so dear to the scientist and unfortunately also to the specialists of the social sciences. There is a need in academe for a new rationality which would make it possible to have an understanding of Man in all the modalities of his expression.

This rationality must make us understand that the Amerindian is not an object, studied within a 'discipline'. He is a person.

The papers that were read and discussed by the Western specialists at the Seminar on Native Religious Traditions, in September 1977, at the University of Alberta, try to reach out to a better appreciation of the complexity of the 'native' traditions. The texts of the discussions the Elders had with the attendants are presented as faithfully as they were taped. The spontaneity and pleasant humour which undergird their statements can be felt by the sympathetic reader.

One cannot help having a feeling that despite all the goodwill of the Western specialists, the religions of the Amerindians remain fenced off from any comparison with any of the major religions of the world. The comparisons unvaryingly refer to the mores and customs of one 'native' people in contrast to those of another, though at times the latter may be located on another continent. It is a pity that none of the descriptions and analyses of the religious traditions of the native peoples succeeds in giving us an inkling of the nature, the form of the actions, the sentiments which the religious beliefs inspire in these 'native' peoples. It would have been highly rewarding to compare the moral or religious actions of these peoples with similar actions on the part of those who follow one or other of the major religions.

It is a whim of history that the 'native' Amerindians came to be called Indians. Yet in some strange ways this term "Indian" seems to be apt. One indeed is struck by the similarity between the wise man of the 'native' traditions and the vedic or upanishadic man of ancient India. The Mohawk cosmology bears striking similarities with the cosmology of the Sāmkhya philosophy.

I invited Elder Emil Piapot to my residence, the day after the seminar was over. It was a pleasure to discover in him an unassuming man, wise and compassionate. He was moved when I read out to him a page from Grant McEwan's "THE TATANGAMANI": he did not know that his father was named in that book. At one moment during our conversation I read out to him parts of the tenth chapter of the Bhagavad Gita where Kṛṣṇa describes himself as the source of all that is in Nature. "Your God is like our Great Spirit", exclaimed Elder Piapot.

Later a sociologist friend of mine came to join us. He asked Elder Piapot to tell him what were the problems which his community is facing for he would be able to convey that information to the officials in Ottawa whom he was meeting a week later. Elder Piapot replied: "Do you want to help us, or do you want to make some money for yourself? If you really want to help us, come and see my reservation for yourself. And you must talk also to the other Elders. I cannot tell you what is wrong or what is right, without consulting my friends".

It is to be hoped that soon the elite of the 'native' peoples will set in print the metaphysical aspirations, the cosmology, the logic, the mythic way of thinking, the ethics which have sustained them and given to them strength and consolation, in good times, in hard times, both before and after the arrival of the European, in the New World. Statements like Leroy Little Bear's 'Concept of Native Title' and 'Jurisprudence' would seem to bear this hope out.

Some questioners at the Elders' seminars were nostalgic about the quaint ways and customs of the indigenous peoples. Their concern was for the possible disappearance of the folk pageantry and colourful festivals. They were not concerned with the growth of the 'native' peoples. Indeed the 'natives' must be allowed to choose their own ways to "be", through the on-going process of time. The outsider must acknowledge that, whatever be the ritual, or the myth, or the legend of the 'native', the latter remains, in all situations, a person, endowed with spiritual good, seeking for meaning in his feelings, in his deeds, and in his relationship to the universe and to man.

D.Prithipaul

About the Participants

Joe Poor Eagle and his wife Beatrice are two of the few religious leaders left in Alberta that can legitimize a sundance. As a consequence, they are much sought after by groups that are attempting to revive the traditional ways. Mr. Poor Eagle, who lives in Cluny, Alberta, was one of the elders who smoked the pipe with Prince Charles at the commemorative ceremonies held at Blackfoot Crossing.

Lewis Running Rabbit is an associate of Mr. Poor Eagle's called upon as a singer at religious events. He also lives in Cluny, Alberta, and is a Blackfoot.

Emil Piapot, a Cree elder, comes from the Piapot Reserve in Saskatchewan. Mr. Piapot is highly regarded among his own people for his spiritual insight and religious knowledge. He travels whenever he can to promote traditional religious ways.

Morris Nanipowisk is an associate of Mr. Piapot who knows many of the songs and rites of the Cree tradition. He lives on Piapot Reserve in Saskatchewan.

Julian Hardisty is a Slavey Indian from Fort Simpson, N.W.T. Now retired, he expresses the values of a man that has stood between two cultures.

Åke Hultkrantz, Chairman of the Institute of Comparative Religion, University of Stockholm, Stockholm, Sweden. Has done field research among Lappo and North American Indians. Author of: *The Indians in Yellowstone Park*; *The North American Indian Orpheus Tradition*; *Prairie and Plains Indians*.

Karl Luckert, Asst. Professor in the Department of Humanities, North Arizona University, Flagstaff, Arizona. Author of: *The Navajo Hunter Tradition*; *Olmec Religion*; *A Key to Middle America and Beyond*; *Coyoteway, a Navajo Healing Ceremonial*.

Joseph E. Brown, Associate Professor of Religious Studies, University of Montana, Missoula, Montana. Author of: *The Sacred Pipe*; 'The Spiritual Legacy of the American Indian'; 'Native American Religion Traditions: An Introductory Survey'.

Sam D. Gill, Asst. Professor of Humanities/Religious Studies, Arizona State University, Tempe, Arizona. Author of: 'Songs of Life: The Ways of Navajo Religion'; 'Navajo Religious Iconography'; 'Theory of Navajo Prayer Acts: A Study of Ritual Symbolism'.

J. W. E. Newbery, Founder and Director, Native Studies Department, University of Sudbury, Sudbury, Ontario. Author of: 'Canadian Responsibility to Native People,' C.A.S.N.P.; 'Kasabonika—A Story of Canadian Neglect,' Laurentian University Review; 'Ethics of Environment: Native American Insights,' University of Wisconsin.

John C. Hellson, Consultant to Museums, Universities and Government Agencies on Artifacts, Films and Oral Interviews with Native Informants. Some of his work: Research Contracts, National Museum of Man, Ottawa, Ontario; Exhibition Consultant & Researcher, Glenbow Alberta Institute, Calgary, Alberta; Field work among the Blackfoot, Cree & Saulteaux.

Appendix

Discussion based on following material:

Blackfoot, Blood, Piegan

"A Blackfoot Sun and Moon Myth" by G. B. Grinnel, *Journal of American Folklore*, Vol. 6, pp. 44-47.

"Beaver Medicine Ceremonial" by McClintock, *The Old North Trail*, pp. 76-102.

"Beaver Medicine Legend" by McClintock, *The Old North Trail*, pp. 103-112.

"Beginning of the Sun-Dance" by McClintock, *The Old North Trail*, pp. 118-183.

"Blackfoot Mythology" by McLean, *Journal of American Folklore*, Vol. 6, pp. 165-172.

"Development of the Sun Dance" by Chief Mountain, *Kainai Chieftanship*, pp. 82-91.

"Legend, Culture and Religion" by Chief Mountain, *Kainai Chieftanship*, pp. 48-50.

"Legend of Poia" by McClintock, *The Old North Trail*, pp. 491-501.

"Medicine Pipe Society" by McClintock, *The Old North Trail*, pp. 251-270.

"Mystical Stories" by McClintock, *The Old North Trail*, pp. 335-351.

"The Blackfoot Creation" by G. B. Grinnell, *Blackfeet Indian Stories*, pp. 145-155.

"The Legend of the Beaver Bundle" by R. Lancaster, *Piegan*, pp. 231-235.

"The Sun Dance—Medicine Lodge and Okon of the Blood Indians" by Chief Mountain, *Kainai Chieftanship*, pp. 74-81.

"The Sun Dance of the Blackfoot Indians" by Clark Wissler, *American Museum of Natural History: Anthro. Papers*, Vol. 16, pp. 229-270.

"The Sun Dance of the Blackfoot Indians" Piegan account of Hundred-Willow Sweathouse — by Clark Wissler, *American Museum of Natural History: Anthro. Papers*, Vol. 16, pp. 251-252.

Cree

"Folk-lore of the Cree Indians" by Swindlehurst, *Journal of American Folklore*, Vol. 18, pp. 139.

"The Cree Legend of Creation" by Charles Clay, *Alberta Folklore Quarterly*, Vol. 2, No. 2, June, 1945, pp. 69-71.

"The Plains Cree" by Mandelbaum, *American Museum of Nature History: Anthro. Papers*, Vol. 37, pp. 251-280 & 288-293.

"The Sun Dance of the Plains-Cree" by Alanson Skinner, *American Museum of Nature History: Anthro. Papers*, Vol. 16, pp. 287-293.

"The Sun Dance of the Cree of Alberta" by Pliny E. Goddard, *American Museum of Nature History: Anthro. Papers*, Vol. 16, pp. 299-310.

Navajo

"A Navajo Medicine Bundle for Shootingway" by Leland C. Wyman, *Plateau*, Vol. 44-45, 1971-73, pp. 131-149.

"Blessing Way, the Core Ritual of Navajo Ceremony" by Charles C. Case, *Plateau*, Vol. 40-41, 1967-69, pp. 35-42.

"Navajo Land" by Hogner, *Navajo Winter Nights*, pp. 3-23.

"Navajo Night Chant" by W. Matthews, *Journal of American Folklore*, Vol. 13-14, pp. 12-19.

"The First Worlds and the Flood" by Link, *The Pollen Path*, pp. 3-14.

"The Navajo Origin Legend" by W. Matthews, *Navajo Legends*, pp. 63-76.

Six Nations

"Legends of the Corn" by Wm. Canfield, *The Legends of the Iroquois*, pp. 51-53.

"Mythologic Explanation of Phenomena" by Erminnie A. Smith, *Myths of the Iroquois*, (no page nos.)

"The Creation Myth" by Hazel W. Hertzberg, *The Great Tree and the Longhouse*, pp. 12-19.

Questions That We Have Requested to be Discussed Are The Following:

September 16

1. Is this a story you remember?

2. Are there details left out or changed?

3. When would such a story be told?

4. Who would tell it?

5. How would he gain the right to tell it?

6. Would there be exchange of goods for the privilege of hearing the story?

7. If so, what gifts would be given and who would give them?

8. Can you describe how you first heard a story like this?

9. Were there problems (ie. rules that you would break) if the story was not recited correctly or at the proper time?

10. Can you tell us what these problems were and how one could overcome the bad created by violating the rule?

September 17

1. Have you ever known a rite like the one described in this selection?

2. Are there responsibilities of important people not discussed here?

3. What elements are missing in the description?

4. Has the writer put proper emphasis on the important points?

5. How often would this ritual be performed? When?

6. Can you tell us what the ritual would mean for someone participating?

7. What religious importance would the ritual have for the individual?

8. Would this be an essential ritual, or one that would depend on the circumstances?

9. Can you describe a ritual like this that seems more true-to-life than this description?

10. Are the parts in this description in the right order?

These Questions And This Material Are Suggestions Only And Elders Are Free To Explore Any Questions Or Issues They Wish.

Index

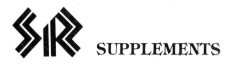 SUPPLEMENTS

1. **FOOTNOTES TO A THEOLOGY: The Karl Barth Colloquium of 1972**
Edited and with an Introduction by Martin Rumscheidt
1974 / vii + 149 pp. / $3.50 (paper)
ISBN 0-919812-02-3

2. **MARTIN HEIDEGGER'S PHILOSOPHY OF RELIGION**
John R. Williams
1977 / 188 pp. / $4.00 (paper)
ISBN 0-919812-03-1

3. **MYSTICS AND SCHOLARS: The Calgary Conference on Mysticism 1976**
Edited by Harold Coward and Terence Penelhum
1977 / viii + 118 pp. / $4.00 (paper)
ISBN 0-919812-04-X

4. **GOD'S INTENTION FOR MAN: Essays in Christian Anthropology**
William O. Fennell
1977 / vi + 56 pp. / $2.50 (paper)
ISBN 0-919812-05-8

5. **"LANGUAGE" IN INDIAN PHILOSOPHY AND RELIGION**
Edited and Introduced by Harold G. Coward
1978 / x + 93 pp. / $4.00 (paper)
ISBN 0-919812-07-4

6. **BEYOND MYSTICISM**
James R. Horne
1978 / x + 158 pp. / $4.00 (paper)
ISBN 0-919812-08-2

7. **THE RELIGIOUS DIMENSION OF SOCRATES' THOUGHT: A Study of the Greek Experience of Life**
James Beckman
1978 / xiv + 274 pp. / $5.00 (paper)
ISBN 0-919812-09-0

8. **NATIVE RELIGIOUS TRADITIONS**
Edited by Earle H. Waugh and K. Dad Prithipaul
1979 / xii + 244 pp. / $5.00 (paper)
ISBN 0-919812-10-4

9. **DEVELOPMENTS IN BUDDHIST THOUGHT: Canadian Contributions to Buddhist Studies**
Edited by Roy C. Amore
1979 / iv + 196 pp. / $5.00 (paper)
ISBN 0-919812-11-2

EDITIONS

1. **LA LANGUE DE YA'UDI: Description et classement de l'ancien parler de Zencirli dans le cadre des langues sémitiques du nord-ouest**
Paul-Eugène Dion, O.P.
1974 / vii + 509 p. / $4.50 (broché)
ISBN 0-919812-01-5

Also published / Avons aussi publié
RELIGION AND CULTURE IN CANADA / RELIGION ET CULTURE AU CANADA
Edited by / sous la direction de Peter Slater
1977 / viii + 568 pp. / $7.50 (paper)
ISBN 0-919812-06-6

Available from / en vente chez:
WILFRID LAURIER UNIVERSITY PRESS
Wilfrid Laurier University
Waterloo, Ontario, Canada   N2L 3C5

Tout chèque doit être fait à l'ordre de Wilfrid Laurier University Press / Make cheques payable to Wilfrid Laurier University Press